A Passion for Vegetables

Also by Vera Gewanter

Home Preserving Made Easy
(with Dorothy Parker)

A
Passion
for Vegetables

Recipes from European Kitchens

Vera Gewanter

THE VIKING PRESS   NEW YORK

Library of Congress Cataloging in Publication Data
Gewanter, Vera.
A passion for vegetables.   Includes index.
1. Vegetarian cookery.   I. Title.
TX837.G46   641.5'636   78-27613
ISBN 0-670-54141-9

ACKNOWLEDGMENT
Atheneum Publishers, Inc.: "Légumes à L'Orientale"
from *Simple French Food* by Richard Olney.
Copyright © 1974 by Richard Olney.
Reprinted by permission of Atheneum Publishers.

Printed in the United States of America
Set in Linotype Baskerville

Acknowledgments

I wish to thank the many friends and relatives who have so freely given me precious suggestions and support during my research in the compilation of this book. I am particularly grateful to my cousin Luciana Alfieri of Rome, Italy, and to my friend Kleopatra Pittas Nathan of Athens, Greece, for their invaluable and assiduous help.

My husband, who offered himself as experimental taster and who for many months patiently subjected himself to repeated tests of the same recipe until it came out to my satisfaction, deserves a special honorable mention.

Contents

Introduction

"Tell me what you eat and I'll tell you how you are" was one of the diagnostic rules of the medical school of Salerno, in southern Italy, established about the ninth century A.D. Considered the first medical school of its kind in the Western world, it successfully merged all the then-known medical science from Arabic, Jewish, Greek, and Latin sources and extolled the virtues of vegetarianism.

The concept of vegetarianism was not new. The beliefs of the Salerno school had obvious Biblical origins and perhaps also reflected the strict vegetarian rules established five centuries before Christ by the Greek philosopher and mathematician Pythagoras. His school had been in Crotona, not far from Salerno, in the section of Italy which was then a Greek colony. Although the Pythagorean school had long since disappeared, its influence, especially among scholars, was still strongly felt when the Salerno school was founded.

The Catholic Church, by then fully established, had promulgated alimentary tenets which were in part based on the ancient Jewish dietary laws but were stricter in curbing the consumption of flesh and fowl. The church provided the religious and ritualistic element that the hygienic principles of the medical scholars could not enforce, acting in effect as a health program for the entire Christian world. At that time it was easier to impose these rules under the guise of religious precepts than as a scien-

1

tific prescription. Today, in the age of science, the opposite is true.

But, while inquiring after somebody's health is still an international form of greeting, by now both the public and the medical profession seem to have largely forgotten the relation between food and health. It is a rare doctor today who shows any interest in his patient's diet or gives advice about food, except when the patient is overweight. In fact, the expression "to be on a diet" has come to mean a reducing diet rather than a regimen to become or remain healthy.

It is hard to pinpoint the moment when the current unbridled passion for meat took over our diets to such an extent that today in most American families meat and/or fish are eaten two or even three times a day. Over the centuries, as the Western world became more and more secularized, the restrictions on flesh eating imposed by the church gradually gave way to political necessities, and the advent of a modern science totally divorced from religion finally obscured the ancient religious and medical reasons that had urged abstention from or parsimonious use of meat.

The eating of flesh has always been much more prevalent among the upper classes. It is therefore not surprising that, as the United States became more and more affluent, the frequent eating of meat became a status symbol, especially as the prices of meat increased, proportionately, much more than those of other foods.

The same phenomenon is taking place in the European countries which have experienced recent economic growth. Yet it is refreshing to find that in those European countries which are considered "underdeveloped" meat is still not eaten more than once or perhaps twice a week. In Greece, for example, a recent television survey conducted in the major cities, where people are more affluent, showed that the average urban Greek does not eat meat more than twice a week. In rural areas, it is eaten even less frequently.

In the United States there are healthy signs that the consumption of meat may be on the decline. In the last ten or fifteen years an increasing segment of the American population has become vegetarian, and more recently many Americans have made a deliberate effort to reduce their consumption of meat. Inflation has been helpful in this decision, and some people may also have been encouraged to reduce their excessive intake of meat by sporadic rumblings from the medical establishment. These are hopeful beginnings, although one wishes that the wise example of the doctors of the Salerno school would find more of an echo in the teachings of present-day physicians and nutritionists. Unfortunately, the public statements of many of these specialists are too often self-serving. Some have tied themselves to various food industries, giving their seal of approval to harmful foods, as recent scandals have shown; others complacently condone, and by their silence foster, the excessive use of certain foods, such as meat, which they have avoided investigating, either out of unquestioned habit or because they are reluctant to check the ill effects of foods they themselves overindulge in.

Although there have been some very vague warnings regarding the fat contained in red meats, we hear precious little from the medical and scientific establishment about other noxious elements contained in animal flesh. The protein drum is being beaten so loudly as to deafen the general public and to counteract the almost absolute silence about the pernicious toxins released in the body by the ingestion of meat. A more honest scientific appraisal is needed.

We live on a constant seesaw of semi-scientific, ill-digested data about food, one fad usually being superseded by its exact opposite. For example, people have become so concerned about sufficient intake of protein that the average American is unaware of the fact that he or she ingests several times the "required" minimum daily amount, with detriment to health. At the same time, the consumption of foods that contain natural vitamins and minerals is inadequate, often to the point of malnutrition.

It is not my purpose to provide the reader with instructions on how to maintain a well-balanced vegetarian diet. The subject has been amply covered by several recent books to which readers can easily refer.

The wave of vegetarianism which started in this country in the mid-1960s, spurred primarily by a resurgence of spiritual ideals, has produced, by and large, a rather bland, uninspired fare closer to asceticism and taste-deprivation than to the enjoyment of the fruits of the earth. This Spartan vegetarian diet was, in more ways than one, "swallowed whole" by a predominantly young population whose appreciation of good food had not yet fully developed and who, with the excessive zeal characteristic of new converts, jumped from one extreme to the other—from the numbing, limited diet of junk food they had known since early childhood to an equally restricted variety of dishes that would in no way excite their taste buds.

Unfortunately, the enthusiastic proselytizing of these young antigourmets, along with the scoffing of a communications media committed to meat-eating, has created all sorts of misconceptions about vegetarianism in the minds of the general public. While I fully endorse a return to healthy, unadulterated foods, I believe that the pendulum has swung too quickly and drastically from too many wrong foods to too few right foods. I hope this book will help fill the gap between the Granola generation and the confirmed carnivores by opening new vistas for both. This selection of European vegetarian recipes should prove interesting not only to vegetarians but to the increasing numbers of Americans seeking respite from the daily meat-and-fish routine and wishing to break the monotony for the sake of variety, out of concern for their health, or for economic reasons.

Vegetarianism—almost unknown in this country except among a few religious sects when I became a vegetarian—by now has become a fact of life, yet it is still considered an aberration, or at least an eccentricity, by the majority of Americans. It is, at best, looked on as a passing fad of the young and has become synonymous with "health foods," usually ridiculed by the larger portion of the public, which believes itself saner and superior by maintaining the status quo of a diet which, by inference, is unhealthy.

This book contains a preponderance of recipes from southern European countries. There are several reasons for this apparent imbalance. Historically, the best European cuisine was born in the south and consequently there is a larger variety of appetizing dishes to choose from. In southern Europe, where the warmer climate and longer growing season provide more abundance and variety, the cuisine has always relied more on the fruits of the earth than the cuisine of northern Europe. Also, until recently, the transportation of fresh produce from southern to northern countries was difficult.

Aside from these considerations, my background is Mediterranean, and therefore I am more familiar with southern European home cooking. Many of the recipes in this book come from my family, and I am grateful to my mother for keeping notebooks filled with recipes I remember from my childhood. She diligently copied not only the family recipes but many others from friends and friends of friends, especially during World War II. Meat and fish were then so scarce that everybody's imagination was put to the test of inventing interesting ways to maintain a nutritious and varied diet using the limited selection of foods at hand.

I have elaborated on a few dishes according to my personal taste; and in some cases I have substituted a few ingredients (especially if the original recipe was not totally vegetarian); other recipes are my own invention but maintain a definite European flavor.

The book is by no means a comprehensive survey of European vegetarian cooking. The present selection comprises for the most part dishes that are seldom found in restaurants but are commonly cooked at home. Occasionally a familiar recipe appears and will, I hope, be accepted as a reminder by those who know how to prepare it. However, I have largely avoided the inclusion of recipes that are so well known as to be boringly superfluous. Ratatouille, stuffed grape leaves, eggplant *alla parmigiana* are but a few such deliberate omissions.

Although many of the dishes I describe have been cooked for centuries, it is only in the last seventy or eighty years, and especially more recently, that the interest in cooking and cookbooks has prompted Europeans to write down recipes. There are still many specialties known only locally, waiting to be discovered and to travel abroad.

Many European recipes are so simple or are cooked so often at home that nobody has ever thought it necessary to write them down. In the relatively few cases in which this has been done, the instructions are often vague. They were intended more as guidelines from one cook to another—both knowing in advance how the dish was supposed to taste and look—than as exact instructions for novices who had never tasted the dish. The recipes that were recorded, even during the many centuries in which cookbooks were practically nonexistent, dealt with the more complicated dishes requiring a certain skill; these were only cooked on special occasions. Written notations were then necessary reminders for the cook. Because meat and fish were important courses at such special holiday meals, those recipes were more often available for inclusion in cookbooks. The same applies to desserts, especially in southern Europe where fruit has always been so abundant that it ends almost every meal. Cakes, pies, and sweets were special holiday treats and the recipes were written down, making them more accessible to the general public, both in Europe and abroad. To this day, ending a meal with a dessert is usually reserved for a special family dinner, for occasions when guests have been invited, or for holidays. The meals consumed daily, even in well-to-do families, end with cheese and fresh fruit of the season.

The casual visitor who has not lived in a foreign country for a prolonged period of time frequently gets a completely distorted view of the food habits of the native population. The restaurant fare in European countries, especially in first-quality restaurants, is quite different from the types of food eaten at home. Unlike Americans, Europeans generally prefer eating at home, and when they go to a restaurant they like to order dishes that are not frequently prepared at home. The average visitor to Europe seldom has an opportunity to eat in private homes. Even when this happens, special dishes are usually prepared in honor of the guest, so that the everyday home-cooked meal remains unknown to most tourists. To confuse the visitor further, European food habits vary, sometimes substantially, from region to region, even from province to province, so that one may receive a certain impression of a nation's food by having visited a portion of a particular country and may have missed a whole array of specialties popular in other parts of the same country. Armed with all sorts of preconceived ideas, the foreigner may order polenta in Naples and pizza in Turin and be totally mystified when no such specialties are available, often returning home with the conviction of having been duped. To add to the general misconception, many dishes imported to America by immigrants were like certain wines: they did not travel well. Oral tradition often suffered by transplantation, and altered or inferior versions of a dish became

popular in the United States. I myself have heard people returning from a trip to Europe declare that the Italians don't know
how to cook pasta (because it was too firm, the way it's supposed
to be but is seldom found in Italian-American restaurants) ; that
the English don't know how to make a pie (because they often
put the crust on top instead of at the bottom) ; or that French
restaurants don't offer authentic food because in France nobody
knows what Vichyssoise is. (It was invented at a famous New
York restaurant by a French chef who came from Vichy, but it is
not a French specialty.)

With the selection of recipes in this book I hope to give a
glimpse of a lesser-known aspect of European home cooking
which better reflects the food habits of countries that until recently, and in some cases to this day, were not nearly as reliant
on meat as the United States is.

A good many of these recipes were created by people who ate
meat and fish so seldom that they were almost vegetarians. And
they certainly were gourmets. Readers who have followed a vegetarian diet for some time will have noticed, among other bene-
ficial physical changes, a sharpening of their senses of smell and
taste. It takes a while for this subtle transformation to become
noticeable because usually all the cells in the body have to be
completely renewed before the new awareness begins. But when
this happens, good, healthy food can be *really* enjoyed, and eating
even the simplest dish can become an astonishing discovery. So
let your newly sensitized taste buds be your guides. First, try these
recipes as they are written; then, if you wish, add your own personal touch, and don't be afraid to experiment. Cooking and
tasting what nature has to offer will then truly become a joy.

Nonvegetarians will perhaps be inspired to follow the example
of our European forefathers who did not overindulge in meat-
eating habits. They have left us an abundant legacy of tasty
culinary preparations that do not entail the use of animal flesh
but employ a wide range of agricultural products inventively
transformed into exciting dishes—sometimes earthy, sometimes
subtly sophisticated—largely forgotten by many of their American descendants. Many of the recipes are of humble origin. A
cursory reading, even by the skilled cook who is unfamiliar with
a specific dish, may not be indicative of the taste, and I strongly

suggest that a recipe be tested before final judgment is passed. Rustic European cooking at times appears deceptively simple, and the combination of certain ingredients may seem quixotic, but these juxtapositions are often the result of centuries of experimentation by people close to the land whose taste buds had not been vitiated by the sophisticated foods of the higher classes. Thrift and self-sufficiency were a securely ingrained way of life. Difficulties of transportation and seasonal and economic limitations taught them to make do with whatever foods were available or even overabundant at a particular time—the temporary abundance of a specific product allowing greater leeway to create new dishes and to perfect them—just as other periods of scarcity or even famine encouraged the invention of seemingly incongruous preparations. But simple cooking—both rural and urban, especially in countries that appreciate good food—is a blending of basic elements. Their unexpected transmutation creates a very special gastronomic alchemy that often cannot be foreseen until a dish is actually tasted.

The book is divided in the conventional way for easier consultation, but in actuality a rigid separation of courses is much less important for vegetarian meals than for meals including meat, fish, or fowl, in which one or more of these foods dominates.

The habit of separating a meal into different courses was first started, in Europe, by the ancient Romans, especially the nobility. This structure still exists in most European countries, though in the last half-century it has become much more flexible than it used to be. Roman banquets traditionally started with an egg dish and ended with fruit, usually apples. The English expression "from soup to nuts," meaning from beginning to end, was probably inspired by the Latin *"ab ovo usque ad mala,"* from egg to apple.

But, except for the almost universal habit of ending a meal with fruit or a sweet-tasting food which would leave a pleasant taste in the mouth, there are many countries in which the meal is not separated into different courses but presented at the table at one time.

The separation of chapters in this book is therefore arbitrary and can be disregarded when planning a meal. Two or three different and even contrasting dishes—provided the tastes don't clash—can be served in lieu of a conventional main course. An "appetizer," when prepared in larger amounts than those indicated in the recipe, can become the central dish, and occasionally a meal can be served smorgasbord style. The order of appearance, or the combination of various dishes, is up to you. Even two or three substantial "side dishes" that complement each other in taste, nutritious properties, and appearance can constitute the main course of a vegetarian meal, perhaps accompanied by a salad. Conversely, a series of different dishes can be served in succession. In this case, you will be wise to serve small amounts of foods that have a distinctive taste and are even better appreciated when eaten alone. This sequential treatment of a meal, especially if variety of taste and appearance has been carefully planned, often astonishes nonvegetarian guests who had reluctantly accepted a dinner invitation with the preconceived idea that there would be little or nothing to eat. Their surprise increases as the meal progresses.

In whichever order or combination you decide to serve the dishes contained in this book, I hope you will use these recipes often and enjoy them as much as have so many people before you.

Notes on Ingredients

Because I am an ovolactovegetarian, the majority of the recipes contained in this book include eggs and dairy products. I hope this will assuage any protein-insufficiency fears on the part of the inveterate meat eater. But stricter vegetarians will also find a number of recipes consonant with their persuasion, and they can also modify other recipes, using this book as a guideline.

Because I don't eat sugar, chocolate, or certain other substances —and I try as much as possible to avoid foods which have been tampered with by additives, synthetic coloring agents, and preservatives—and because I don't drink coffee, tea, or carbonated drinks, this book reflects my beliefs.

In Europe the habit of using seasonal fresh foods is fortunately still prevalent, and since most of these recipes preceded the advent of canning and refrigeration, fresh foods are usually recommended, not only for the sake of authenticity but because I personally believe in following the seasonal habit. You will seldom find a suggestion to use canned foods. Because most vegetables are low in acidity, they require a long canning process, with considerable alteration of taste and texture. Vitamins are also lost, especially because the liquid in which the vegetables were processed is usually discarded. In a few cases, certain canned vegetables may be substituted, but even these allowances are to be interpreted as suggestions for shortcuts in the preparation of a dish rather than as recommendations. These exceptions are almost exclusively made when the recipe calls for a food that needs long cooking even when fresh, such as beets, or when the specified ingredient subsequently has to be mashed or added to a dish that needs further cooking. In these cases firmness, looks, and texture are less important, and the nutritious elements stay in the finished dish. In other cases—notably tomatoes—the quality available to the general public in the United States has become so tasteless and unappealing that the canned food is at times even suggested because canneries can obtain better varieties. The tomatoes sold fresh on the market are new strains which have been produced to resist mishandling in transit and to withstand longer shelf life, to the detriment of taste. It is understood, however, that the reader who has access to the better varieties should definitely choose fresh produce.

Vegetables

The following list includes vegetables that are either uncommon or require special care in preparing them for cooking. The more common vegetables are omitted, since I assume that the reader knows how to handle them.

In root vegetables, the greatest amount of vitamins and other nutrients are contained in and directly under the skins, so it is advisable not to peel these but to scrub them with a stiff brush under cold running water, removing any stubborn residue of dirt with the point of a small knife. If sometimes they seem to need a deeper cleaning, scrape them lightly with a sharp knife instead of peeling them. Beets are an exception, and details on their preparation are given in this list.

Except for leafy vegetables, which tend to mat, steaming is preferable to boiling, as in this way most of the nutrients remain in the vegetable. Large vegetables, or those that take a long time to cook, can be boiled in a small amount of water, or if more water is needed—as in the case of potatoes—the liquid should be saved and used in other dishes. More specific instructions are often given in the recipe.

ARTICHOKES. Because artichokes easily oxidate (become dark when they come in contact with the air after they are cut), an anti-oxidant is needed to prevent discoloration. This is purely for appearance, as oxidation in no way affects either taste or edible safety. The most common anti-oxidant is lemon juice. Prepare a bowl with about one cup of cold water mixed with the juice of one lemon, and roll the cut artichokes into this acidulated water. Or, rub wedges of lemon on each cut portion of the artichoke as soon as you finish cleaning it.

Artichoke stems are also edible, provided you peel off a thin layer all around to get rid of the bitterness. In Europe, especially in the country, artichokes are often sold with three or four feet of stem, and the stems are eaten with the rest of the artichokes. But, whatever the length of the stems, do not discard them. Just cut them off at the base of the "flower," slice off a thin portion at the other end, where it had been previously cut, peel them, and rub them with a cut lemon or plunge in lemon-and-water mixture. Only overgrown artichokes are likely to have stems which are too tough to eat.

With a very sharp knife, cut off about an inch from the top of each artichoke. If you are preparing whole artichokes to be eaten by stripping each leaf at the table, remove only a few outer leaves, cut off the thorny tips of the remaining leaves with a pair of scissors, and with the knife slice off a thin layer all around the bottom. Plunge in acidulated water, and steam. The peeled stems can be steamed at the same time and served on the side.

For many dishes small, young artichokes should be selected. At this stage the choke is small and soft and can be removed easily when the artichokes are halved or quartered. If whole artichokes are called for, gently spread the leaves and cut out the choke with a small, sharp knife, turning the artichoke as you maneuver.

A few recipes call for artichokes so small and young that the choke has not even started to form. Although artichokes of this size are almost impossible to obtain in the market—except perhaps in California—do not be discouraged. Test the recipe by using one or two sample artichokes as small as you can find them, remove more outer leaves, and clean them of their chokes as previously described.

Do not discard the leaves you are not using but save them in your soup bag. Wrapped in cheesecloth for easy removal, these leaves add flavor to soups, stews, broths, sauces.

To prepare artichoke bottoms, cut off the stems and rub the cut surface with a lemon wedge. Slice the leaves off the bottom in one neat cut parallel to the base, scoop out the choke, and again rub with lemon. Or, if the dish allows it, steam the artichoke whole, then pluck off the leaves or cut them off at the base, and scoop out the choke. You will find it easier to cut off the bottom of a cooked artichoke.

ASPARAGUS. Cut off a portion of the woody part of the stem. Wash the stalks under cold running water, checking for grit under the scales. (If the stalks are very dirty, remove the scales with a small knife.) Tie in a bunch with a string, keeping the bottom end of the stems level. Put in a tall pot (a large coffee pot may be used), tips up, with about three inches of boiling salted water. Cover tightly, and steam-boil until the tips are cooked but not limp.

Or, if you have a fish steamer—also called an asparagus steamer—place the washed asparagus on the slotted tray, all facing in one direction to simplify later removal to a serving platter.

For dishes in which only the tenderest part of the stalk is to be served, snap each raw asparagus stalk, holding it with thumb and index finger of both hands. The woody part will break off naturally at the right spot.

BEANS, DRIED. Dried beans of all types should be soaked in cold water to rehydrate them. Because they swell during this process, cover them with at least twice their volume of water. Presoak them for several hours, preferably overnight. (Check water absorption after a couple of hours and add more water if needed.) Or put them in a pot with water, cover tightly, and slowly bring the water to a boil. As soon as it boils, turn off the heat and let sit for about one and a half hours. Overnight soaking in cold water is preferred for dishes in which the beans should maintain a good appearance. The more violent rehydration in hot water tends to crack the skin and sometimes separate it from the bean.

Beans must be cooked very slowly. To obtain the lowest simmer, use an asbestos pad or metal "flame tamer." Salt should be added only after the beans have cooked for about 45 minutes, because with some varieties the addition of salt at the beginning may slow the cooking process and even prevent the beans from ever softening.

BEETS. Unless very young, beets, unlike other root vegetables, usually need to be peeled. To avoid "bleeding," cut the stems one inch above the base and leave the root tip; then rinse the beets in cold water. Perhaps the best way to cook beets is to bake them in a slow oven, but they can also be boiled. In either case, they are peeled after they are done. Beets require a considerable amount of time to cook, perhaps an hour or longer, depending on their size and quality.

BROCCOLI. Many people use only the tips and discard the stems, even though they are very healthful and tasty. However, the tips will cook very quickly, while the stems take a little longer. If you don't want to have limp, overcooked broccoli and if the dish you are making allows it, cut the larger stems into bite-sized pieces or strips, and cook them separately for a few minutes before adding the tips.

If you prefer to leave the stems attached to the flowerets, separate chunks of stems and flowerets by cutting the entire stalk lengthwise; then cut slits in the stems. Broccoli steams very easily.

CABBAGE, WHITE. With closed-head cabbage, wash the head and remove one or two of the outer leaves if these are tough or damaged. Slice off the stem.

With open-head cabbage, remove more of the outer leaves if they seem tough.

The core of the cabbage can be cooked in soups, then fished out and discarded before serving.

Shredded cabbage cooks very quickly. It is usually boiled in very little water, just enough to prevent sticking, with or without the addition of butter and/or oil. It can also be pan-fried.

CABBAGE, RED.   Follow the preceding instructions. If it is to be cooked, it preserves more of its color if some vinegar is added to the cooking liquid, though it always tends to discolor.

CARDOONS.   Cardoons are thistles, belonging to the same botanical family as artichokes, although they have no flowers. The prickly leaves at the top and along the sides of the stems should be cut off and discarded. Cardoons are not very popular in the United States, although they grow very easily. They can be found in specialized stores but are sometimes huge by the time they reach those markets. When they are so large, the outer stems are often bitter and should be discarded. If you grow cardoons yourself, pick them when the stems are no taller than two feet, preferably much shorter.

Like artichokes, cardoons oxidate quickly. To prevent this, they are usually submerged in plain water, which also removes their slight bitterness, and the water changed after about 20 minutes. Before you submerge them, remove the stringy tips of the ribs with a knife held between thumb and index finger, starting from the bottom of the stalk.

Cardoons are usually boiled in water (cooking time depends on size), strained, and defuzzed by rubbing with a cloth. Then cut them into 2- or 3-inch pieces and cook either breaded and sautéed, or according to the recipes in this book.

CHARD.   Chard is also called Swiss chard (nobody knows why, as it did not originate in Switzerland), and the stems are usually cooked separately from the leaves. The leaves should be cooked like spinach. The stems can be steamed whole if they are small, or cooked like asparagus if they are large. They can be cut into bite-sized pieces and sautéed in oil or butter without any previous cooking, especially if they are fairly young and tender.

CHESTNUTS.   Chestnuts are usually boiled or roasted. To boil, remove the outer shells with a sharp knife, then put the chestnuts in a pot with twice their volume of water, and a little salt. Bring to a boil and cook for about 15 to 20 minutes, when they should be done. (Taste for doneness after about 15 minutes, to make sure.) Remove from heat, drain, and peel off the second skin. Discolored chestnuts or those that show signs of having been penetrated by an insect should be discarded. Tasting a small piece of a chestnut you are in doubt about should easily tell you whether it is good or bad.

There are no recipes calling for roasted chestnuts in the book, but if you wish to make them, you must first cut a long slit, crosswise, through the outer shell. This step is very important, as the chestnuts would otherwise explode while cooking. The best way to roast them is on an open fire. They can be put on a closely woven grill or in a special pot with holes, and should be shaken frequently, so that they roast evenly. They can also be placed directly in the embers, among the hot ashes. In this way they pick up a delicious smoky taste. Taste one for doneness after about 10 minutes, and gauge roasting time accordingly. If the fire is very hot, keep moving them, and taste them after about 5 minutes.

If an open fire is not available, they can be roasted under the broiler, at least 5 inches away from the source of heat. Shake the tray frequently to turn them as they cook.

CHICK-PEAS. See BEANS, DRIED.

EGGPLANT.   This strange name is used only in the United States. Actually it has become a misnomer, since the recent and more popular American strains are nearer the size of a football than that of an egg. In Europe, there are several varieties—one of them white, which may have inspired the American name—but these eggplants are much smaller and the skin thinner, making it more easily edible than the skin of American varieties. The advantage of the new larger strains is that all the bitterness has been removed, so that it is no longer necessary to use salt to draw out the bitterness and then rinse the eggplant, as some recipes still suggest.

The small, thinner-skinned varieties are available here in some specialized markets and are preferred for dishes that call for cooking the whole eggplant. If you can find them, or if you grow them yourself, do not peel these eggplants.

When eggplant is sautéed, it absorbs a considerable amount of oil during the first few minutes of frying. To cut down the amount of oil without losing the taste, slice and peel the eggplant, then pass the slices quickly under the broiler before frying. Eggplant tends to become mushy even after it has been removed from heat, so gauge doneness accordingly.

If only the cooked pulp is needed, bake the eggplant whole in a 450° oven until soft and wrinkled; then peel it.

FINOCCHIO or FLORENCE FENNEL. In the last few years this old European favorite has become popular in the United States and is now frequently found even in supermarkets.

To use in salads, wash it, then cut off a thin slice from the bottom of the "bulb." Remove one or two of the outer sections, including the hollow stems attached to them. Slice thinly, starting from the bottom; do not discard the feathery part, which is very tasty. The toughest portions of the hollow stems may have to be discarded, but the tender stems can be used.

To prepare it for cooking, remove two or more outer sections, slice off the bottom, and cut off the stems, keeping only the bulbous part of the vegetable. According to size, finocchio is then left whole or halved or quartered before cooking.

JERUSALEM ARTICHOKES. As most people know, this is not an artichoke, though it has a similar taste, nor does it come from Jerusalem. Although the word Jerusalem may be a transliteration of the Italian *girasole,* which means sunflower, in Italy this tuber is called either *carciofo di Giudea* (artichoke from Judea) or *topinambour,* from the French. *Girasole,* the sunflower, has a root that nobody would dream of eating. The Jerusalem artichoke seems to have originated in Canada, and in England it is called Canadian potato. Whatever its name, it is an excellent vegetable, strangely more popular in Europe than in America.

Because the American varieties are much more knobby than the European ones, take great care in washing this vegetable. The grit often hides at the base of the bumpy parts, but soaking briefly in cold water loosens some of it. Then use a stiff brush under running water to remove any residual dirt.

Jerusalem artichokes are steamed or boiled until barely tender and are much easier to peel after they are cooked. Make sure not to overcook, because they lose both taste and consistency. If you use them raw in salads, however, they must be peeled first.

KOHLRABI.   Unless this vegetable is very young and small, it must be peeled. It is easier to peel after having been either steamed or boiled. The leaves are also edible.

LEEKS.   For those who are preparing leeks for the first time, a word of caution about washing. Almost invariably, leeks hide dirt inside, and this is impossible to detect. Slice them first, and check for grit as you slice. Chances are you will soon see the internal mud appear. Rinse the cut portions that need it in cold water, preferably by quickly submerging a strainer full of the vegetable into a bowl. There is almost no other way to remove dirt from leeks.

Both the root and the top of the green portion should be discarded.

LENTILS. See BEANS, DRIED.   However, the presoaking period can be shorter, just two or three hours. The small red lentils (also called Egyptian lentils) do not require presoaking.

MUSHROOMS.   Wild mushrooms (uncultivated) are very common in Europe and are available in the markets, fresh in the summer and fall, dried at other times. Because wild mushrooms are infinitely tastier than the cultivated kind and have a different texture, they should be used, if at all possible, in the mushroom recipes in this book, either fresh or dried. In the dishes that really require this special taste, "imported dried mushrooms" are listed in the ingredients. Avoid dried "cultivated" mushrooms, which are a very poor substitute even for fresh cultivated mushrooms. When the recipe simply calls for "mushrooms," use the common cultivated fresh type, unless you are lucky enough to have fresh wild mushrooms at hand; in the United States, they are hard to come by.

When rehydrating dried mushrooms, take special care to get rid of all the grit without at the same time losing any of the flavor. The best way is to rinse them quickly under cold running water, in a sieve, then put them in a small pot with just enough water to cover, and slowly bring to a boil. Cover the pot tightly, switch off the heat, and allow the mushrooms to swell up for about thirty minutes. Place a piece of cheesecloth, folded three times, in a sieve, and strain the mushrooms, reserving the liquid, which you can add to the mushrooms when you cook them or use in other dishes. Because the dried pieces are usually very uneven in size, cut the larger pieces with a sharp knife after soaking but before cooking them.

PEAS, DRIED. See BEANS, DRIED. Handle the same way. If the peas are small, presoaking time can be shortened to two or three hours. For any size of dried peas, always soak in cold water, unless you are cooking them for purée or similar further treatment.

SPINACH. Spinach and similar leafy vegetables need to be washed very thoroughly, as the curly leaves hide a considerable amount of dirt. The best way is by submersion. Cut off a bit of the stem, remove any yellowed or browned portion of leaves, and put the vegetable in a large strainer or colander. Fill the sink or a large bowl with cold water, and slosh the sieve up and down in it. Lift the sieve and drain the water from the sink or bowl, rinsing the dirt from the bottom. Refill and repeat at least one more time, or until you no longer find any grit at the bottom of the basin. Drain well, shaking the sieve to remove most of the water. Put the spinach in a large skillet, uncovered, and cook without adding any more liquid, turning the leaves several times until all are wilted.

If you are cooking the spinach as a side dish, after it has wilted check the amount of water left at the bottom, draining some if there is still too much; then continue to cook, uncovered, either without adding anything except perhaps a little salt, or by sautéing quickly in either oil or butter over fairly high heat, adding salt, pepper, and nutmeg, and shaking or stirring the spinach often in the pan.

If you need the spinach for another type of dish, strain it when wilted, then squeeze it gently against the colander. If the dish requires it to be even drier, squeeze the "ball" of spinach between your hands as soon as it is cool enough to handle.

Of course, all liquid should be saved and used in other dishes. It is very nourishing.

SQUASH BLOSSOMS. Squash blossoms are not easy to find in markets here, but so many people now grow their own vegetables that this treat is not difficult to come by. Since you will probably have to pick your own squash blossoms, choose only the males, which are easily recognizable because they are elongated on thin stems while the female blossoms are rounder. Obviously, if you eat the female blossoms, you will have no mature squash to eat later on. In Europe squash blossoms are sold in the markets during late spring and summer. Since they are a delicacy, and a bonus for anybody who grows squash, they are strongly recommended.

Squash blossoms are rather perishable. They bruise and wilt easily, and this must be the main reason why they are not usually sold in markets here.

Plan to pick them either in the early morning or late afternoon. If they are not to be prepared for a few hours, put them in a shallow dish with some water at the bottom, sprinkle some more water on them, and cover with plastic wrap, suspended so that it does not touch them. Before cooking, rinse them gently, by submersion, and drain them on a cloth rather than in a sieve.

The stamens, inside the flowers, should not be removed, as they have a taste reminiscent of shellfish. For this reason, and because their shape and color resemble goldfish, in Europe squash blossoms are sometimes called "little fish."

TOMATOES. Tomatoes can be peeled very easily if they are plunged very briefly in boiling water, then immediately removed to a bowl filled with ice water. Start peeling at once.

Other Foods and Ingredients

BREAD. The absence of a bread-baking section in this book reflects European habits that go back to ancient Greece, where the first guild of professional bakers was formed. The ancient Greeks were master bakers, both for bread and pastry, and their art, through the Romans—who at first hired Greek bakers and later became experts themselves—gradually spread throughout Europe. Even the tiniest village in Europe has a bakery shop. Professional baking ovens are very large, are made with special materials designed to retain the right amount of heat and distribute it evenly, and can achieve higher temperatures than home ovens. The result, therefore, is completely different from home-baked breads, and cannot be duplicated at home. I am, of course, talking about the kinds of breads that are very crusty outside and fluffy inside.

The American habit of baking bread at home was necessitated by the vastness of this country, the distances between settlements, and by the constant migration of the first European settlers from east to west. Because so many of the early settlers were English, the English way of baking bread, like many other culinary habits, was adopted, and these breads are easier to duplicate at home. In pioneer conditions, Old World habits had to be abandoned, and the home, rather than the village or town, became the center of daily life. The kitchens were provided with large ovens in which bread and pastries could be baked.

Today's society, predominantly urban, relies on external sources for its daily existence. But the homes of the settlers were self-sufficient units where all the most important needs of the household could be satisfied. Bread baking at home became the proud symbol of a good housewife, and to this day is considered a sign of a good homemaker.

Recently the habit of baking bread at home has attained new momentum—rightly so, considering the adulteration and depletion in commercial breads—and dozens of books on baking bread have been published. The reader who wishes to bake European breads at home can consult those books, but the results are bound to fall short of professionally baked European breads for many reasons, especially because the size of today's home ovens has shrunk considerably.

While the following comments may seem superfluous in a book that does not deal with bread baking at home, it might be interesting and perhaps useful to home-baking enthusiasts to know that the addition of sugar or any sweetener is unnecessary, as is amply proved by what is known here as French bread. Sweeteners are mild leavening agents, but the reason they are usually added to bread in this country is that they quicken the action of the yeast. If you are willing to wait longer—up to twice the time—for some doughs to rise, you can accomplish the same results without sweeteners, with benefit to your health and palate.

To Europeans, American breads, aside from their rubbery, crustless texture which is considered uninviting, taste like cake because of their sweetness. Bread should complement the taste of the foods eaten with it, and the European palate finds even the slightest sweetness distracting.

Because the addition of sweeteners shortens the leavening process, commercial bakers took advantage of this profit bonus which was unfortunately also made easier by the American penchant for sweet foods.

With very few exceptions, therefore, even the most reputable American books about baking European breads almost invariably list sugar or other sweeteners, and this unauthentic infiltration is still followed by home bakers. Even in health food stores it is very difficult, if not impossible, to find breads that do not contain any sweetener.

I can only hope that the advice to omit sweeteners in bread baking will find some adherents. If you bake bread at home regularly, try at least to reduce the amount of sweeteners gradually each time you bake until you reach a minimum amount. You may be surprised at the good results you can obtain even by completely omitting any sweetener.

BUTTER. In this book butter means unsalted butter, unless specified otherwise. I suggest using butter rather than margarine because the original recipes called for it and because, in spite of the propaganda to the contrary, nothing else tastes like butter. Another reason for not substituting margarine is that the chemical substances added to it in abundance to make it look and taste like butter and to preserve it are quite harmful. However, whenever it seemed feasible, I have cut down the original amount of butter. People who are concerned about cholesterol levels should realize that, when there is zero intake of meat or fish, one can be more lenient with dairy products.

Because in Europe people eat their bread plain rather than buttering it—with the exception of the English, who taught the butter habit to the Americans—the total intake of butter is substantially less than it would be in the United States. If you serve tasty, crunchy breads with your meals, there is no need to butter them; in fact, you may find that a good, fresh bread tastes much better without, so try to eliminate this superfluous intake of fats, and use butter only for cooking.

FLOUR. Because of the substantial devitalization that results from processing wheat into white flour, many people are now returning to whole-wheat flour, which can easily be found either in regular markets or in health food stores, and others prefer to grind their own flour at home. Both the quality of whole-wheat flour and the type of grinding vary considerably from brand to brand, and at this writing there is no standardization of this product. For these reasons, I do not specify the amounts or proportions in which whole-wheat flour could be used, if one opts for it over the regular flour. White flour was originally intended for the majority of these recipes; if you wish to substitute whole-wheat flour, experimentation will be the best guide.

If whole-wheat flour does not seem appropriate, always use unbleached flour rather than the lily-white powder ("enriched" or not). The addition of bran flour and/or wheat germ to unbleached flour can reinstate the most important nutrients that have been taken out while processing it, if the particular dish allows it. For baking purposes, it is best to experiment with a mixture of whole-wheat flour and white flour until you find proportions that give good results.

For sauces, whole-wheat flour does not have the binding properties of white flour, aside from the fact that in delicate or light-colored sauces the dark specks and coarser texture would ruin the appearance. But there is no rule that states you have to have *all* your nutrients in the same dish. People who are very exacting about daily nourishment can add bran or wheat germ to such other dishes as stews, soups, or casseroles, or serve these at other meals, and still use white flour whenever it seems more appropriate.

and summer, then bring the plants indoors when the weather turns cool, you will be able to use these herbs throughout the winter. In the spring, if the plant is still vigorous, put it out in the sun, then bring it in again at the end of the summer.

Experiment with a few basic herbs. You may be surprised by the ease with which they grow, and you will almost always have fresh herbs. Even if they become a bit leggy and don't do too well, it is still rewarding to have your little herb garden in the winter months.

Appetizers

RAW VEGETABLES
Crudités

This classic French medley can be made in any season, but must be prepared with fresh, top-quality vegetables. Of course, the fare will change according to the season. A minimum of five or six vegetables should be served as an appetizer, a side dish, or a main dish, and for this reason no quantities or servings are indicated. Prepare approximately the same amount of each vegetable.

The word *crudités* means raw foods, and that is exactly what these are. Occasionally, an exception may be made, as for asparagus or green beans (although very young and tender green beans may be served raw). Peas are usually excluded because of their small size, as the vegetables are cut into bite-sized pieces. Although the sauce is served separately and each person dips the vegetable pieces in it, certain vegetables, such as artichokes, should be dipped briefly in lemon juice and water (about half and half), to prevent oxidation. If you can obtain very young, small, tender artichokes, preferably at the beginning of the season, they are delicious raw, but you might prefer to slice them thinly lengthwise instead of just quartering them, to make chewing them easier. Or you may steam them very briefly, and allow to cool. Celery, carrots, and other long vegetables may be cut into strips about ½ inch thick, rather than cubed. A variety of tastes is of the essence, but these should not clash (as, for example, tomatoes and beets do). Raw beets or turnips should be sliced thin rather than cubed. Tomatoes should be red but firm, not too ripe. They should be quartered, sprinkled with salt, and allowed to drain for about ½ hour before serving.

The choice of vegetables is up to you, and to the season. Try to combine a contrast of color as well as tastes.

The classic sauce used to dip crudités is Vinaigrette, but you may want to choose another cold sauce such as Cold Green Sauce, Italian or French Garlic Sauce, or Green Mayonnaise (see index).

VEGETABLES ORIENTAL STYLE
Légumes à l'Orientale

Although this is a French dish, its origin is specified in the title. It is uncertain when or how the French adopted (and perhaps adapted) it, or even what is meant by *"orientale."* It may have been invented in France. But whatever its origin, it is an excellent dish and well known throughout France. Here I am inspired by Richard Olney, whose version simply cannot be improved upon.

This can be served either as a first or as a main course. Some of the vegetables, of course, vary according to the season. In the summer, finocchio can be replaced by celery, parsley by fresh basil, and so on.

Practically any non-leafy vegetable can be used; the variations are infinite. In the spring you can add asparagus tips; in the summer small zucchini; in the fall cauliflower or broccoli; in the winter chard ribs.

> *1 large sweet onion (4 to 5 ounces), chopped*
> *1 cup olive oil (in all)*

2 cups preserved tomatoes, juice drained off
4 large garlic cloves, crushed, peeled, finely sliced
Salt
1 healthy pinch cayenne
1 teaspoon sugar
1 mounded teaspoon finely crumbled mixed herbs
  (thyme, savory, oregano)
1 bay leaf
4 tender artichokes (2 pounds), pared, quartered,
  chokes removed, immersed immediately in
  remaining ¾ cup olive oil
1 ounce dried currants (or other seedless raisins),
  soaked 1 hour in tepid water, drained
8 ounces small garnish onions (25 or 30), peeled
8 ounces whites of leeks, cut into 2-inch lengths
1 pound hearts of fennel bulbs, trimmed, quartered
10 ounces firm, unopened mushrooms (whole, halved,
  or quartered, depending on size)
2 cups dry white wine
1 large pinch coriander seeds (about 30)
Juice of 1 lemon
About 20 peppercorns
Chopped parsley

"Cook the chopped onion with ¼ cup olive oil in a large, heavy copper saucepan or earthenware *poëlon* for from 20 to 30 minutes without permitting to color, add the tomatoes and the garlic, stew gently for about 10 minutes, stirring, until nearly all liquid has evaporated, salt lightly, add the cayenne, the sugar, the herbs, and the artichoke quarters with their olive oil. Stir well together, add the raisins or currants and, a handful at a time, the remaining vegetables, stirring so that all are evenly coated with the tomato mixture. Add the wine, the coriander, and the lemon juice, bring to a full boil over a high flame, reduce the heat, and simmer, covered, for about 40 minutes (the acidity of the cooking liquids prevents the vegetables from softening—they will remain firm and even slightly crunchy despite the length of cooking time).

"Remove the vegetables with a large wire skimming spoon to a non-metallic serving utensil, add the peppercorns to the cooking juices, and reduce at a high heat for 5 to 10 minutes, stirring all the while. About 1½ cups—or slightly more—should remain, just enough to barely cover the gently packed vegetables. Taste for salt (the vegetables will be somewhat undersalted if correctly done and the sauce should be relatively salty—without exaggeration). Leave, uncovered, to cool and then refrigerate, covered. Serve either chilled or at room temperature, generously sprinkled with parsley."

Serves 8.

MARINATED BEETS

1 pound beets, fresh or canned
3 tablespoons olive oil
2 tablespoons wine vinegar
1 teaspoon fresh tarragon leaves (or ½ teaspoon
   dried tarragon)
½ teaspoon onion powder
½ teaspoon dried thyme
salt and pepper

Boil the fresh beets (see page 14), or drain the canned beets, reserving the liquid in either case. Slice them. In a bowl, whip the rest of the ingredients into a dressing. Add the beets, mix thoroughly, put in a jar, and pour in enough of the reserved liquid to reach the top. Seal, and shake well, then reopen and adjust taste. If too much of the liquid must be used to reach top of the jar, more salt and vinegar may have to be added. Seal again and marinate at least 24 hours in the refrigerator, but remove about one hour before serving. Drain, and serve at room temperature.

Sealed in a jar, and covered with their liquid, these will keep for at least 2 or 3 weeks in the refrigerator.

Serves 4.

MARINATED ZUCCHINI

4 medium-sized zucchini
4 tablespoons olive oil
1 clove garlic, left whole
salt and pepper
½ teaspoon fresh dill (or ¼ teaspoon dried)
3 tablespoons wine vinegar (approximately)

Slice the zucchini in thin rounds, and fry in the oil, with the garlic clove. If the garlic becomes too dark while frying the zucchini, remove it; otherwise, discard it after frying. Keep stirring and flipping the zucchini, removing them as soon as they turn a light golden color. Put them in a bowl, sprinkle salt, pepper, and dill on them, and add the vinegar a little at a time, tossing them gently. They should be just moistened in the vinegar, not drenched. Taste one and add a little more vinegar if necessary. Cover the bowl, and let rest at least 4 hours before serving. They marinate better if not refrigerated, but choose a fairly cool place. They are even better the following day. In a sealed jar, in the refrigerator, they will keep for about 2 weeks.

Serves 4.

CELERIAC IN SOUR SAUCE

A variation of the French celeriac in Vinaigrette Sauce.

1 pound celeriac
4 tablespoons olive oil
2 tablespoons lemon juice
salt and white pepper
2 tablespoons yogurt

Scrub or peel the celeriac and cut it in long, thin strips. In a bowl, whip oil, lemon, salt, and pepper together, then mix in the yogurt. Coat the celeriac well with the dressing, and marinate at least one hour at room temperature before serving.

Serves 4.

ONIONS IN SWEET-AND-SOUR SAUCE
Cipolline in Agrodolce

Sweet and sour (*agrodolce*) is one of the oldest taste combinations in Italian cooking. In fact, it goes back to ancient Roman times, and onions in agrodolce is a very old, classic Italian recipe.

> *16 to 20 small white onions (number depending on size)*
> *2 tablespoons olive oil*
> *1 tablespoon butter*
> *1 medium-sized onion, chopped fine*
> *1 clove garlic, minced*
> *2 tablespoons dry or sweet white wine*
> *1 tablespoon honey*
> *dash of powdered coriander*
> *water*
> *white wine vinegar*

Arrange the peeled onions in one layer in a fairly large saucepan where they will fit snugly. Add oil, butter, chopped onion, and garlic, then pour the wine all over, and blanch the onions. Add the honey and coriander, then barely cover the onions with a mixture of water and vinegar (half and half). Cover tightly, and simmer until the liquid is considerably reduced and the onions are cooked. The sauce should be thin but not runny.

Serves 4.

BELL PEPPERS

Interesting dishes can be made with peppers of any color—red, yellow, or green—provided they are very fresh. Most of these dishes are quite simple and quick, and can be served as an appetizer, a first course, or one of the tidbits in a buffet-type meal. In the summer, peppers can be grilled outdoors.

Quantities and servings are not specified, because they depend on how you are going to use the peppers. A good rule of thumb is to serve 1 medium-large pepper per person as an appetizer, 1½ or 2 for a more substantial course.

FRIED PEPPERS. Seed and core the peppers, cut them into fairly wide strips, and dip them in deep, very hot olive oil for 3 or 4 minutes. Remove them, shaking off the excess oil, sprinkle with salt, and serve.

PEPPERS WITH CAPERS AND OLIVES. Follow the preceding recipe, but fry only 2 minutes. Drain, pour off most of the oil, and return the peppers to the skillet. For every 3 peppers, add 1 clove garlic, lightly pressed, 2 tablespoons capers, and 1 tablespoon green olives, coarsely chopped. Pan-fry until peppers are done but still chewy. Sprinkle with salt and pepper, remove from heat, and sprinkle about ½ tablespoon chopped parsley on top.

ROASTED PEPPERS. Roast the peppers whole, on a grill or in a very hot oven, until the skin has blackened. Some people don't mind the burned taste of the pepper skin, in which case roasting peppers is even simpler, since you can serve them unpeeled. Otherwise, as soon as you remove them from the grill or oven, wrap the peppers in heavy paper (or put in a clean paper bag) and allow to cool; this will simplify peeling them. Peel with a small paring knife or with your fingers, dipping the knife or fingers in cold water frequently. Cut into strips and remove seeds and membranes. Season with olive oil, salt, and pepper and add chopped fresh parsley or fresh basil, if you wish.

COLD STUFFED PEPPERS
Pepper Zakuski

In Russian *zakuski* means appetizer. A habit imported from the Scandinavian countries, various types of zakuski, hot or cold, precede the main meal, accompanied by a glass of vodka. Here is a sample.

> *4 medium-sized green peppers*
> *½ cup oil*
> *¼ teaspoon mustard seeds*
> *1 large onion, chopped*
> *3 medium-sized carrots, shredded*
> *2 stalks celery, chopped*
> *½ cup thick Tomato Sauce (see index)*
> *½ teaspoon salt*
> *pepper*
> *1 tablespoon sour cream*
> *½ cup water*

Cut off the pepper tops and remove seeds and membranes without disturbing the walls of the pepper.

For the stuffing, heat the oil in a skillet, and cook the mustard seeds just until heated. Add and sauté the onion, carrots, and celery. When done but still a bit chewy, add the Tomato Sauce, salt, and pepper and remove from heat. Stir in the sour cream.

Stuff the peppers with the mixture, then stand them in a saucepan. Pour the water into the bottom of the pan, cover, and simmer for about 20 minutes, or until cooked. (A little more hot water might be needed after about 15 minutes.)

Allow to cool, and serve at room temperature.

Serves 4.

DEVILED EGGS WITH CHERRY TOMATOES

If you plan to serve these eggs at a cocktail party or other type of large gathering allow 1½ eggs per person.

> *4 small cherry tomatoes*
> *4 large hard-cooked eggs, chilled*
> *1½ tablespoons mayonnaise*
> *½ teaspoon prepared mustard*
> *¼ teaspoon salt*
> *pinch of white pepper*
> *pinch of paprika*
> *few drops of Tabasco sauce (optional)*
> *capers for garnishing*

Cut the tomatoes exactly in half, across. Sprinkle the cut side with salt.

Shell the eggs and cut in half lengthwise. Scoop out the yolks and mix them with all the other ingredients except the tomatoes and the capers. Mash well with a fork to make a smooth paste. Refill the egg whites gently, making a slight mound, which you push down slightly in the center to level it a bit. Press in the tomato halves, round side up, then surround them with capers, also slightly pressed down into the filling. Or put 2 or 3 capers on each side of the tomato along the length of the egg.

Serves 4.

EGG-FILLED TOMATOES

4 medium-sized ripe tomatoes, round and of similar size
salt
2 eggs
2 tablespoons heavy cream
1 tablespoon chopped parsley
1 teaspoon fresh basil, chopped (or ½ teaspoon dried)
2 teaspoons grated Romano or Parmesan cheese
1 finely chopped chive
olive oil

Cut tomatoes in half, horizontally. With a small knife, spoon, or your fingers, remove the seeds and central pulp. Reserve. Sprinkle the cavity with salt, upturn each tomato half, and put on a plate for about 30 minutes, to release most of the watery liquid. Strain the pulp, and discard the seeds.

Preheat oven to 325°. Beat the eggs with the tomato pulp and all the other ingredients except the oil. Pour the mixture into the tomato halves.

Grease a baking dish large enough to accommodate the tomatoes fairly snugly. Dribble some olive oil on top of each stuffed tomato. Bake for 15 or 20 minutes, or until the eggs have set. The tomatoes should be barely softened. Serve warm, or let cool. This is good either as an appetizer or a luncheon dish.

Serves 4.

MELTED CHEESE CANAPÉS

The simplest canapés to serve at a cocktail party or to precede a dinner.

4 slices dark bread, lightly toasted
4 slices semi-soft cheese (two different
varieties may be used)
ketchup, capers, or prepared mustard

Preheat oven to 425°. Cut the bread slices into four equal pieces and cover each piece with a slice of cheese, cut slightly smaller than the bread pieces, so that it will not overflow while melting. Dot the center of each canapé with a tiny blob of ketchup or mustard or with 1 caper.

Heat for 5 minutes, preferably in an oven-proof platter, to simplify serving.

Serves 4.

GOAT CHEESE AND HERB SPREAD

This tasty appetizer comes from Rumania.

½ pound feta cheese (or similar goat's milk or
sheep's milk cheese)
6 tablespoons butter, at warm room temperature
3 tablespoons chopped parsley
1 teaspoon powdered or crushed fennel
(not fennel seeds) or dill
1 teaspoon paprika
1 teaspoon caraway seeds
15 black olives (Greek type)
15 medium-sized red radishes
4 or 5 scallions
2 medium-sized tomatoes

Drain the cheese if it has been preserved in salted water. Put it in a bowl. Add the softened butter and mix with a fork very thoroughly, then add the herbs and spices.

Pit the olives, trim the radishes, slice the scallions, and cut the tomatoes in small wedges. Arrange the cheese paste on a platter, with olives, tomatoes, scallions, and radishes on top and around it.

Serve at room temperature.

Serves 4 to 6.

GORGONZOLA SPREAD

This spread can become a dip by adding more yogurt or a little milk. It can also be used as stuffing for whole celery stalks or scooped-out tomatoes (small size, or even cherry tomatoes) by increasing the amount of cream cheese and ricotta. The proportions in this recipe may have to be adjusted as you prepare it, because both taste and consistency of the various cheeses and yogurt vary.

> *2 tablespoons Gorgonzola, Roquefort, or blue cheese*
> *4 tablespoons yogurt*
> *2 tablespoons cream cheese*
> *2 tablespoons ricotta*
> *¼ teaspoon dry mustard*
> *1 tablespoon brandy (optional)*
> *paprika (for stuffed celery stalks)*

With a fork, mix the Gorgonzola or similar cheese with a little yogurt, adding more yogurt as the paste blends. In a separate bowl, work the cream cheese with yogurt in a similar way, reserving a tablespoon or so of yogurt. Mix in the ricotta. Whip the reserved yogurt with the mustard, and thoroughly mix everything together, brandy (if used) last. If you prefer to use a blender, crumble the cheese first.

Celery stalks stuffed with this spread will look very attractive sprinkled with paprika.

Serves 4.

CHICK-PEAS AND SESAME PASTE
Húmmus Mé Tahíni

A Middle Eastern specialty. If sesame seed paste (*tahíni*) is unavailable where you live, crush sesame seeds very fine and allow to stand for 2 days covered and at room temperature, then add to the recipe, together with whatever oil the crushing may have released. Although not the real thing, this is a reasonable approximation.

1½ cups chick-peas, dried or canned
4 tablespoons lemon juice
2 cloves garlic
4 tablespoons olive oil
liquid from the chick-peas
2 tablespoons chopped parsley
½ teaspoon ground coriander
½ teaspoon salt
¼ teaspoon ground pepper
4 teaspoons sesame paste
½ teaspoon paprika
additional chopped parsley

Soak dried chick-peas and cook very well (see Beans, Dried, page 13), or use canned chick-peas. For this recipe they should be overcooked. Drain, reserving the liquid. Put chick-peas and ½ cup of their liquid in the blender, and mash. Blend with the other ingredients, except the sesame paste, the paprika, and the additional parsley. In a small bowl, mix the sesame paste with a little more of the chick-pea liquid, add it to the blender, and mix very briefly.

Serve sprinkled with the paprika and the additional parsley, and provide crackers, toast, or pitta (Middle Eastern bread) to scoop out the mixture. In a covered jar, this keeps in the refrigerator for at least 2 weeks.

Serves 4 to 6.

CUCUMBER DIP
Tsatsíki

Variations of *tsatsíki* are to be found in many Middle Eastern and Balkan countries. This is the Greek recipe. It can be used as a salad dressing (you may have to thin it with milk), a sauce for vegetables, or a spread. In Greece it is often served in a bowl, at the table, so that each person may spread it on bread or add it to the other dishes served.

> 2½ *cups yogurt*
> 2 *small cloves garlic, crushed*
> 3 *tablespoons olive oil*
> 1 *tablespoon wine vinegar*
> 1 *tablespoon chopped fresh dill* (*or* 2 *teaspoons dried*)
> 2 *teaspoons chopped fresh mint* (*or* 1 *teaspoon dried*)
> *salt and white pepper*
> 1½ *medium-sized cucumbers, peeled and chopped*

Mix all ingredients except cucumber, whipping them with a fork or whip. Add the cucumber, and mix well. Refrigerate for a few hours before serving, to allow the cucumber to marinate.

This dip can be made thicker by using yogurt which was strained through a folded cheesecloth for about 1 hour, to remove some of the whey (which can be used in other dishes). It can also be made in a blender, by adding all ingredients at once and blending at medium speed for just 1 minute. It will keep for at least 2 weeks in the refrigerator.

Serves 4.

GREEK EGGPLANT APPETIZER

Melitsanosaláta

Practically every Middle Eastern country has its own version of this cold eggplant dish, usually served as an appetizer. It is geographically natural that Greece, bordering on the Middle East, would also have one of its own. This is the Greek recipe, but the ingredients vary little in other versions. Sesame seed oil is often substituted for olive oil outside of Greece, and spices are sometimes added.

2 medium-sized eggplants (about 3 pounds)
3 medium-sized tomatoes, peeled and coarsely chopped
  (if canned, drained)
3 cloves garlic
3 tablespoons chopped parsley
½ teaspoon oregano
1 teaspoon fresh mint, chopped (or ½ teaspoon dried)
1 teaspoon salt
¼ teaspoon pepper
3 tablespoons olive oil (approximately)
5 tablespoons lemon juice or wine vinegar

Cook the eggplants in their skins (see page 17). Peel them or scoop out the pulp. Mix the pulp with the tomatoes, garlic, herbs, salt, and pepper. Put into blender (if too large an amount, mix well and divide in half). Add the oil a little at a time, blending at low speed. Then add the lemon juice or vinegar, and switch to a higher speed for a few seconds until mixture is smooth.

The consistency should be that of a thick dip or a spread. Serve with pitta (Middle Eastern bread), crackers, or small pieces of toast, and lemon wedges. This can also be used as a sandwich spread.

In a well-sealed jar, with a little olive oil on top, this appetizer will keep in the refrigerator for several weeks.

Serves 4.

SICILIAN EGGPLANT APPETIZER
Caponatina

An old reliable classic. The authentic original *caponatina* was made with the addition of chocolate, which I consider an abomination. Here is a more recent version. Some recipes omit the tomato sauce but substitute a little water; other recipes call for a thinly sliced onion to be sautéed with the celery.

> *3 medium-sized eggplants*
> *olive oil*
> *4 or 5 small celery stalks, from the heart, diced*
> *4 tablespoons Tomato Sauce (see index)*
> *4 tablespoons wine vinegar*
> *½ teaspoon honey*
> *4 or 5 green olives, pitted and halved*
> *4 or 5 black olives (Sicilian or Greek type),*
> * pitted and halved*
> *4 tablespoons capers*
> *1 tablespoon pine nuts*
> *½ teaspoon pepper*
> *salt (optional)*

Cube the eggplants without peeling them, and fry in olive oil in a skillet. In another skillet, fry the celery in olive oil until it begins to brown, then add it to the eggplant. Pour the Tomato Sauce into the empty skillet and mix in the vinegar, honey, olives, capers, and pine nuts, stirring. As soon as they are blended, pour over eggplant, add pepper and salt, and simmer for about 10 minutes. If needed, add a little water or red wine, but only if the sauce is too thick. Stir often. Allow to cool before serving.

Sealed in a jar, caponatina will keep a long time in the refrigerator.

Serves 4.

LENTIL "PÂTÉ"

The recipe for this appetizer comes from England. The "pâté" should be served on a leaf of lettuce, on individual plates, with a slice of lemon for each person to squeeze onto the "pâté," and a few pieces of dark-bread toast.

In the summer, it can be served as a cold main course.

1½ cups lentils
1 bay leaf
vegetable broth or water
2 eggs, lightly beaten
1 cup chopped onions
3 tablespoons butter
1 clove garlic, minced
2 medium-sized tomatoes, peeled (if canned, drain),
 coarsely chopped
1 cup grated hard cheese
4 tablespoons chopped parsley
¼ teaspoon dried basil
¼ teaspoon paprika
pinch of nutmeg
pinch of turmeric
pinch of powdered cumin
1 teaspoon salt
¼ teaspoon pepper
1 cup breadcrumbs, plus additional breadcrumbs

Simmer the lentils with the bay leaf in just enough broth or water to cover. Stir a few times while they cook to make sure they don't stick to the bottom. A little more hot broth or hot water may be needed, but after about 40 minutes, all the liquid should be absorbed and the lentils cooked. Taste them to be sure. Allow to cool for a while, then add the eggs, and mix.

Preheat the oven to 375°. Sauté the onions in the butter, and add the garlic when the onions are half done. Add to the lentils, together with all the other ingredients including 1 cup of the breadcrumbs, and mix thoroughly.

Grease a square or rectangular baking dish about 3 inches deep, sprinkle with additional breadcrumbs all around, fill with the lentil mixture, and bake at 375° for about 1 hour, or until a knife inserted into the pâté comes out clean.

Allow to cool about 10 minutes, then unmold onto a platter.

Serves 4.

Soups

The preparation of a tasty soup does not require the use of meat, chicken, or fish, as the recipes in this section amply prove. Aside from the selection given here, experiment on your own with soup recipes you already have, using one of the basic vegetable broths suggested in this section instead of a beef or chicken broth.

If you have been meaning to invent a few dishes of your own but never dared, soups are an excellent testing ground. Within certain limits—which you will soon figure out by trial and error—practically anything can be thrown into a soup: leftovers from stews, casseroles, or other vegetable dishes; mushrooms that are beginning to wilt; milk that just started to turn sour; and so on.

And, when you prepare other dishes, remember the soup, and fill a plastic bag with peels or portions of vegetables to be used in soups or broths. For example, when a recipe calls for peeled potatoes, scrub the unpeeled potatoes well, peel them, and put the peels in the bag. The hard core of a cabbage or cauliflower, the tougher stems or stem portions of broccoli or asparagus, the outer leaves of artichokes, and many parts of other vegetables can be put in the "soup bag." Keep the bag in the refrigerator for a few days, until enough scraps are collected. You can then make a separate broth by gently boiling the scraps in water until about half the liquid is absorbed. Strain the broth, and add it to whatever soup or broth you are preparing. If you prefer, gather all your vegetable odds and ends into a muslin bag, or make a bag with two or three layers of cheesecloth, tightly tied. Boil the bag right in the soup or broth you are making and remove it before serving. An amazing variety of interesting tastes can be produced in this way.

Some of the soups in this section can be a meal in themselves, perhaps followed by a salad.

In the summer, if a hot soup is not desired, gently reheat, covered, whatever soup you previously made, stirring once in a while to mix the different temperatures in the pot, until the soup is barely lukewarm. You'd be surprised how good many soups taste at this temperature. "Cold" minestrone was one of my father's favorites. Of course, by "cold" I mean at room temperature, or barely heated.

VEGETABLE BROTH I

This is a basic recipe, given in a fairly large quantity because it can be used repeatedly. Refrigerated, this broth keeps for at least 2 weeks; omitting the oil and the first step of sautéing, it can be frozen. The oil can be added when you reheat it.

It is an excellent base for soups, stews, and other dishes. You can make a purée with the vegetables, to be used as a pie filling or in a soufflé, or added to other dishes, especially those that need a boost in taste. For more delicate-tasting dishes, or if you need a clear broth as a base, you might prefer the following recipe for Vegetable Broth II.

> *3 medium-sized onions, chopped*
> *½ cup chopped celery*
> *1 cup chopped carrots*
> *2 leeks, or 5 or 6 scallions, chopped*
> *4 tablespoons chopped parsley*
> *4 tablespoons oil*
> *5½ quarts water*

6 or 7 walnuts, finely minced
3 cloves
1 tablespoon peppercorns
½ cup beans, presoaked if dried
½ cup lentils, presoaked
1 small cabbage, shredded (the core can be added)
½ teaspoon thyme or marjoram
salt to taste
1 tablespoon soy sauce

In a very large pot, sauté the onions, celery, carrots, leeks or scallions, and the parsley in the oil. When the onions are transparent, pour the water on the vegetables, adding the cloves and peppercorns. Then add the beans. Bring to a boil and simmer for 30 minutes. Add the lentils, cabbage, walnuts, and the thyme or marjoram, together with the salt (go easy with the salt, as this broth will become concentrated). Bring back to a boil, then lower the heat, and simmer until the liquid is reduced to about half its original amount. Strain the liquid and add the soy sauce.

If you are making a purée with the vegetables, remove the peppercorns and cloves.

VARIATION. Add 2 fresh tomatoes, chopped, or 1 tablespoon of tomato paste to the broth when you add the lentils and cabbage. At this point, you can also pour in some red wine.

VEGETABLE BROTH II

This is a lighter broth than the preceding one, more indicated for use in soups with delicate flavors, or in cream of vegetable soups.

3 quarts water
1 pound onions
½ pound carrots
½ pound turnips
1 medium-sized parsnip
4 stalks celery
½ pound potatoes (omit if you wish a clear broth)
2 leeks, or 4 or 5 scallions
1 teaspoon tomato paste
4 sprigs parsley, whole
1 bouquet garni (see below)
salt to taste

Bring the water to a boil, and while you wait, wash, trim, and cube the vegetables. Add all the other ingredients, and simmer for at least 1½ hours.

Remove the bouquet garni, and strain the broth through several layers of cheesecloth in the strainer.

Makes about 2 quarts of broth.

BOUQUET GARNI
1 teaspoon thyme
1 teaspoon oregano
½ teaspoon sage
½ teaspoon savory
1 bay leaf
1 teaspoon mustard seeds
6 peppercorns

All these herbs and spices are dried, not fresh. If you have any that are fresh, double the amount, and chop. Pack all in a small bag made of muslin or of several layers of cheesecloth and tie securely with string.

CEREAL BROTH

This broth is usually served plain and is a rather gentle dish which was originally recommended for "indisposed" people.

The cooked vegetables strained from the broth can be made into a purée and then into excellent croquettes or vegetable burgers. If the purée is not sufficiently dry, you may have to spread it onto a flat ovenproof dish or cookie sheet and dry it a little in a very low oven.

5 quarts water
½ cup barley
½ cup whole-wheat grains
½ cup rye grains
½ cup oats
½ cup cornmeal
½ cup brown rice
1½ cups diced carrots
1 cup diced celery
few sprigs fresh parsley
1 bay leaf
½ teaspoon thyme
¼ teaspoon nutmeg
2 tablespoons butter
1 tablespoon soy sauce
salt to taste

Bring the water to a boil, add all the ingredients except the butter and soy sauce, and simmer. When the liquid is reduced to less than half its original quantity, strain through a sieve lined with cheesecloth. Stir in the butter and soy sauce. Adjust salt if needed.

Makes about two quarts of broth.

CORSICAN VEGETABLE SOUP

Red beans have a different taste and texture from white, black, and other beans. There are several varieties of red beans to choose from in making this dish and any one will do.

> 2½ *quarts vegetable broth or water*
> 1½ *cups red beans (rehydrated if dried)*
> *3 large potatoes, peeled and cubed*
> *3 stalks celery, coarsely chopped*
> *1 clove garlic, sliced*
> *salt and pepper*
> *1 cup coarsely chopped fresh mushrooms*
> *3 tablespoons olive oil*
> *1 tablespoon fresh basil (or 1½ teaspoons dried)*
> *4 wide, long strips lasagne*
> *grated Romano cheese*

In a large pot, bring the broth or water to a boil with the beans, potatoes, celery, and garlic. Cook for about 1½ hours, adding salt and pepper after about 1 hour.

In a skillet, quickly sauté the mushrooms in the oil, then add to the soup, together with the basil. Bring to a boil, and add the lasagne, cut in large pieces; bring back to a boil, and simmer for an additional 20 minutes, or until the lasagne are cooked.

Serve hot, with the grated cheese on the side.

Serves 4.

GENOESE VEGETABLE SOUP

Minestrone alla Genovese

5 or 6 stalks and leaves chard
10 or 12 leaves spinach
1 cup large fresh beans (dried beans, rehydrated,
*   may be used)*
2 large potatoes, peeled and diced
1 small onion, coarsely chopped
½ small cabbage head, shredded
2 quarts water or broth
2 tablespoons olive oil
salt and pepper
1 cup rice
2 tablespoons Pesto Sauce (see index)
grated Parmesan cheese

Chop chard and spinach coarsely. Put all the vegetables in a pot. (If you use dried beans, cook them for about 40 minutes before adding to the other vegetables; the liquid in which they cooked can also be added.) Add the water or broth to the vegetables, bring to a boil, add oil and seasoning (but not the Pesto), cover, and simmer for about 45 minutes. Bring back to a full boil, add the rice, and cook for 15 minutes. Stir in the sauce, and continue to cook until the rice is tender, about 3 to 4 minutes longer.

Serve with grated Parmesan cheese.

Serves 4.

FRENCH VEGETABLE SOUP
Pistou Savoyard

This soup from the Savoy region on the Riviera is derived from Genoese Minestrone. The name *pistou* is derived from *pesto,* which in Italian means something that has been pounded, as in making the famous Genoese Pesto Sauce. In this recipe the two main ingredients in Pesto—garlic and basil—are still present, but in crossing the border, pistou has become a soup, rather than a pounded sauce.

1 medium-sized onion, chopped
3 cloves garlic, pressed or minced
4 tablespoons olive oil
4 large tomatoes, peeled, seeded, and coarsely chopped
1 medium-sized potato, peeled and diced
1 large leek, chopped
2 stalks celery, diced
1 cup chopped spinach or chard leaves
1 small zucchino, diced
1 cup fresh peas or diced green beans
1½ cups whole fresh small beans
5 cups water (approximately)
1 tablespoon fresh basil, chopped (or 2 teaspoons dried)
½ teaspoon thyme
salt
¼ teaspoon pepper
¼ pound spaghettini
1 cup grated Gruyère or Swiss cheese

In a large pot, sauté onion and garlic in the olive oil, then add the next eight ingredients and stir, adding a little of the water. Raise the heat, add the rest of the water and the basil, thyme, salt, and pepper, and bring to a boil. Simmer, covered, for 30 minutes.

Break the spaghettini into short lengths, and stir into the soup. Boil for about 10 minutes, or until the pasta is cooked but still firm. Add about half the cheese when you remove the soup from heat, and serve the rest on the side.

Serves 4.

SPANISH VEGETABLE SOUP

The actual origin of this soup is unclear. It may have been first made in South America, then found its way into Spain, and by now it is a dish often prepared at home in both parts of the world. It is a whole meal rather than just a soup.

> *1 small cabbage, quartered, core removed*
> *4 large potatoes, peeled*
> *4 medium-sized carrots, scraped*
> *4 medium-large onions, outer skin removed*
> *4 kohlrabis, peeled*
> *2 quarts vegetable broth*
> *2 ears fresh sweet corn, halved*
> *4 pieces of pumpkin (size to match the potatoes),*
>   *peeled and seeded*
> *½ cup rice*
> *2 tablespoons olive oil*
> *salt*

Simmer all the vegetables except the corn and pumpkin for about 15 minutes in the broth, bring to a boil, add corn, pumpkin, rice, and oil, adjust salt, and cook, covered, for about 18 minutes, or until the rice is tender, stirring a few times gently.

Divide the vegetables on individual plates, one of each vegetable per person. Serve the broth in cups on the side. Or you can strain most of the broth, pour it into individual bowls, and serve as a first course, followed by the vegetables which have been kept hot in the covered pot.

This dish can also be served in large individual bowls, together with all the broth, and eaten with fork and spoon.

Serves 4.

BEET SOUP

Borscht

There are many versions of this well-known Eastern European soup, the variations often depending on the particular country of origin. Mine is a Russian recipe, but borscht is made not only in Russia but in other European countries adjacent to its borders. This soup is sometimes served cold, especially in the summer.

> ½ *small red cabbage*
> 2 *medium-sized leeks (whites only) , or*
>   1 *medium-sized onion*
> 3 *medium-sized beets*
> 2 *quarts water or broth*
> 1 *medium-sized carrot*
> 2 *white celery stalks*
> 1 *small turnip*
> *salt and pepper (preferably white pepper)*
> 3 *tablespoons butter*
> 1 *cup sour cream, at room temperature*
> 2 *teaspoons dill*

Thinly shred the cabbage, chop the leeks or onion, and cut all the other vegetables into julienne (thin strips, about 1 inch long). Simmer the beets in the water or broth for 20 minutes and then add all the other vegetables except the cabbage, with the salt and pepper. Bring back to a boil, and simmer for another 20 minutes. Add the cabbage, bring to a boil again, and simmer for about 10 minutes, or until the cabbage is cooked but still firm. Remove from heat and stir in the butter.

Sour cream and dill are usually added at the table, individually, according to taste, and stirred into the soup.

Serves 4 to 6.

1 pound spinach, coarsely chopped
3 tablespoons yellow cornmeal
salt and pepper
grated Parmesan cheese

Heat the water or broth. In a large pot, sauté the garlic in the butter, then add the flour, stirring until blended. Add the spinach, and sauté for 5 or 6 minutes, turning the spinach often. Add the boiling water or broth, a little at a time at first, stirring vigorously, then in larger amounts, always stirring.

Cook for about 20 minutes, then mix the cornmeal with a little cold water, and add to the pot, stirring. Add salt and pepper, and continue to cook, stirring almost constantly, for another 20 minutes.

Serve the soup with grated cheese on top.

Serves 4.

GREEN SOUP

Caldo Verde

This is a delicious Portuguese soup. It is much tastier made with kale, but if kale is unavailable, spinach or chard makes a good substitute.

1 medium-sized onion, chopped
4 tablespoons olive oil
5 cups water
3 medium-sized potatoes, peeled and cubed
1 pound tender fresh kale
2 teaspoons wine vinegar
1 teaspoon salt

In a soup pot, sauté the onion in the oil, add the water and the potatoes, bring to a boil, and simmer, covered, for about 20 minutes.

Discard any tough leaves from the kale, and shred it very fine.

Pass the potatoes and onion through a sieve or food mill, and put them back into the pot, with their liquid. Add the kale, vinegar, and salt, bring to a boil, and cook for about 10 minutes, or until the kale is tender but still chewy. Adjust salt, if needed, and serve immediately.

Serves 4.

CREAM OF LENTIL SOUP

While this soup originated in Egypt, it is also made in some Mediterranean islands, such as Malta and Pantelleria, and has found its way onto the mainland of at least two European countries, where it has become European by adoption.

> *2 cups red lentils (the small orange kind also*
> *   called Egyptian lentils)*
> *2 medium-sized onions, finely chopped*
> *2 medium-sized carrots, finely chopped*
> *2 stalks white celery, finely chopped*
> *salt and pepper (white pepper preferred)*
> *½ cup flour, cornstarch, or arrowroot*
> *1 quart milk (approximately)*
> *½ teaspoon curry powder*
> *croutons*

Cook the lentils in enough water to cover, plus 1 inch, together with the onions, carrots, and celery. Simmer, and stir once in a while. The vegetables should be done when the water has been absorbed, about 30 minutes, but you may have to add a little hot water toward the end. Salt and pepper should be added during the last 15 minutes.

Pass the lentils and vegetables through a sieve or food mill. Mix the flour (or cornstarch or arrowroot) with a little cold milk, then add the rest of the milk and the curry powder. Put the lentils back into the pot, stir in the milk, and heat slowly, almost but not quite to boiling point.

Serve with croutons.

Serves 4.

CREAM OF NETTLES SOUP

A specialty from the Balkan countries, this soup, of course, can be made only if you can get hold of some fresh nettles and if you can catch them at the moment in which they produce flowers (although the flowers are not absolutely essential). Handle these stinging plants with gloves! They lose their potency when cooked and will not harm you, but the uncooked plant should be handled with care.

> *2 or 3 cups of flowering nettles*
> *3 small potatoes*
> *1½ quarts vegetable broth*
> *salt*
> *pepper*
> *4 tablespoons heavy cream*
> *pinch of nutmeg*
> *croutons*

Wearing gloves, wash and drain the nettles, then chop them coarsely. Peel and chop the potatoes. Cook both in the broth, adding salt to taste.

When the potatoes are cooked, pass the broth with the potatoes and the nettles through a sieve or food mill, and add the pepper. Return the soup to the heat, and warm briefly. Stir in the cream, add the nutmeg, and serve with croutons.

Serves 4.

TOMATO AND GREEN-PEPPER SOUP
Sopa de Sofrito

A classic Spanish soup, often served with sautéed croutons.

3 medium-sized onions, chopped
2 medium-sized green peppers, chopped
3 tablespoons olive oil
3 medium-sized tomatoes, peeled and chopped
2 cloves garlic, minced
¼ teaspoon pepper
¼ teaspoon saffron
6 cups boiling water
1 teaspoon salt
sautéed croutons (optional)

In a large pot, sauté the onions and peppers in the oil for about 10 minutes. Add the tomatoes, stir, and simmer about 5 minutes. Stir in the garlic, pepper, and saffron. Add the water and salt. Bring to a boil, stir, and simmer for about 15 minutes, or until the flavors seem to blend.

Serve with sautéed croutons, or with pieces of crusty bread.

Serves 4.

SQUASH BLOSSOM SOUP

3 medium-sized onions, chopped
2 medium-sized carrots, chopped
2 celery stalks, chopped
1 tablespoon chopped parsley
4 tablespoons butter

4 tablespoons olive oil
4 tablespoons dry white wine
½ cup imported dried mushrooms, rehydrated
  (reserve liquid)
1½ quarts water
2 tablespoons celery leaves, chopped
1 clove garlic, minced
salt and pepper
½ teaspoon fresh dill, or ¼ teaspoon dry
¼ teaspoon saffron
pinch nutmeg
1½ cups coarsely chopped squash blossoms

Sauté the onions, carrots, celery, and parsley in the butter and oil, and add the wine. When the vegetables begin to turn golden, put them through a sieve or food mill. Chop the rehydrated mushrooms. Heat the water and add the vegetable purée, together with the liquid in which the vegetables were sautéed and the liquid in which the mushrooms were rehydrated. Add the celery leaves, mushrooms, and garlic to the water, and boil for 20 minutes, uncovered, with the salt, pepper, dill, saffron, and nutmeg.

Add the squash blossoms, adjust the seasoning, return to a boil, and simmer for 15 minutes.

SUGGESTIONS.   For an elegant soup, serve with croutons. Or, if you prefer, add rice or small pasta to cook for the last 15 minutes.

Serves 4.

PANZANELLA

A specialty from Tuscany, where it is sometimes referred to as "poor people's soup," though it is debatable if it can really be considered a soup.

1 pound Italian bread, preferably whole-wheat,
*   at least 1 day old*
1 pound fresh tomatoes, very ripe, chopped
1 large onion, sliced thin
4 tablespoons olive oil
2 tablespoons fresh basil, coarsely chopped
salt and pepper
1 tablespoon wine vinegar

Cut the bread in chunks, or tear it with your hands. Soak it in cold water for about 30 minutes, then squeeze dry with your hands. Mix all the other ingredients with the bread, vinegar last.

Tuscan gourmets maintain that this dish is even better if allowed to rest several hours or overnight, without the vinegar, which is added just before serving.

Serves 4.

BREAD AND TOMATO SOUP

Pappa al Pomodoro

This soup is another old Tuscan favorite, sometimes called *pancotto,* which, translated literally, means "cooked bread." Pancotto and Panzanella (see preceding recipe) are quite similar; however, this one is cooked and the other is not. Since it is made primarily in the country, the bread usually used is very rustic, sometimes homemade. Whole-wheat Italian bread would be a good substitute.

2 garlic cloves, chopped
1 medium-sized onion, chopped
⅔ cup olive oil
1 pound very ripe fresh tomatoes, chopped
2 tablespoons fresh basil leaves, or 1 tablespoon
*   fresh sage leaves (or 2 teaspoons dried basil,*
*   or 1 teaspoon dried sage)*

*1 pound stale Italian bread, preferably whole-wheat,
    in chunks*
salt and pepper
6 cups boiling water (approximately)

In a large pot, sauté the garlic and onion in half the oil, then add the tomatoes and herbs. Stew, uncovered, until the tomatoes are almost done. Add the bread, stir, and sprinkle with salt and pepper to taste. Pour the boiling water on top, adding slowly at first, letting the bread absorb the liquid, simmering for a few minutes, then adding more water. This soup must be very thick; that's why it is called *pappa* (pap). Add the rest of the water if needed, and adjust the salt and pepper to taste. Simmer, covered, until the soup is the desired consistency. When ready, allow to cool somewhat, then serve. Trickle the rest of the oil over the individual servings at the table.

This soup is usually eaten lukewarm, or even at room temperature, and is even better if left to soak overnight, then warmed slightly the following day.

Serves 4.

RICE AND MILK SOUP

Riso e Latte

A very simple, healthful soup, eaten at home in Italy but never found in restaurants. It is a great favorite of Italian children, who must often be coaxed to drink milk.

1¾ quarts milk (approximately)
2 cups long-grain rice
salt to taste

Divide the milk in half into two pots, one larger than the other. Start heating the milk in the larger pot, and when it is warm, turn the heat on low under the smaller pot. When the milk in the large pot comes to a boil, add the rice, stir, and cook it, stirring once in a while to make sure it does not stick at the bottom. Add the milk from the other pot—now hot—a little at a time, as the rice swells. Add salt, and continue cooking until rice is done but still firm.

The result should be a fairly thick soup.

Serves 4.

TUSCAN RICE SOUP
Riso alla Toscana

A thick soup known only in coastal Tuscany, where my father's family originates, and even there not to be found in restaurants, but only in private homes. The taste is very distinctive and in no way similar to the Greek egg-lemon soup (see Greek Egg and Lemon Sauce in index), as some of the ingredients deceptively suggest.

> *⅔ cup long-grain rice or brown rice*
> *6 cups (approximately) Vegetable Broth II*
>   *(see index), or about double the amount of*
>   *liquid you would use for cooking rice*
> *1 egg yolk, lightly beaten*
> *2 strips lemon peel, twisted*
> *4 tablespoons grated Parmesan cheese*
> *¼ teaspoon freshly grated nutmeg*
> *dash of pepper*
> *salt if needed*

In spite of the simplicity of this soup, you must adhere strictly to the listed ingredients or it will not taste the way it should.

Cook the rice in the broth. (If brown rice is used, cook it in about 2 cups of water for about 40 minutes, then add some broth.)

While the rice is cooking, put the beaten egg yolk into a tureen, add the other ingredients, and mix vigorously with a metal whisk.

When the rice is cooked, add a ladleful of broth to the ingredients in the tureen and whip, then pour in the rest of the broth and the rice, and mix well. If you are not sure about the proportions of rice and broth, strain the rice, add it to the other ingredients, then add the broth a little at a time until the soup reaches the desired thickness, which should be that of a fairly loose porridge. Cover, and let stand a few minutes. Additional grated cheese may be added individually after the soup is served. The lemon peel can either be discarded before serving or left in the tureen to continue flavoring the soup to the last minute.

Serves 4.

RICE AND ASPARAGUS SOUP
Zuppa di Riso e Asparagi

A Milanese soup, very delicate in taste. It must be made only with fresh, thin asparagus.

> *1½ quarts vegetable broth*
> *1 pound very fresh, green, thin asparagus*
> *1 cup rice*
> *2 tablespoons butter*
> *grated Parmesan cheese*

Make or heat the vegetable broth. While it is getting hot, slice the asparagus in 1-inch-long pieces, discarding any tough portions of the stems. When the broth begins to boil, add the asparagus and bring to a full boil; then add the rice, bring back to a boil, stir, and cover, lowering the heat. Simmer for about 18 minutes, or until rice is cooked but still firm. Remove from the heat, stir in the butter, and serve with grated cheese on the side.

Serves 4.

RICE AND PEAS
Risi e Bisi

A specialty of the Venetian cuisine but popular all over northern Italy, this is not really a soup, being much thicker. The density should be closer to that of a very loose risotto than that of even a thick soup. Fresh peas are far superior to frozen, but if you must, you may substitute the latter.

> *1 quart vegetable broth (approximately)*
> *1 medium-sized onion, chopped fine*
> *4 teaspoons finely chopped parsley*
> *1 tablespoon olive oil*
> *3 tablespoons butter*
> *1 pound fresh peas (or 1 10-ounce package frozen)*
> *salt and pepper*
> *1 cup rice*
> *3 tablespoons grated Parmesan cheese,*
> *plus additional cheese*

Heat the broth. In a large pot, sauté the onion and 2 teaspoons of the parsley in the oil and 2 tablespoons of the butter. When almost ready, add the peas, with a little cold water, salt, and pepper, and bring to a boil. Try to judge cooking time according to the size of the peas. If they are young and tender, you can add the rice at the same time; if larger, cook them for 5 to 10 minutes before adding the rice. Keep the broth very hot, and add it a little at a time, stirring the rice and peas constantly. After about 10 minutes from the time the liquid has returned to a boil, taste and adjust seasoning, if needed. Add the rest of the parsley. Only enough broth should be added to give the soup the right consistency. When the peas and rice are cooked, stir in the remaining 1 tablespoon butter, and about 3 tablespoons grated cheese. Serve additional cheese at the table.

Serves 4.

RICE AND TURNIP SOUP

Riso e Rape

An old northern Italian favorite. The tastes of rice and turnip go together very well.

1 quart vegetable broth
1 pound turnips
½ medium-sized onion, chopped fine
1 clove garlic, minced
4 tablespoons butter
⅔ cup rice
½ cup grated Parmesan cheese
2 tablespoons chopped parsley

Heat the broth. Scrub or peel the turnips, and cut them in about ¼-inch cubes. In a large, heavy pot, sauté the onion and garlic in the butter, then add the turnips and sauté for a few minutes, stirring often to get everything well coated. Pour the hot broth on top, and bring to a boil. Lower the heat, and cook, covered, for about 40 minutes. Add the rice, bring back to a boil, and cook until the rice is done, about 18 minutes.

Remove the pot from the heat, add the cheese and parsley, and mix well.

Serves 4.

TRAHANÁ

Trahaná is a very old Greek dish. However, the basic idea must have originated in North Africa or the Middle East, for, in spite of the completely different taste, it is made by rubbing pieces of dough between the hands, in the same way that bulgur is prepared for couscous. Throughout the winter, trahaná is a staple fare, especially in the Greek villages, where it is sometimes eaten in the morning, for breakfast, as well as being used in soup. It is usually prepared in the month of August, when the wheat has just been harvested and milk is available in large quantities. Practically every village in Greece has its own recipe. Sour trahaná is made by adding curdled milk; a sweeter variety calls for fresh milk; and some recipes even substitute yogurt. The addition of eggs is optional.

It is now prepared commercially (like pasta in Italy) and can be bought in stores; even in the United States, Middle Eastern specialty stores carry it. However, homemade trahaná is still preferred everywhere in Greece, although it can seldom be found in larger centers.

The following recipe makes a fairly large amount, which can be preserved almost indefinitely, and used as needed.

> *2 quarts milk*
> *1 tablespoon salt*
> *5 pounds bulgur or whole-wheat flour*
>   *(more may be needed)*
> *3 eggs (optional)*

Pour the milk into a large bowl, cover it with a thin cloth, and allow it to curdle at room temperature. When ready, add the salt, mix, and add enough bulgur or flour to make a rather firm dough. Knead, add the eggs (if used), then more bulgur or flour, until the paste no longer sticks to your hands. Break the dough into pieces the size of large walnuts, flatten these into patties, and spread them out to dry. In the countryside of Greece, trahaná is dried in the sun and taken indoors at night, but the drying process can also be done in a warm, well-ventilated place. Turn the patties once or twice during the first drying period. After a few hours, when the outer portions of the dough have formed a slight crust, cut the patties into rather small pieces and spread out to dry a few hours longer. When the pieces are sufficiently dry to crumble, rub them with your hands (this is the old-fashioned method still used by many), or, to accelerate the process, rub the pieces through a sieve or colander. The final pieces should be very small, like coarse breadcrumbs (some pieces may be a little larger, some smaller). Spread out on a wide surface for the final drying. If you plan to use a batch immediately, it should be ready after a few hours. The rest should be dried completely, moving the pieces once or twice a day, until very hard. This last drying may take 3 or 4 days. Store in glass jars, tightly covered.

In addition to the soup which follows, an excellent mush can be made with trahaná, using water, milk, or broth. The ratio of liquid to trahaná is about 2 cups for each cup trahaná. The mush should be stirred often.

TRAHANÁ SOUP

1 large tomato, coarsely chopped
2 tablespoons olive oil
3½ cups water or vegetable broth
½ cup dried trahaná
½ cup milk
salt and pepper
4 tablespoons grated cheese, plus additional cheese

Put the tomato and the oil in a pot, add the water or broth, and bring to a boil. Mix the trahaná with the milk, add to the boiling liquid, and bring back to a boil, adding salt and pepper to taste. Simmer for about 30 minutes, stirring in 4 tablespoons grated cheese about 5 minutes before the soup is ready. Serve with more grated cheese on the side.

Serves 4.

Pasta and Dumplings

HOMEMADE PASTA

This is the basic recipe for making simple pasta, such as egg noodles (*tagliatelle* or *fettuccine*), lasagne, cannelloni, ravioli, and so forth.

> *4 cups flour*
> *4 eggs, lightly beaten*
> *1½ teaspoons salt*
> *3 tablespoons cold water (approximately)*

Make a mound of the flour. Hollow out a depression in the center and add the eggs, salt, and water. With a fork, beat in a little flour, gradually adding more flour until you cannot mix with the fork any longer. Using your hands, knead until smooth, about 10 minutes. Cut the dough into three or four pieces, and roll out one piece at a time on a lightly floured board. Make it as thin as you can (for larger pieces of pasta, such as ravioli or cannelloni, you may leave the pasta a little thicker).

For egg noodles, fold the dough into a flat roll, and cut into strips of the desired width, then toss each strip to separate, and spread the strips out in one layer to dry, covered with a towel, at least 1 hour, or up to several hours.

For cannelloni or lasagne, cut the rolled-out dough into the desired shape and allow to dry in one layer, as for noodles.

For ravioli, use two large sheets of pasta. On one, spoon out small blobs of filling about 1½ inches apart in both directions, then lay the other sheet of pasta on top. With a pastry wheel, cut into squares, by cutting in long straight lines in both directions. Let dry, as for other pasta, and separate the squares when dry. To cook, drop the ravioli into boiling water; when they float, they are done.

Homemade pasta is cooked in large quantities of boiling water. It cooks much more quickly than the store-bought varieties, and cooking time varies according to size, so check it after about 3 or 4 minutes. It should always be cooked *al dente*—that is, on the chewy side—and should never be allowed to overcook. Drain and use as you would commercial pasta.

Serves 8–10.

EGG NOODLES WITH PEAS AND MUSHROOMS
Tagliatelle ai Piselli e Funghi

> *1 cup mushrooms, sliced*
> *4 tablespoons butter*
> *1½ cups fresh peas, small size*
> *salt and white pepper*
> *½ cup heavy cream*
> *1½ pounds egg noodles (tagliatelle),*
> *preferably homemade*
> *3 tablespoons grated Parmesan cheese*

Sauté the mushrooms in the butter for a few minutes. Steam the peas to a firm consistency, then add to the mushrooms, add salt and pepper, and stir in the cream.

While you are making the sauce, cook the noodles *al dente,* and drain. Bring the sauce almost to a boil, stirring, and pour it on the noodles. Mix together, sprinkling with 3 tablespoons grated cheese as you mix. Serve additional cheese at the table.

Serves 4.

PAN-FRIED NOODLES

Fettuccine in Padella

1½ pounds egg noodles (homemade or store-bought)
salt
3 tablespoons olive oil
grated Parmesan cheese

Boil the noodles in salted water until about three-quarters done and drain immediately. Shake the colander to make sure they are completely dry, but do not let them cool too much.

Heat the oil in a large heavy skillet and spread the noodles in it in a fairly thin layer (no more than 1-inch deep). You may have to use two skillets. Lower the heat a few seconds after you put the noodles in the pan. Press the noodles gently with a spatula and level the top. The noodles should come out with a golden crisp crust on the bottom but must not burn, so gauge the heat accordingly. Check after a few minutes by sliding a spatula underneath and lifting. When the crust has acquired its golden color, cover the skillet, and cook about 5 minutes longer.

If the crust is not too hard, the noodles can be folded like an omelet. If you prefer to have a crust on both sides, cover the skillet for only 2 or 3 minutes; then uncover, brush the top with more oil, and pass the skillet briefly under the broiler, making sure the surface does not burn. In this case, you will serve the noodles flat, instead of folded.

Sprinkle abundantly with grated cheese before serving.

Serves 4.

PUMPKIN TORTELLI
Tortelli di Zucca

This is an Italian dish often served as a first course on Christmas, especially in the region of Parma, where it originated. *Tortelli* is the local word for ravioli.

Because the filling of these tortelli is very delicate in flavor, do not serve them with any sauce that could distract from their basic taste. The butter and cheese of this recipe is the most suitable.

> *2½ pounds pumpkin, peeled, seeded, and cut into chunks*
> *6 amaretti (Italian almond cookies) ; if unavailable*
>   *use 4 macaroons*
> *6 or 7 sage leaves*
> *½ cup light red wine (preferably Lambrusco)*
> *1 teaspoon honey*
> *salt and pepper*
> *1 tablespoon grappa, aquavit, or similar liqueur*
>   *(gin may be substituted)*
> *¼ teaspoon nutmeg*
> *¼ teaspoon cinnamon*
> *juice of 1 lemon*
> *2 cups grated Parmesan cheese*
> *breadcrumbs, if necessary*
> *1 recipe Homemade Pasta (see index)*
> *8 tablespoons (1 stick) butter, melted*

Bake the pumpkin at 350° until done, about 45 minutes, then pass it through a food mill, mashing it well. In a pot, crush the *amaretti* with the sage leaves, and add the wine, honey, salt, and pepper. Simmer, uncovered, until most of the liquid has evaporated. Add the pumpkin, liqueur, nutmeg, cinnamon, and lemon juice, heat briefly, always stirring, and remove from heat. Allow the mixture to cool a few minutes, then stir in 1½ cups of the grated cheese. Cool a little longer. The mixture should have the consistency of mashed potatoes; if it seems too soft, add a couple of tablespoons of breadcrumbs.

Prepare the dough and add the filling as for ravioli, but make larger squares (about 4 inches). Cook in a large amount of salted water. Like ravioli, these tortelli cook in just a few minutes, sinking to the bottom of the pot at first, then coming to the surface. Remove with a slotted spoon as they float.

In a heated tureen, make a layer of tortelli, then one of melted butter and grated cheese, then repeat, finishing with butter and cheese. Cover, allow to rest a few minutes, then serve.

Serves 4.

GERMAN "RAVIOLI"
Maultaschen

This is the southern German version of ravioli, perhaps derived from an Austrian recipe, which, in turn, must have been adapted from Italian ravioli. The long Austrian occupation of Italy in the eighteenth and part of the nineteenth centuries yielded a bonanza of recipes for the Austrian cuisine.

DOUGH
1 recipe Homemade Pasta (see index)

FILLING
*1 pound stale French or Italian bread
  (approximately)*
water or milk
1 large onion, minced
1 leek, chopped (optional)
4 tablespoons butter
1 clove garlic, minced
*1 cup chopped spinach, partially cooked,
  drained, and squeezed*
3 tablespoons chopped parsley

1 tablespoon vegetable broth
3 eggs, lightly beaten
salt and pepper
breadcrumbs, if necessary

Soak the bread in water or milk, and while it is soaking, sauté the onion (and the leek, if you are using it) in the butter. When the onion is transparent, add the garlic, spinach, parsley, and vegetable broth. Continue to cook over low heat, uncovered, about 5 or 6 minutes, stirring often. Remove from heat. Squeeze the liquid from the bread and add it and the eggs to the spinach mixture. Add salt and pepper to taste, and mix well. If the mixture seems too soft, add some breadcrumbs.

Roll out the dough; then cut it into 3-inch squares. On half of the squares, place 1 tablespoon of the filling in the middle. Cover each with another square and pinch the edges together on all sides. If the dough does not close properly, dip your fingers in water and pinch again. (For a quicker system, see method of cutting ravioli under Homemade Pasta.)

Drop the maultaschen in a large quantity of boiling salted water, bring back to a boil, and remove them with a slotted spoon after about 8 minutes.

Serve with melted butter on top, or with any sauce of your liking.

Leftovers can be sautéed in butter, about 5 minutes on each side.

Serves 4 to 6.

PASTA WITH GARLIC AND OIL
Pasta all'Aglio e Olio

This way of serving pasta is very common in central and southern Italy, yet almost unknown here, although it is of the utmost simplicity. The pasta most frequently used is linguine or vermicelli, but any other long type will do.

1½ pounds pasta
4 cloves garlic, sliced (more, if you want
* a stronger flavor)*
6 tablespoons olive oil
salt and pepper
grated Parmesan cheese

Cook the pasta in salted water until *al dente,* and drain well. While the pasta is cooking, sauté the garlic in the oil in a skillet until well browned but not burned. Add salt and pepper, and stir. Pour the oil over the pasta. Mix well, and serve with cheese on the side.

Serves 4.

SPAGHETTINI WITH PEAS AND EGGS

1½ pounds spaghettini or linguine
1½ cups fresh, tender peas
3 tablespoons butter
3 tablespoons grated Parmesan cheese,
* plus additional cheese*
salt and white pepper
2 eggs, lightly beaten

Cook the pasta in boiling, salted water, and while it is cooking, steam the peas to a firm consistency, then remove them to a large pot, and add the butter. When the pasta is *al dente,* drain. Turn the heat on low under the peas and butter, add the pasta, 3 tablespoons grated cheese, salt, and pepper, then the eggs, and mix quickly. Turn off the heat and serve immediately with additional grated cheese.

Serves 4.

VERMICELLI SICILIAN STYLE

2 cloves garlic, chopped
½ cup olive oil
5 large ripe tomatoes, peeled, seeded, and
   chopped coarsely
2 small eggplants, cubed, unpeeled
2 yellow peppers (if unavailable, 2 sweet
   red peppers)
3 tablespoons pitted black olives,
   Sicilian or Greek style
2 tablespoons capers
2 tablespoons fresh basil, chopped (or
   1 tablespoon dried)
abundant pepper
1½ pounds vermicelli or spaghetti
grated Romano cheese
salt (optional)

Sauté the garlic in the oil; add the tomatoes and eggplant. While they are cooking, roast the peppers, whole, either directly over a flame (by sticking with a fork and turning slowly, a few inches from the flame) or under the broiler, fairly close to the heat, turning them every half-minute, for about 2 minutes. Remove the seeds and burned skin; then cut peppers into small bite-sized pieces.

Add the peppers, olives, capers, basil, parsley, and pepper to the sauce, bring to a boil, cover, and cook for a few minutes. If it seems too thick add a little water or red wine. The olives should provide enough salt, but taste, and add more if necessary.

Cook the vermicelli or spaghetti *al dente*. Drain, and mix well with the sauce. Serve with grated cheese on top.

Serves 4 to 6.

PASTA WITH RICOTTA

This dish calls for fresh Roman ricotta, made of goat's or sheep's milk (see page 279), which is a rare ingredient here and rather difficult to find. If you live in or near a Greek neighborhood, you might substitute the Greek cheese *mizíthra* or fresh *anthótiro,* which is somewhat similar to Roman ricotta. Otherwise you can use the combination of cheeses listed.

> *1½ pounds pasta of any shape*
> *½ cup milk*
> *1½ cups Roman ricotta, or 1 cup ricotta and*
> *½ cup feta or similar goat's or sheep's milk*
> *cheese, crumbled*
> *½ teaspoon honey*
> *½ teaspoon powdered cinnamon*
> *pinch of nutmeg*
> *abundant pepper*
> *salt (optional)*
> *½ fresh hot pepper, seeded and minced, or a*
> *pinch cayenne (optional), or ½ teaspoon*
> *paprika*
> *grated Romano cheese*

Cook the pasta in boiling, salted water. While it is cooking, warm the milk in a small pot, and stir in the Roman ricotta or whatever cheese you are using. Add the honey, cinnamon, nutmeg, and pepper. Taste, and if the mixture is sufficiently salted, proceed; otherwise, add salt and/or more seasoning. If you like spiciness, add the hot pepper or the cayenne; for a milder taste, add the paprika. Keep the sauce warm, but do not cook it.

Drain the pasta well, put it in a serving bowl or platter, and add the ricotta sauce. Mix well. Serve grated Romano cheese on the side.

Serves 4.

PASTA WITH RICOTTA AND BROCCOLI

A specialty from Sicily.

> *¾ pounds fresh broccoli*
> *1 pound short pasta, such as ziti, shells, rigatoni,*
>   *and so forth*
> *½ cup olive oil*
> *salt and pepper*
> *½ cup grated Romano cheese (approximately)*
> *½ cup ricotta*
> *½ cup mozzarella, thinly sliced*
> *2 eggs*

Preheat the oven to 425°. Chop the broccoli coarsely, separating stems from flowerets. Bring a large pot of salted water to a boil, drop in the broccoli stems, bring back to a boil, let cook for a few minutes, then add the flowerets. With a slotted spoon, scoop out all the broccoli after a couple of minutes, keeping the water boiling. Throw the pasta into the boiling water, and cook only until still very chewy.

While the pasta is cooking, heat about 3 tablespoons of the oil in a heavy skillet, and pan-fry the broccoli quickly, adding salt and pepper. Remove the skillet from the heat when the stems are still very chewy.

Grease a baking dish approximately 10 inches wide and 4 inches deep and sprinkle some of the grated cheese all over the bottom and sides. Arrange a layer of pasta, then one of broccoli, on which place blobs of ricotta, and then put slices of mozzarella on the ricotta. Sprinkle with more grated cheese, dribble some oil all over, and continue to make similar layers, ending with pasta. Beat the eggs with about 3 tablespoons of the grated cheese, and spread on top. Dribble some more oil on top, and bake at 400° for 20 minutes, or until the top turns golden.

Serves 4.

BAKED PASTA AND CHEESE
Pasta al Gratin

1½ pounds short pasta, such as rigatoni, shells,
  ziti, and so forth
thin White Sauce (see index), made with
  3 tablespoons butter, 2 tablespoons flour,
  and 3½ cups hot milk
5 tablespoons grated Parmesan cheese
¼ teaspoon nutmeg
salt and pepper
2 tablespoons butter
breadcrumbs (optional)

In a large pot of salted water, cook the pasta *al dente,* adding about 2 cups of cold water as soon as you remove the pot from the heat, to halt the cooking. While the pasta cooks, preheat the oven to 450° and make the White Sauce, using the amounts of butter, flour, and milk indicated in the list of ingredients.

A couple of minutes before the sauce is ready, add the grated cheese, nutmeg, salt, and pepper to it. Remove from heat, and stir for another minute or so, until all the cheese has been mixed into the sauce.

Grease a wide oven-proof dish with fairly low sides. Drain the pasta well. Mix it with the 2 tablespoons butter, then arrange it in the dish. Pour the sauce in as you fill the dish, making sure it penetrates throughout and reserving quite a bit to pour on top. Breadcrumbs may be sprinkled on top before putting the dish in the oven.

Bake for about 15 minutes, or until the top layer of pasta is becoming golden brown.

Serves 4.

PASTA WITH CAULIFLOWER
Pasta alla Gangitana

1 medium-sized cauliflower
1½ pounds short pasta, such as rigatoni,
shells, ziti, and so forth
salt
2 cups Tomato Sauce (see index)
½ cup raisins
½ cup pine nuts
pepper
grated Romano or Parmesan cheese

Clean the cauliflower, cut off flowerets, and boil flowerets and core in about 4 quarts of salted water. When the cauliflower is cooked but still very chewy, remove the flowerets with a slotted spoon or strainer, leaving the core in the water. Cook the pasta in the same water.

Make or heat the Tomato Sauce, and add raisins, pine nuts, and the flowerets (you may cut them into smaller pieces, if you wish).

Drain the pasta well, discarding the cauliflower core, and mix it with half the sauce. Remove to a serving platter or bowl, and pour the rest of the sauce on top, sprinkling with pepper and cheese. Additional cheese may be added individually at the table.

Serves 4.

PASTITSIO

The word *pastitsio* is a Greek phonetic transliteration of the Italian word *pasticcio,* which, in culinary terms, means a mixture of various foods, often including pasta, baked with or without a crust. The Greek pastitsio is no doubt a variation of the Italian dish, quite probably picked up and adapted, like so many other dishes, during the Venetian occupation of some of the Greek islands, which lasted for several centuries.

Since both Pastitsio and Pasticcio traditionally contain meat, I am giving here my own version of Pastitsio, which is very tasty, and in the following recipe my rendition of the Italian Pasticcio di Maccheroni.

> *2 medium-sized eggplants*
> *4 cups Tomato Sauce (see index)*
> *thin White Sauce (see index), using 2 tablespoons*
>   *butter, 2 tablespoons flour, and 3 cups milk*
> *1 cup grated Romano cheese*
> *½ teaspoon ground cinnamon*
> *¼ teaspoon grated nutmeg*
> *1 pound plus ½ cup short pasta, such as ziti or*
>   *short macaroni*
> *4 tablespoons butter*
> *5 eggs*
> *3 tablespoons feta cheese (or any other semi-hard*
>   *goat's milk cheese), crumbled*
> *5 tablespoons ricotta*
> *salt and pepper*
> *olive oil*

Start the broiler and while it is heating, peel the eggplants and cut them in slices ½-inch thick. Brush both sides with olive oil, put the slices on a cookie sheet or shallow baking dish, and brown them under the broiler. About 3 minutes on each side will be sufficient if the slices are placed 4 or 5 inches from the heat. Now, cut the slices into bite-sized pieces. Warm the Tomato Sauce, and add the eggplant. Simmer for a while, uncovered, to allow the eggplant to finish cooking and absorb the flavor of the sauce.

Put a large amount of salted water in a pot, and as you wait for the water to boil, make the White Sauce. As it thickens, add 2 tablespoons of the grated Romano cheese, and part of the cinnamon and nutmeg, reserving a little of each. Remove from heat. Boil the pasta for about 12 minutes, or until still very chewy. Pour some cold water in the pot to stop the cooking process, then drain.

Melt the butter and let cool. Lightly beat 3 of the eggs in a large bowl. Add the feta cheese to the eggs, then the ricotta, the melted butter, salt, and a little freshly ground pepper. Mix well. If the pasta is sufficiently cooled, add it now. Mix everything very well, using two large spoons. One at a time, lightly beat the other 2 eggs, adding one to the White Sauce and the other to the eggplant sauce, both of which should be cooler by now.

Preheat the oven to 400°. Grease a large baking pan, about 4 inches deep, preferably square or rectangular. Add half of the pasta mixture, then make a layer of the eggplant sauce, and cover with the rest of the pasta. Pour the White Sauce on top, making sure it penetrates underneath. Sprinkle with the remaining grated Romano cheese, then with the rest of the cinnamon and nutmeg.

Bake for 15 minutes, then peek to be sure a crust is forming. If it is, continue baking for another 15 minutes; if not, raise the temperature to 450° and bake 20 minutes longer, or until top is dark and crusty.

Allow to cool about 15 minutes after removing from the oven.

Serves 4.

PASTICCIO DI MACCHERONI

This is my own version, without meat, of course, of the classic Italian dish.

CRUST
½ *cup butter*
2 *cups flour*
3 *egg yolks*
3 *teaspoons honey*
½ *teaspoon salt*

Cut the butter into the flour until you have a crumbly mass. Stir egg yolks, honey, and salt together, and add to the dough. Knead a little on a floured surface, wrap in cloth, and chill for 1 hour. (If dough is too dry, add a little cold water, a few drops at a time.)

FILLING
2 small onions, chopped
2 small carrots, chopped
½ cup butter
1½ cups fresh tomatoes (peeled, seeded, and chopped)
    or canned tomatoes, drained and chopped
2 tablespoons tomato paste
½ cup dry white wine
½ pound fresh mushrooms, sliced thin
12 black olives (Greek), pitted and chopped coarsely
30 capers
1 tablespoon chopped fresh mint (or 2 teaspoons dried)
1 tablespoon chopped fresh basil (or 2 teaspoons dried)
½ teaspoon thyme
salt and pepper
1 pound short pasta, preferably ziti or mostaccioli
½ cup grated Parmesan cheese

First make a sauce by sautéing the onions and carrots in one third of the butter. Add tomatoes, tomato paste, and wine, and simmer a few minutes. Add mushrooms, olives, capers, herbs, salt, and pepper, and continue to simmer, uncovered, about 20 minutes, or until the sauce begins to thicken.

Meanwhile, cook the pasta until very firm. Drain well, and mix thoroughly with the sauce and the grated cheese. Grease a rather deep baking dish. Roll out a little more than half the dough for the crust to about ½ inch thickness, and line the dish. Fill with the pasta mixture. Preheat the oven to 350°. Roll out the rest of the dough, and cover the baking dish with it, pressing all around with fingers to seal. Prick several holes on the upper surface with a fork. Bake for 50 minutes, or until surface is golden.

Serves 4.

BAKED PASTA AND TOMATOES

The peculiarity of this dish (which also simplifies its preparation) is that the pasta is not previously cooked but is put into the oven raw. You should use only types of short pasta that are neither too thick nor too big, otherwise the cooking time will vary. Canned tomatoes cannot be substituted in this dish, as they would also affect the cooking time and would change the taste considerably.

> *4 pounds fresh tomatoes, very ripe and of even size*
> *4 tablespoons parsley, chopped*
> *2 tablespoons fresh basil, chopped (or 1*
> * tablespoon dried)*
> *2 teaspoons oregano*
> *4 cloves garlic, pressed or minced*
> *salt and pepper*
> *1 pound short pasta, preferably ziti or mostaccioli*
> *1 cup olive oil (approximately)*

Peel the tomatoes. With a very sharp knife, cut them exactly in half horizontally; spoon out seeds and liquid, reserving both.

Grease a deep mold or baking dish that has a tight lid and can be used for serving. Preheat the oven to 375°. Put one layer of tomatoes on the bottom, cut side down, then another layer, cut side up, filling the shallow areas of the first layer. Sprinkle parsley, basil, oregano, garlic, salt, and pepper on top, then add a layer of uncooked pasta and dribble some olive oil on it. Continue to make layers finishing with tomatoes with cut side down. This top layer must cover the entire surface without any pasta showing. Dribble more oil on top. Press through a sieve whatever liquid and pulp was left from the tomatoes, discard the seeds, and pour the purée on top. Cover the dish tightly, and bake for about 1¼ hours, checking after 45 minutes and pressing the top surface of tomatoes gently with a fork. At this point you may taste a piece of pasta to gauge how much longer it should cook.

Remove from the oven and allow to rest, still covered, for about 15 minutes. This will help the timbale (as molded dishes are sometimes called) to solidify. Unmold on a warm platter, or serve in the baking dish, if one was used.

Serves 4.

POTATO GNOCCHI

A Roman specialty of humble origin, this dish was formerly prepared only in private, often modest households or in very inexpensive trattorie. In the last fifty years or so, these gnocchi have gained popularity throughout Italy, and now they are frequently found in good Italian restaurants in the United States, as well as in Italy.

Select a sauce from the Sauces section (see index). My favorites are Tomato Sauce or Pesto.

> *3 pounds mealy potatoes*
> *2 cups flour (approximately)*
> *¼ teaspoon salt*
> *1 tablespoon olive oil*
> *grated Parmesan cheese*

Cook, drain, peel, and mash the potatoes. Mix the flour and salt, and shape into a mound. Make a depression in the top, pour the oil into it, then add the potatoes. Knead well with your hands, then sprinkle some flour on the table and pull out pieces of dough, then, with the palms of your hands, roll fairly long pieces of dough, the thickness of one finger. Cut these cylinders into 1-inch pieces, then take a fork and pass each piece lightly on the curved tines, so that these make little depressions. Use your index finger to help the gnocchi curl up. Once you pick up the knack, you'll be able to make them very fast, but don't be discouraged if your first few attempts fail.

Bring a large amount of water to a full boil. Keep the heat high as you plunge about a dozen gnocchi at a time into the pot. At first they will sink. As they float back to the surface, remove them with a slotted spoon, and place them on a warm platter to keep them warm as you cook the rest.

Gnocchi can be made a couple of hours in advance. Spread them out so that they do not touch one another, and cover with a cloth to prevent excessive dryness (a little dryness is good, as their texture, when cooked, should be rather firm). No need to refrigerate; in fact, the moisture they would pick up in the refrigerator would make them sticky.

Serve with grated cheese on the side.

Serves 4 to 6.

GREEN GNOCCHI
Gnocchi Verdi

This recipe, similar to the preceding one, is another Italian favorite. Again, choose a sauce from the Sauces section. One of the best for these gnocchi is Pink Sauce (see index).

> *2 pounds potatoes*
> *1 pound spinach*
> *2 egg yolks*
> *2 tablespoons grated Parmesan cheese*
> *pinch of nutmeg*
> *1/4 teaspoon salt*
> *5 tablespoons flour*
> *grated Parmesan cheese*

Boil, drain, peel, and mash the potatoes. While the potatoes are boiling, cook the spinach (see page 19). When it is cool enough, squeeze it with your hands. At this point the ball of spinach should be the size of a large orange. Pass the spinach through a sieve or food mill.

Bring 3 cups of the milk to a boil and mix the remaining cup with the semolina. When the milk boils, add the semolina mixture and stir. Add salt to taste. Keep stirring, scraping the thickening paste from the bottom and sides of the pot. After about 10 minutes, add the 3 tablespoons of grated cheese, 2 tablespoons of the butter, and the egg yolks, and stir well until thoroughly mixed. Cook for a couple of minutes longer, until semolina is almost done.

Pour the semolina mixture onto a slightly wet, smooth surface, such as a large serving platter, and spread it out to a thickness of about 1/2 inch. Smooth the surface with a wet spatula, and allow to cool for at least 1 hour.

Preheat the oven to 450°. Grease a large square or rectangular baking dish that is no more than 2 inches deep. Cut the cooled semolina into 2-inch squares, or preferably into disks 2 inches in diameter (as a cutter use a small glass dipped in cold water).

Lay several rows of gnocchi in the pan, overlapping one on another by half, and keeping the rows very close together. Sprinkle with more grated cheese, and align another layer of rows in between the rows of the previous one. If you have enough gnocchi, finish with one central row, but this is not essential. However, try to make even rows. In a small saucepan, melt the remaining 2 tablespoons of butter. Sprinkle the gnocchi abundantly with grated cheese, and pour the melted butter on top.

Bake for about 15 minutes, or until the edges of the gnocchi have turned golden brown. Serve in the baking dish.

Serves 4.

POTATO DUMPLINGS
Kartoffelkloesse

A close relative of Italian Potato Gnocchi, these dumplings are from Germany. Use as a side dish.

8 medium-sized potatoes of the mealy type
½ cup flour
2 eggs, lightly beaten
salt to taste
1 tablespoon chopped onion
2 tablespoons butter
1 slice of any type bread, cut into small cubes

Steam or bake unpeeled potatoes until tender. Peel and mash. Let stand overnight, uncovered and spread out, but not in the refrigerator. Put the mashed potatoes into a bowl, add the flour, eggs, and salt, and mix well. Sauté the onion in the butter in a skillet, add the bread cubes, and brown. Flatten a spoonful of the potato mixture in the palm of your hand, and put a few bread-and-onion cubes in it. Roll into a ball about 3 inches in diameter. Repeat until all the mixture is used. Because both potatoes and flour vary considerably, the proportions given here may need adjusting. It is a good idea to roll one dumpling and cook it according to the following instructions; if it doesn't hold together, add more flour to the mixture before rolling the dumplings.

Drop the dumplings into a large quantity of salted boiling water. Boil, uncovered, for about 15 minutes. Drain well, and serve at once.

Serves 4.

GERMAN DUMPLINGS
Spaetzle

These dumplings are usually served with a stew but they can also be served alone as a first course. This dish, or close variations, can also be found in Austria, Hungary, Yugoslavia, Czechoslovakia, and other Middle European countries.

2½ cups flour (approximately)
1 teaspoon salt
dash of nutmeg
dash of paprika
3 eggs, lightly beaten
½ cup water (approximately)
4 tablespoons butter, melted
breadcrumbs (optional)

Sift the flour with the salt, nutmeg, and paprika, then add the eggs. Add almost all the water, and beat the batter until thick and smooth. If it gets too thick, add the rest of the water. Sprinkle some flour on a board, place about 1 cup of the dough on it, and roll it out, not too thin. If the dough seems sticky, add some more flour. Cut into small strips or squares, then throw the spaetzle into a large quantity of salted boiling water, making sure the pieces of dough don't stick together. (Water at a rolling boil helps to keep the pieces separate.) Boil for about 5 minutes. If you prefer, you can cook the dumplings in three or four batches, removing each batch with a slotted spoon to a warm platter before you start boiling the next.

Serve with melted butter on top. You can also brown some breadcrumbs in butter and mix with the dumplings.

The dough can be prepared ahead of time, refrigerated, and rolled out when needed. It will stay fresh for several days.

Serves 4.

Grains

Polenta

The Italian word *polenta* is derived from the Latin *pulmentum,* a dish eaten by the ancient Romans. Their polenta was a dense pap (that's what the word means) made with whole wheat, as corn had not then reached the Old World. Russian Kasha (see index) resembles the old Roman *pulmentum,* though it is more versatile.

Today, wheat polenta is still sometimes cooked in northern Italy, but cornmeal polenta is much more common, though only in the north. In the Italian Alps it is a staple eaten almost every day, especially by the poor. The cornmeal is always made from yellow corn, although it varies in grind from medium to rather coarse, with the latter usually preferred.

In small Alpine villages, polenta is still cooked in a heavy copper caldron hanging from the fireplace, which gives it a delicious smoky taste, but this habit is now disappearing. The Italians still insist, however, that polenta must be cooked, stirring almost constantly, for a good long time—from 1 to 2 hours. While the flavor improves considerably with longer cooking, few people now have either the time or the physical strength to cook it this way. When polenta thickens, it is quite a job to stir it, especially a large quantity.

However, if the amount of water is reduced, about 30 or 40 minutes' cooking, depending on the quality of the cornmeal, are sufficient. The stone-ground types of cornmeal available in health food stores, are, unfortunately, better suited to American cornmeal mush than to polenta, as they turn out very gooey. I recommend using either cornmeal imported from Italy or nationally distributed American commercial brands. While the grain of the latter is not very coarse, these types give better results than the stone-ground cornmeal.

In Rumania, the peasants eat a cornmeal dish similar to polenta. Yellow corn is ground rather coarsely, then toasted dry on the fire, and when it has changed color, a large amount of water is added, and cooking is continued. This procedure changes both taste and consistency, and the dish is darker and considerably more liquid than Italian polenta. The Rumanian word for this mush is *mamaliga,* and it is usually eaten with milk. It is strange that the habit of eating a cornmeal mush has remained limited to these two small sections of Europe and is practically unknown elsewhere.

The Alpine Italians eat polenta with milk, usually when it is time to milk the cows. They first make a big batch of polenta and then make a well in a mound of piping hot polenta and pour in milk still warm from the cow.

In Italy, polenta has been elaborated in numerous ways, as the following recipes show.

Note: A pot in which polenta or any other mushy preparation such as kasha, semolina, and so on has been cooked is very easy to wash if you fill it with cold water and let it rest for a couple of hours or overnight. Then the film will slide off the pot by itself.

BASIC POLENTA

4 cups water (approximately)
1½ teaspoons salt
1½ cups yellow cornmeal

Bring 3 cups of salted water to a boil, in a heavy pot with a long handle (this helps you get a good grip while stirring). In a bowl, mix the cornmeal with the remaining cup of water. This prevents lumps from forming when you add the cornmeal to the boiling water. Have another pot of simmering water ready, in case you need to add some.

When the water in the large pot comes to a furious boil, plop in the cornmeal mixed with the cold water, and start stirring immediately with a wooden spoon, keeping the heat very high to bring the water back to a boil as quickly as possible. When it starts to boil again, lower the heat to medium, and stir constantly for 10 minutes or so. When the mixture begins to thicken considerably, stir frequently, especially scraping from the sides and bottom. If the type of cornmeal you are using absorbs a lot of water, add a little boiling water one or more times as needed, but remember that the greatest absorption takes place during the first 10 or 15 minutes. On the other hand, if you want a firmer polenta (especially to make some of the dishes suggested here), either cook it a little longer, or use less water.

It will take 30 to 40 minutes to cook the polenta. A good test is to stand the wooden spoon in the middle of the pot. If it doesn't tilt, the consistency is right and the polenta is done. Turn it out onto a large wooden board so that it retains its round loaf shape —this is the way it is often served in Italy.

Serves 4.

SERVING SUGGESTIONS. Polenta can be sliced with a large knife or, as more often in Italy, by holding a thread taut in both hands and sliding it between the board and the polenta, then cutting with the thread through the middle and into individual wedges.

There are countless ways to serve polenta. Since the Italian peasant method of serving it with milk still warm from the cow is not often possible today, the next simplest is to put large blobs of fresh butter in the central cavity of the hot polenta and sprinkle the mound with abundant grated Parmesan cheese, before you cut it.

POLENTA WITH CHEESE. Practically all types of cheese go well with polenta. One of my favorites is polenta with Gorgonzola. Make a creamy, thick sauce with 1 part Gorgonzola to 1 part butter and 1 part milk; pour it over the polenta loaf or slices. Cheeses that melt easily, such as Bel Paese, Bonbel, Fontina, can be put on top of the hot polenta and worked in individually at the table.

COLD POLENTA. When making polenta, it is a good idea to double the basic recipe and set aside half for a dish to be prepared a few days later. Cold polenta, covered, keeps several days in the refrigerator. For certain dishes in which a firmer consistency is desirable, a dryer polenta may be suggested. If you are making one of these with leftover polenta, cook the second half a little longer; you might keep it in the pot, covered, while you eat the first half, and then uncover and cook it a little longer.

The portion to be set aside must be shaped while the polenta is still hot. If the polenta is thick enough, after you have removed the amount needed for the current meal, pour the rest into a shallow dish with straight sides, and level the top surface. Leave uncovered until cool, then cover and refrigerate.

POLENTA FRITTERS. Slice off thin rectangles of cold polenta (about 1/2-inch thick), and pan fry on both sides in a little oil or butter on a heavy griddle or pan. The outer surface should be crisp and golden, but keep the heat rather low until the fritters have warmed up. Served with grated cheese, they are a delicious accompaniment to many vegetable dishes.

BROILED POLENTA. If you like a burned taste, brush polenta slices with butter or oil, then put under the broiler and broil on both sides.

POLENTA WITH ONION AND PEA RAGOUT

For a more substantial meal, we suggest the following accompaniment or sauce, which may inspire you to invent one of your own.

18–20 very small onions or pearl onions
1 pound very small tender fresh peas, or 10-ounce package
frozen (petits pois preferred)
2 cups tomato purée or Tomato Sauce
6 tablespoons olive oil
2 teaspoons chopped fresh basil (or 1 teaspoon dried)
1 teaspoon fresh tarragon leaves, chopped
(or ½ teaspoon dried)
salt and pepper
2 or 3 tablespoons milk (optional)
1 recipe Basic Polenta

Leaving onions whole, remove ends and outer skin, and place in a pot or saucepan with the peas, where they should fit in one layer. In a bowl, mix the other ingredients, except the milk, and add to the onions and peas, so that they are just more than covered. Bring to a boil, and simmer for about 20 minutes, until onions and peas are cooked and the sauce has been reduced to a nice density. Depending on the rate of absorption of the liquid, you may have to cover the pot from time to time. If you use Tomato Sauce rather than purée, the sauce may become too thick; in that case simply add a little milk and continue cooking.

Pour over polenta and serve.

Serves 4.

POLENTA WITH SAGE AND ROSEMARY

This dish is excellent if you can use fresh rosemary and sage, which are very easy herbs to grow on your windowsill. Both are perennial, thriving in all seasons. If you don't have fresh herbs, you can use the dried varieties, but the dish will not be nearly as good.

> *1 recipe Basic Polenta*
> *1 stick butter (8 tablespoons) , approximately*
> *3 or 4 fresh rosemary branches, each about 3 inches*
>   *long, or 2 teaspoons dried rosemary leaves (whole)*
> *12 to 14 fresh sage leaves, or about 6 dried*
>   *sage leaves (whole)*
> *4 tablespoons grated Parmesan cheese (approximately)*

Make Basic Polenta, flatten it on a rather shallow dish, and let cool. When cold, cut it into rounds, using a glass as cutter.

Preheat oven to 425°. In a small saucepan, sauté the fresh sage and rosemary in half the butter. If you use dried herbs, simmer the butter with the herbs without letting it brown, but for a shorter time; then remove the rosemary by draining through a sieve, and proceed with the recipe, omitting the rosemary on top.

Grease a shallow baking dish. Place the polenta rounds, slightly overlapping, with one piece of sage and some butter between each two slices. If any sage remains, add to the next layer (try not to make more than two layers) . Stick rosemary tufts on top, and pour the butter in which the herbs cooked all over the top surface. Sprinkle with the grated Parmesan cheese, and bake about 15 minutes, or until polenta begins to brown.

Serves 4.

POLENTA PASTICCIATA

1 recipe Basic Polenta, cooked and cooled
2 cups Tomato Sauce (see index)
3 tablespoons red wine
2 medium-sized onions, chopped
1 medium-sized carrot, chopped
1 celery stalk, chopped
3 tablespoons olive oil
½ cup imported dried mushrooms, rehydrated
    (see page 18)
salt and pepper
1 bay leaf
12 juniper berries
1 cup mozzarella (about 1 package), sliced thin
½ cup chopped Fontina, Muenster, or similar cheese
½ cup grated Parmesan cheese

Slice the cooled polenta or cut it into chunks. If the Tomato Sauce you have is already made and is fairly thick, dilute it with the red wine or with water. In a separate saucepan, sauté the onions, carrot, and celery in the oil. Add the mushrooms, salt, and pepper, sauté a few more minutes, then add the Tomato Sauce, the bay leaf and juniper berries, wrapped in cheesecloth, to be retrieved later.

When the sauce has simmered for a few minutes, add the wine, if you haven't already done so, and continue to simmer for about 10 minutes. Remove the bay leaf and juniper berries.

Preheat the oven to 400°. Grease a rectangular or square baking dish, not too shallow, and fill with layers, alternating polenta, sauce, and a mixture of the mozzarella, the Fontina or similar cheese, and the grated Parmesan. End with sauce, and sprinkle generously with grated cheese.

Bake for 20 minutes, or a little longer.

Serves 4.

VARIATIONS. This version is more elegant-looking than the preceding one, so you may want to reserve it for a special dinner. Use 1 cup grated Parmesan cheese instead of the three kinds of cheese. In a round baking dish, place a layer of polenta squares on the bottom, cover with sauce, and sprinkle with grated cheese. Start a second layer, making it smaller in circumference, and continue making smaller layers, alternating polenta, sauce, and grated cheese, to form a dome-shaped mound. Pour the rest of the sauce on top (you may need ½ cup or so more Tomato Sauce than for the previous recipe), dot the top of the mound with butter, and sprinkle additional grated cheese all over.

Bake in a 450° oven for 15 minutes, or until the curved surface has formed a light crust.

POLENTA AND CHEESE CROQUETTES

1 recipe Basic Polenta
1 cup (approximately) Fontina or
  similar cheese
1 egg, lightly beaten
breadcrumbs
oil for deep-frying

Make the polenta, using a little less water than called for. Turn it into a bowl and allow to cool a little, stirring once in a while to speed up the process. Make croquettes or small balls about 2½ inches in diameter. As you form each ball with your hands, enclose a small piece of cheese inside, making sure it is completely surrounded with the polenta. Dip the balls in the egg, then roll them in breadcrumbs, and fry in deep, very hot oil for 2 or 3 minutes. Remove with a slotted spoon, and drain on absorbent paper for a couple of minutes. Serve hot.

Serves 4.

Bulgur

BULGUR AND SPINACH

This dish is from southeastern Europe and is also common in the Middle East. The Greek version is very similar, although no spices are used. Sometimes the bulgur, which in Greece is called *plíguri,* is replaced by rice and more liquid is used. The dish is then called *spanakórizo.*

> *2 large onions, chopped*
> *5 tablespoons butter*
> *4 cups water*
> *1 cup coarse-grain bulgur*
> *1 teaspoon salt*
> *pinch pepper*
> *pinch ground cumin*
> *pinch nutmeg*
> *1 pound spinach, cleaned and drained*

In a heavy pot, sauté the onions in the butter until golden. Meanwhile, separately, bring the water to a boil and keep it hot without letting it evaporate. Add the bulgur to the onions, stirring over medium heat for a few minutes. When the bulgur begins to fry, add a little hot water, and stir. When the bulgur has absorbed the water, add a bit more, then add the rest of the water and the salt, pepper, cumin, and nutmeg. Continue to simmer, covered, on very low heat, for about 15 minutes. Mix in the spinach, and continue to simmer for another 15 minutes, or until bulgur and spinach are cooked.

Serves 4 as a main dish.

BULGUR AND LENTIL PILAF

This dish, originally from Armenia, has found its way into the Balkan countries, where it is usually cooked at home.

1 cup lentils
4 cups vegetable broth or water
1 bay leaf
3 tablespoons butter
1 large onion, chopped
salt and pepper
1 cup coarsely ground bulgur

Rinse the lentils, and put them in a pot with enough broth or water to cover. Add the bay leaf, bring to a boil, and keep covered. Turn off the heat and let stand for about 30 minutes.

While the lentils are soaking, melt the butter over medium heat in a fairly large heavy pot. Add the chopped onion, salt, and pepper, and sauté until the onion pieces are transparent.

Bring the lentils to a boil, then lower the heat, and simmer for about 20 minutes. Heat the rest of the broth in a separate pot.

When the onions are ready, keeping the heat medium, stir in the bulgur and continue stirring with a quick motion, so that the butter is absorbed. After 3 or 4 minutes, lower the heat to a simmer, add a little of the hot broth, and continue stirring. Then add the rest of the broth and the lentils in their broth. Bring to a boil, lower the heat to a bare simmer, stir one last time, cover tightly, and continue to cook until all the liquid is absorbed, or until the lentils and bulgur are cooked. Ideally, the bulgur and lentils are cooked and properly thick when all the liquid is absorbed. However, you may have to add a bit of liquid toward the end. Conversely, if the mixture is too loose, cook uncovered and stir often during the last 15 minutes. Remove the bay leaf before serving.

This is an excellent side dish to a vegetable stew.

Serves 4.

Kasha

BASIC KASHA

This cereal dish is the staple of Russia and of some bordering Middle European countries. While the most common version is made with buckwheat groats, in Russia, where *kasha* means pap or mush, it is often made with barley, oats, semolina, or even rice. The peasants often eat one of these dishes for breakfast.

5 tablespoons butter
2 cups buckwheat groats
1 egg, lightly beaten
3 cups boiling water, or a little more
1 teaspoon salt

Melt 3 tablespoons of the butter in a pot. Add the buckwheat, and increase the heat, stirring constantly to prevent the grain from sticking. After about 3 minutes, lower the heat, add the egg, and continue stirring for a minute or so. Add the boiling water, the salt, and the remaining 2 tablespoons butter, cover, and simmer for about 30 minutes.

Kasha is often eaten with cottage cheese or similar fresh cheeses, on the side or mixed in.

Serves 4.

KASHA WITH SPINACH AND EGGS

This simple home-cooked dish comes from southern Russia and bordering countries; it is more prevalent in the southern Middle European countries.

3 medium-sized onions, coarsely chopped
3 tablespoons oil
2 cups chopped spinach
1½ cups buckwheat groats
¼ teaspoon paprika
½ teaspoon salt
pepper
4 eggs
2 tablespoons butter

Sauté the onions in the oil, then add the spinach. After a few minutes, when the spinach is wilted, stir in the groats. Boil 3 cups of water and pour it on. Add paprika, salt, and pepper to taste, and stir well. Cover tightly, and simmer about 30 minutes, or until the grain is tender and fluffy.

During the last few minutes of cooking, lightly scramble the eggs in the butter, adding a little salt to the mixture. Mix the scrambled eggs into the kasha just before serving.

Serves 4.

Rice

Rice was first imported to Europe from the Orient by way of the Middle East, at the time of the Crusades. For about two centuries it was used only as a dessert. Various versions of rice puddings, rice with honey and milk, and other sweet dishes were eaten long before rice became a staple for soups, a first course, or an accompaniment to main dishes.

Almost a thousand years ago, the Po Valley in northern Italy (where most Italian rice is still grown) became the most important rice center in Europe, and from there rice was exported abroad. Thomas Jefferson found Italian rice so good that he imported some as an experiment for possible extensive cultivation, and grew it successfully. Much of the rice eaten today in the United States is a descendant of Italian rice.

The Italian rice growers successfully developed a strain of rice that grew larger than the Far Eastern rice, did not become mushy while cooking, and whose grains remained separate. Even today, while there are many different varieties of rice, the basic types fall into either of two categories: the Italian large, long-grain rice, the result of the growers' experiments, and the roundish, smaller grain. The former is used for risotto or for dishes accompanying the main courses. In this country Italian long-grain rice has been closely approximated by what is known as "converted rice," whose grains remain so separate, in fact, that it cannot be used for croquettes or molds, as they will not hold together. The smaller-grain rice is best suited for soups, puddings, croquettes, molds, and the like.

In this book, whenever the recipe specifies long-grain rice, the converted type is meant. Of course, if you can find imported Italian rice in your neighborhood, you will obtain even better results. If no mention is made of the type of rice to be used, the smaller grain would be preferable.

Brown rice is now available in specialized stores, as well as in some supermarkets. This has been processed only minimally—just enough to remove the hulls—to retain all its nutrients, but it is not a different variety. The same two basic categories apply also to brown rice. Many of the recipes contained in this book can be made with brown rice, if you prefer, although the result may not be quite the same, and, of course, you will have to cook it much longer.

As mentioned for flour (see page 23), while most nutrients are retained in brown rice and not in white rice, this is a matter of fewer nutrients rather than of added harmful substances. The depletion in white rice is not nearly as radical as that in white flour. You can decide which rice you want to use, keeping in mind that these recipes were originally meant for white rice.

Rice is such a versatile grain that additional rice recipes are given in other sections of the book.

BASIC RISOTTO

The basic method for starting any risotto is as follows: Use long-grain rice of the converted type (or imported Italian rice), calculating that 1½ cups of rice will be amply sufficient for four people if the risotto is to be a separate course or a substantial portion of the meal; 1 cup if it is to be used as a side dish.

Either water or vegetable broth can be used; of course, vegetable broth gives more flavor.

> *1 quart hot vegetable broth or water (approximately)*
> *1 medium-sized onion, finely chopped*
> *4 tablespoons butter, or 2 tablespoons butter and*
>   *2 tablespoons oil*
> *1½ cups long-grain rice*
> *salt*
> *grated Parmesan cheese*

Have the broth or water very hot or slightly simmering as you start the risotto in a separate pot. Sauté the onion in the butter or the oil and butter over low heat. When it is beginning to turn a very light golden brown, raise the heat to medium, and add the rice, mixing constantly with a wooden spoon for 2 or 3 minutes, until the rice turns yellowish-golden. Make sure it does not stick to the bottom of the pot. Now add a little broth or water, and continue stirring. The rice will absorb the liquid very quickly. Add a little more liquid as soon as the rice begins to look dry.

From this point on, there are two ways to continue. The traditional way is to keep adding liquid several times, though in greater quantities than the first couple of times, always stirring after the liquid has been added, until the rice is done. The other method is to add a little liquid two or three times at the beginning, then pour on the rest all at once, stirring. Cover the pot, and check after 10 minutes, at which point a little more liquid may have to be added. If the rice seems too liquid, remove the cover and let some moisture evaporate.

Total cooking time varies slightly according to the quality of the rice, but it is usually about 18 minutes from the first addition of liquid. Taste the rice after about 15 minutes. A good risotto should be *al dente* and should also have enough liquid in it to make it rather creamy. Since rice will continue to absorb some liquid even when removed from the heat, by the time it is served it will be just right.

Usually a few tablespoons of grated Parmesan cheese are stirred into the risotto when it is removed from the heat. This is one more reason to leave a little liquid in the rice. The cheese will make it drier and bind it together. More grated cheese can be added at the table, individually.

There are infinite varieties of risotto, some of which follow. You can also invent your own.

Whatever you add to the risotto, follow the steps indicated here up to the first two or three additions of liquid. Then continue according to the individual recipe.

Serves 4.

RISOTTO ALLA MILANESE. Add a small envelope (about $1/4$ teaspoon) of saffron to the rice about 5 minutes before the risotto is ready.

RISOTTO WITH MUSHROOMS. Presoak about $1/2$ cup imported dried mushrooms, chop them coarsely, and briefly sauté them. (If you don't have imported mushrooms, use double the amount of fresh cultivated mushrooms.) Add the mushrooms to the rice about halfway through the cooking.

Use vegetable broth rather than water for a much tastier dish. A little dry white wine can be substituted for broth during the last 5 minutes of cooking.

RISOTTO WITH BRANDY. Make Basic Risotto, using broth rather risotto. You will need two pots in addition to the one in which you cook the risotto. Heat the broth in one, and in the other heat 1 cup of beer, without letting it boil.

Proceed as for Basic Risotto, adding beer instead of broth when the rice is about half cooked and more liquid is needed.

RISOTTO WITH BRANDY. Make Basic Risotto, using broth rather than water, and add about 4 tablespoons good brandy a few minutes before the rice is ready. Make sure the rice returns to a boil quickly after you add the brandy, and let it cook at least 2 or 3 minutes, but not much longer, before removing from heat.

RISOTTO WITH VEGETABLES
Risotto Tutto Giardino

Literally, the Italian name means "risotto with the whole garden." With fewer vegetables, it is usually called *alla paesana* (country style). This risotto and similar versions are made throughout northern Italy. You can substitute your own choice of vegetables, especially if you grow them yourself and have a different selection from the ones listed here, but try and maintain similar proportions.

The vegetables should be chopped rather coarsely.

> *1 small onion, chopped*
> *1 shallot or 3 scallions, chopped*
> *3 tablespoons olive oil*
> *1½ cups long-grain rice*
> *3 tomatoes, peeled and chopped*
> *1 small zucchini, chopped*
> *½ cup fresh peas*
> *½ cup fresh beans (lima, pinto, navy, or similar variety)*
> *1 medium-sized carrot, chopped*
> *2 stalks celery, chopped*
> *½ cup dry white wine*
> *3 cups vegetable broth (approximately)*
> *2 teaspoons fresh basil, chopped (or 1 teaspoon dried)*
> *½ teaspoon fresh sage, chopped (or ¼ teaspoon dried)*
> *salt and pepper*
> *3 tablespoons butter*
> *½ cup grated Parmesan cheese*

In a large pot, sauté onion and shallot or scallions in the oil. Add the rice, raising the heat a little, and coat well in the oil by stirring. Add the tomatoes, zucchini, peas, beans, carrot, celery, wine, and seasoning. Bring to a boil, start adding the broth slowly, and proceed as for Basic Risotto. Add the herbs, salt, and pepper when the rice is half cooked.

Season with the butter and about 3 tablespoons of the cheese, remove from heat, and serve. The rest of the cheese can be sprinkled on individual portions at the table.

Serves 4.

GREEN RICE
Arroz Verde

A Spanish rice specialty. Similar versions of green rice are also found in Italy, where it is usually not baked and is made without peppers, and in Greece, where it is even simpler and is called *spanakórizo*.

> *4 tablespoons chopped green peppers*
> *7 tablespoons olive oil*
> *1½ cups long-grain rice*
> *½ cup chopped spinach*
> *½ cup chopped parsley*
> *2 tablespoons fresh chopped chives*
> *2 eggs*
> *1 cup light cream*
> *1 teaspoon salt*
> *¼ teaspoon pepper*
> *5 tablespoons grated Parmesan cheese*

Preheat the oven to 350°. Sauté the green peppers in the oil in a fairly large skillet for 5 minutes. Stir in the rice, spinach, parsley, and chives. Beat the eggs with the cream, salt, and pepper, and mix in. Put the mixture in well-greased 1-quart casserole, and sprinkle the cheese on top.

Bake for 35 minutes, or until browned and set.

Serves 4.

RICE SPANISH STYLE

Arroz Español

½ *pound mushrooms, sliced*
4 *tablespoons butter*
salt and pepper
2 *tablespoons sweet wine or sherry*
1 *small onion, chopped*
1 *clove garlic, pressed or minced*
2 *tablespoons olive oil*
1½ *cups long-grain rice*
1 *medium-sized green pepper, chopped*
4 *medium-sized tomatoes, fresh or canned, chopped*
3 *cups hot water* (*approximately*)
3 *whole cloves*
1 *bay leaf*
dash of cayenne or ¼ *teaspoon paprika*
parsley for garnish

Sauté the mushrooms in 2 tablespoons of the butter for a few minutes. Add salt and pepper, cover and remove from heat.

Sauté the onion and garlic in the oil and the remaining 2 tablespoons butter, raise the heat a little, add the rice, stirring until well coated, then add the green pepper, tomatoes, hot water, cloves, bay leaf, cayenne or paprika, mushrooms in their sauce, salt, and pepper. Stir, cover the pot, reduce the heat to simmer, and cook for 15 minutes or a little longer, adding the wine after about 10 minutes. All the liquid should have been absorbed by the rice at the end, but make sure not to overcook the rice. Check the liquid after you add the wine, and if there is too much, leave the lid off the pot, and continue cooking uncovered. If rice is too dry, add a little hot water. Remove the cloves and bay leaf and sprinkle with parsley before serving.

Serves 4.

FEATHERED RICE

For a different taste in rice, you may wish to try this basic recipe for pre-toasted rice. Use either brown or white rice, but it must be good-quality long grain. To the water or broth you may add sautéed chopped onions, carrots, celery, mushrooms, peas, or almost any other vegetable you have on hand. You many also add a pinch of saffron.

> *1½ cups rice*
> *4 cups boiling water or broth*
> *2 teaspoons salt*

Preheat oven to 425°. Have the rice perfectly dry, and spread it in a shallow pan so that it makes a very thin layer. Bake in the oven, stirring occasionally, until well toasted and golden brown.

Pour the rice into a heavy oven-proof casserole with a tight-fitting lid, add the salted boiling water or broth, and mix. Reduce the oven temperature to 400°, and bake, covered, about 25 minutes if you are using white rice; about 50 minutes for brown rice.

Serves 4.

PAN-FRIED RICE

Riso al Salto

The Italian verb *saltare* and the French verb *sauter* both mean "to jump," but in European kitchens they have long been used to mean "to fry quickly in a skillet," usually in butter—in other words, to make the food jump in the pan. The terms actually used are *al salto* or *saltato* in Italian and in French *sauté*, which is familiar around the world. Saltato and sauté can also mean flipped with a quick motion of the arm, as adept cooks do when turning pancakes or omelets, in which case the food actually jumps out of the pan and falls back again.

Although Pan-Fried Rice can be turned by flipping, more often this very simple dish is made by frying it as you would a frittata. In Italy, the dish is frequently made with leftover risotto, so I have used that method in this recipe.

> *leftover risotto or leftover rice (enough*
> *to fill one or more 9-inch skillets)*
> *3 tablespoons butter (more if you used more*
> *than one skillet)*
> *grated Parmesan cheese*

Whether you choose to make this dish with leftover risotto or with leftover rice, you must decide in advance and increase the quantity accordingly. You cannot use converted rice, as the grains will separate and it will be impossible to cook the Pan-Fried Rice in one piece. Instead use Italian long-grain rice or a nonconverted long-grain rice. If you use risotto, a plain one such as Risotto alla Milanese (see index) is best.

When the original risotto or rice is done, pour the warm rice to be used later for the Pan-Fried Rice onto a plate the approximate size of the skillet you will use, pressing it down gently to a thickness of 1 inch while still hot. Level the top. Allow it to cool, uncovered; then refrigerate, also uncovered, to allow the rice to form a slightly dry film. If you have more than enough to fill a 9-inch skillet, divide the rice onto two plates; you can then cook it in two skillets.

To make the Pan-Fried Rice, heat 2 tablespoons of the butter in a heavy skillet. Slide the pre-shaped rice into the skillet, taking care not to break the flattened shape, and start pan-frying over fairly high heat, then reduce heat to medium without letting the rice brown too much. It should form a nice crunchy crust on the bottom. Gently press with a spatula once in a while to flatten the rice a little more and to quicken the cooking process, but try not to allow the "caked" rice to separate into chunks. When the rice is golden and crusty on the bottom, flip it if you can. Unless you are an expert, it's safer to put a plate the same size as the skillet, or slightly larger, on top, remove the skillet from the heat, and, holding the plate and skillet together, turn them over with a quick motion. The rice should drop cleanly onto the plate. Put the skillet back on the stove, heat the remaining 1 tablespoon butter, slide the rice into it, and cook the other side.

Serve with lots of grated Parmesan cheese.

1 skillet serves 4.

RICE AND CHEESE BAKE

12 ounces mozzarella (about 1½ small packages)
4 tablespoons butter
2 cups rice
2 eggs, lightly beaten
4 tablespoons grated Parmesan cheese or more
4 tablespoons milk
white pepper to taste
breadcrumbs

Leave the mozzarella and butter at room temperature for about 30 minutes.

Preheat the oven to 400°. Cook the rice in 3½ cups of salted water (or slightly less than the amount of water specified on the package) for 12 to 14 minutes, depending on the quality of the rice; it should be undercooked. Remove from heat, pour into a bowl, and allow to cool somewhat. Meanwhile, cube the mozzarella very small, and add it to the warm rice with all the other ingredients, except the breadcrumbs. Mix it very well, until it becomes a thick pasty mass.

Grease a deep baking dish, sprinkle the bottom and sides with breadcrumbs, and fill it with the rice mixture, leveling the top. Sprinkle lightly with a little more grated cheese, and bake for 30 minutes.

Serves 4.

Casseroles

Vegetable casseroles, molds, pies, and similar dishes constitute the backbone of many vegetarian meals, and are quite satisfying. They can be served hot in the winter and lukewarm or at room temperature in the summer. Quite a few of them taste even better the following day.

Whether you cook them at the last moment or prepare them several hours or even a day in advance, there is no need to refrigerate, as the food is already cooked and will not spoil if not refrigerated for such a short time. Just cover the plate or oven dish with plastic film when the food has cooled to lukewarm. This makes it easier to reheat for a few minutes in the oven (without the plastic) if you plan to serve it warm, and it is already at room temperature if you plan to serve it cold.

If you prefer to refrigerate but would like to serve the dish at room temperature—always advisable, as the flavor is better than when a pie or casserole is too cold—take the dish out of the refrigerator at least 1 hour before mealtime.

The best pots to use for many types of dishes that contain a mixture of vegetables, eggs, grains, cheese, and so on are skillets or casseroles made of cast iron, without enamel coating. They absorb and distribute the heat very well, and if you heat the oil thoroughly before adding the mixture and let it run all around the sides as well as over the bottom, the mixture will sear quickly without sticking. Casseroles or pans of other materials may give you a lot of trouble.

Since cast-iron pots don't usually have plastic or wooden handles, the kind of dish described here can often be started on top of the stove and finished in the oven or under the broiler. When the dish is cooked, remove it from the heat and allow it to cool for at least 5 minutes before unmolding. Then pass the blade of a blunt-tipped knife all around the sides, as close to the pan as possible, place a serving dish on top of the skillet, and turn both dish and skillet, holding them close together. Gently lift the skillet to see if the food has loosened from the bottom (usually it has). If it does not fall whole onto the plate, let cool a few minutes, then tap the bottom of the pan with the handle of a large knife in several spots.

For molds and crustless pies the same system should be used, but cooling 5 to 10 minutes before unmolding is recommended. Because most molds are made of a metal thinner than cast iron, putting a wet cloth on the bottom of the upturned mold and around it usually helps to unmold the filling intact, after you have used the system previously described.

Vegetable pies without crusts are included in this section; those with crusts in the following section.

MIXED-VEGETABLE MOLD

With this dish you can really use your imagination. Consider the recipe as only a guide, and choose any vegetables that you find compatible in taste, juiciness, and texture, according to the season in which you are preparing this mold. If cabbage is out of season, make the outer bed with grape leaves or any other large edible leaves. Increase the variety of herbs if you wish.

> 2 small zucchini
> olive oil
> 3 medium-sized tomatoes, very ripe
> 1 small eggplant
> 2 medium-sized potatoes
> ½ pound green beans (approximately)
> 2 large carrots
> butter
> 1 fairly large cabbage
> 4 eggs
> 4 tablespoons grated cheese of your choice
> 1 tablespoon chopped parsley
> 1 tablespoon fresh basil, chopped (or 1½ teaspoons dried)
> salt and pepper

Each vegetable must be precooked separately. Slice the zucchini in thin rounds, and sauté them in a little oil. Peel the tomatoes, remove the seeds, cut them in wedges, then sauté them in some oil for a few minutes on fairly high heat, adding a little salt, and making sure they don't overcook and fall apart. Peel and slice the eggplant and fry it in oil (if the slices are too large, halve or quarter them). Peel the potatoes and cut them into slices about ½-inch thick, then sauté them in oil on low heat in a large skillet, being careful that they don't stick to the bottom and turning them once or twice. Steam the green beans. Cut the carrots in fairly thin strips about 2 inches long, removing the inner woody portion if necessary. Simmer them in a little butter and water, adding some salt, or, if you prefer, steam them. Parboil the cabbage whole. As soon as you think the outer leaves have loosened, lift the cabbage out of the boiling water and remove four or five large leaves, from the bottom up, without breaking them. You may have to put the cabbage back in the pot and boil it a little longer, but don't let it overcook, as the leaves you need should be barely softened. (The rest of the cabbage can be used in another dish, such as Bubble and Squeak, see index.)

Preheat the oven to 400°. Grease the bottom and sides of a fairly large deep mold very well with butter and oil. Lay the cabbage leaves at the bottom and sides, overlapping them slightly, to make a container inside a container.

Beat the eggs lightly with the grated cheese, parsley, basil, salt, and pepper.

Arrange a bottom layer of eggplant slices, distributing them well over the bottom and pressing them a little. Dribble a little of the egg mixture on top. Make layers of the other vegetables, dribbling some of the egg mixture on top of each layer. Stir the egg mixture before you pour it, as the cheese tends to settle on the bottom of the bowl. Finish with a layer of potatoes, and pour the remaining egg mixture on top. If some portions of the cabbage leaves stick out, either fold them toward the center, or cut them off. Dot with butter.

Bake for 30 to 40 minutes. Allow to rest at least 5 minutes before unmolding onto a hot platter.

Serves 4 to 6.

VEGETABLE BAKE

This is my grandmother's specialty, and an easy dish to prepare. It is similar to the preceding recipe; the types of vegetables can be changed according to the season, but you must have at least five different ones. The following version is excellent in the fall or winter.

breadcrumbs
1 medium-sized potato
1 medium-sized carrot
8 or 9 thin slices pumpkin or squash
4 or 5 small salsify (parsnips may be substituted)
3 small turnips
2 eggs, separated
salt and pepper
1 cup Tomato Sauce (see index)
grated Parmesan cheese
butter

Preheat the oven to 400°. Grease well a fairly deep baking dish, and sprinkle breadcrumbs all around inside.

Precook each vegetable separately, just until chewy; whenever possible, steam the vegetables. Cube them. Beat the egg whites until almost stiff, then lightly beat the yolks and fold them into the whites. Add salt and pepper at the same time.

Fill the baking dish, starting with a layer of potato cubes, adding some beaten egg, a few blobs of Tomato Sauce, and a sprinkling of cheese. Continue to layer in this way with the other vegetables. Cover with breadcrumbs, dot with butter, and bake for about 45 minutes or until the top begins to brown.

This can be served in the baking dish or can be unmolded onto a plate, as the bottom layer of potatoes, which when upturned becomes the top layer, is very attractive.

Serves 4 to 6.

FRENCH VEGETABLE MOLD

Far du Poitou

This is an excellent vegetable pudding from the Poitou region of France.

1 pound cabbage coarsely chopped, core removed
1½ pounds leeks, coarsely chopped
2 pounds sorrel or spinach, coarsely chopped
2 medium-sized onions, chopped
4 tablespoons butter
4 eggs
1 cup heavy cream
1 teaspoon salt
¼ teaspoon pepper
¼ teaspoon nutmeg
4 tablespoons grated Gruyère or Swiss cheese
breadcrumbs (optional)

Preheat oven to 375°. Cook cabbage and leeks in a tightly covered pot with just a little salted water. Stir once in a while, and add a little more hot water, if needed. Remove from heat after 20 minutes. Cook the sorrel or spinach in a large uncovered skillet for just a few minutes, stirring often. Squeeze out any liquid that may be left. Now drain the leeks and cabbage.

Sauté the onions in 2 tablespoons of the butter, then add the rest of the butter and the other vegetables, stirring constantly over high heat to allow all the liquid to evaporate.

Beat the eggs, cream, and seasoning together, then stir in the cheese. Add the vegetables, and mix well.

Grease a bread-loaf pan or deep mold and sprinkle with bread-crumbs or line with pieces of waxed paper to facilitate unmolding. Pour in the vegetable pudding and set the pan in a larger pan. Fill the outer pan with boiling water to reach about halfway up the mold. Bake for about 1 hour, or until a knife inserted in the pudding comes out clean. Remove from the oven, and allow to rest 5 to 10 minutes, then unmold.

Serve with Sauce Aurore (see index) either on the side or poured over the mold.

Serves 4.

SPANISH VEGETABLE STEW WITH EGGPLANT
Sanfaina

Similar to the well-known French *ratatouille, sanfaina* is very popular all over Spain. It is usually served with boiled potatoes or rice on the side.

> *5 tablespoons olive oil*
> *4 medium-sized onions, coarsely chopped*
> *4 large green peppers, coarsely chopped*
> *4 large tomatoes, chopped*
> *1 medium-sized eggplant, peeled and cubed*
> *⅛ teaspoon cayenne pepper*
> *¼ teaspoon paprika*
> *salt*

In a heavy skillet with a lid, heat the oil and sauté the onions, then add the other ingredients, stirring well so that all are coated with the oil. Cover, and simmer for about 15 minutes or until the green peppers are cooked but firm. At this point if the stew seems too liquid, remove the cover and continue cooking, stirring once in a while, until most of the liquid has evaporated. If the tomatoes are not very juicy, you may have to add a little water.

Serves 4.

SPANISH VEGETABLE STEW WITH SQUASH
Pisto

The preceding stew and this one are very similar, both being derived from the French ratatouille. *Pisto,* however, has taken its name from the ubiquitous Genoese Pesto, which had already traveled to France where it was transformed from a sauce into a soup called *pistou* (see French Vegetable Soup in index). Pisto, though, has ended up as a stew instead of a sauce or soup. The basil has totally disappeared, and the garlic and olive oil are the only ingredients left from the original inspiration. Pisto is often served as an appetizer, warm or cold, but the amounts of this one from Valencia are sufficient for a main dish.

3 large onions, chopped
4 large green peppers, coarsely chopped
4 large tomatoes, peeled and coarsely chopped
1 pound yellow squash, peeled, seeded, and cubed
2 medium-sized potatoes, peeled and cubed
5 tablespoons olive oil
2 cloves garlic, minced
2 tablespoons chopped parsley
1½ teaspoons salt

Follow the directions in the preceding recipe, but simmer, covered, on very low heat, for about 40 minutes, stirring a few times while it is cooking. You may have to adjust the liquid by adding water if the stew is on the dry side or by reducing by removing the lid if you have too much liquid when the vegetables are nearly done.

Serves 4.

GREEK VEGETABLE STEW
Bríami

A dish popular all over Greece. Some of the vegetables change with the season, but because both tomatoes and potatoes are abundant in Greece throughout the year, these are always included. You may wish to follow the Greek habit and prepare *bríami* with whatever vegetables are in season. Here is a summer version.

> 2 medium-sized zucchini, sliced
> 1 medium-sized eggplant, peeled and sliced
> 2 medium-sized onions, peeled and sliced
> ½ pound small young okra, stems removed
> 1 cup green beans, cut in half
> 1 large potato, peeled and sliced thin
> 3 or 4 medium-sized fresh tomatoes, peeled and sliced
> olive oil
> 2 tablespoons fresh basil leaves, chopped (or
>   1 tablespoon dried)
> 2 cloves garlic, minced
> salt and pepper

Preheat oven to 350°. In a deep casserole with a lid, which will double as a serving dish, make a layer of each vegetable. Dribble a little oil over each layer and sprinkle lightly with basil, garlic, salt, and pepper. Layer the vegetables in any order you wish, but put the potatoes in the middle, so they won't stick to the bottom, and end with tomatoes.

Bake, covered, for about 1½ hours, basting once or twice. The vegetables should be simmered, so if you see that they are bubbling too much, lower the temperature, even though this may lengthen cooking time. If some of the vegetables you have included are rather watery, bake uncovered for the last 10 minutes or so.

Serves 4 to 6.

IMÁM BAIALDÍ

A Mohammedan import that has become a very popular dish in Greece and is fast becoming well known in America. The secret is in the quantity of onions—you can hardly use too many. There

are two ways of cooking this—on top of the stove or in the oven.
I prefer the oven version.

> *3 pounds small eggplants (the European variety*
> *with thinner skin is preferable)*
> *6 cloves garlic*
> *½ to ¾ cup olive oil*
> *7 or 8 medium-sized onions, sliced thick*
> *1 tablespoon chopped parsley*
> *1 teaspoon salt*
> *pepper*
> *3 large fresh tomatoes or 2 cups canned*
> *(fresh preferred)*

Cut the stems from the eggplants. Make a deep slit along the
length of each eggplant. Cut the garlic cloves in halves or quarters according to their size, and insert a couple of pieces inside
each slit.

Fry the eggplants briefly in the olive oil, until the outer skin
wrinkles and the pulp just underneath begins to cook. Remove
the eggplant and in the same skillet sauté the onions over medium
heat, stirring constantly. They should not be completely cooked,
but if they are a little browned it's all right. Stir in the parsley,
salt, and pepper.

If you plan to cook this on top of the stove, add the tomatoes
to the onions, and cook, uncovered, for about 10 minutes; then
put the eggplants on top, add a little water, cover, and boil for
about 5 minutes. Reduce the heat and continue cooking for
about 40 minutes longer. Shake the skillet once in a while, or
move the vegetables around to make sure they don't stick to the
bottom.

If you bake it, preheat the oven to 400°. Oil an oven-proof dish
in which the pre-fried eggplants will fit snugly. Put the eggplants
in it, cover with water, then with the sautéed onions, and finally
with the tomatoes. Bake for about 30 minutes. If the vegetables
seem undercooked, raise the temperature to 450°, and bake 15
minutes longer.

Serves 4–6.

JERUSALEM ARTICHOKE CASSEROLE

2 pounds Jerusalem artichokes
½ cup imported dried mushrooms, rehydrated
*   (see page 18)*
3 tablespoons butter
3 large onions, coarsely chopped
pinch of nutmeg
pinch of ginger
salt and pepper
6 tablespoons Swiss cheese, shredded or grated

Boil the Jerusalem artichokes in water, including that in which you have rehydrated the mushrooms, and 1 tablespoon of the butter. Do not overcook, but remove from the heat when still very chewy. (Reserve the cooking liquid, which is excellent as a base for soups, sauces, and other dishes.) Peel the Jerusalem artichokes, and chop them coarsely. Add the onions and seasoning.

Preheat the oven to 450°. Grease a baking dish, put in one layer of artichokes and onions, and sprinkle with some of the cheese. Coarsely chop the mushrooms, and add some of them. Continue layering until the casserole is almost full, ending with cheese. Dot with the remaining 2 tablespoons of butter.

Bake for about 20 minutes.

Serves 4.

BROCCOLI CASSEROLE

3 pounds broccoli (approximately)
1 large onion, sliced very thin
1 whole clove garlic
½ cup olive oil (approximately)
5 or 6 black olives, Sicilian or Greek type
½ cup feta cheese or similar goat's milk cheese,
  crumbled
8 tablespoons grated Romano cheese
1 cup capers
½ cup dry red wine

For this dish to cook evenly it is best to use only the top portions of the broccoli, including the tender part of the stems (you can use the stems in other dishes). Cut off the flowerets and if the tender stems are too thick, cut them in half, since they take longer to cook than the flowerets. Keep separate.

Put the onion and garlic in a deep cast-iron pot or a heat-resistant dish that has a lid, and sauté very gently in a little of the oil.

Pit the olives and chop them coarsely, then put them in a bowl with the crumbled feta cheese, 6 tablespoons grated Romano cheese (reserve 2 tablespoons), the capers, and a little more oil. Mix well. Discard the garlic. Add a layer of broccoli to the pot (the cut stems on the bottom). Make another layer with the cheese and olive mixture, pour in a little oil, and continue layering, ending with the cheese mixture. Pour the wine on top, then the rest of the oil, sprinkle with the reserved grated cheese, and cover tightly.

Cook very, very gently over low heat for about 40 minutes. Do not uncover, but shake the pot once in a while, so that the bottom layer will not stick. Serve in the same pot.

Serves 4.

CHICK-PEA AND SPINACH CASSEROLE

This tasty dish comes from France.

2½ pounds spinach
1½ cups chick-peas
1 teaspoon thyme
2 medium-sized carrots, each cut into 4 or 5 pieces
2 small onions, each stuck with 2 cloves
1 clove garlic, chopped
salt and pepper
2 medium-sized tomatoes, chopped (if canned, drain
*   after chopping)*
5 tablespoons olive oil
3 tablespoons chopped parsley
1 teaspoon savory
12 almonds, blanched
¼ teaspoon saffron
dash cayenne pepper
breadcrumbs

Wash the spinach and wilt it in a saucepan for a few minutes. Squeeze dry, saving whatever liquid may be left.

In a large saucepan, cover the chick-peas with water and the liquid from the spinach, bring to a boil, turn off heat, and soak for about 1 hour. Then add the thyme, carrots, and onions. Simmer for about 1 hour, or a little longer. During the last half hour, add salt and pepper.

While the chick-peas are cooking, simmer the tomatoes, uncovered, in about 2 tablespoons of the oil, adding the garlic, parsley, savory, and a little salt.

Preheat oven to 400°. Chop the almonds in a blender, then remove to a mortar, and pound them to a paste. Add the saffron, a pinch of black pepper, and the cayenne, and pound some more. If the paste becomes too dry, add a little liquid from the chick-peas. When the chick-peas are cooked, the little liquid left in the pot should have the consistency of a sauce. If there is too much liquid, drain out some. Remove the carrots and onions and pass them through a sieve, discarding the cloves. Add the purée to the chick-peas, then stir in the tomato mixture and the almond paste, and bring to a boil, stirring constantly. Add the spinach, adjust seasoning, and pour into a greased baking dish, leveling the surface. Sprinkle with breadcrumbs, and bake for 30 minutes.

Serves 4.

RUTABAGA AND CARROT CASSEROLE

From Scandinavia. Rutabagas are yellow turnips, sometimes called swedes, presumably because they were first introduced in this country by Swedish immigrants.

> *2 pounds rutabagas*
> *1 pound small carrots*
> *4 tablespoons butter*
> *4 tablespoons heavy cream*
> *⅛ teaspoon powdered coriander*
> *¼ teaspoon nutmeg*
> *¼ teaspoon fennel seeds, crushed*
> *salt and pepper to taste*

Steam the rutabagas and carrots separately, as cooking time is different. They should both be rather firm when you remove them from the steamer. Cut both into bite-sized pieces. Preheat the oven to 375°. Melt 2 tablespoons of the butter in a skillet, and add the vegetables. Finish cooking, stirring so that every piece is coated. Add the other ingredients, and pour the mixture into a heat-resistant baking dish, dotting with the rest of the butter.

Bake for 20 minutes. If at the end of this time the surface still looks pale, pass under the broiler for a minute or so.

Serves 4.

SORREL AND LEEK BAKE
Smeazza Ticinese

This excellent dish from the Ticino canton, the Italian-speaking section of Switzerland, is a successful blend of northern Italian and Swiss cooking. The vegetable most often used, aside from the leeks, is sorrel, but since sorrel is not as common as it used to be, spinach or chard is often substituted. You may also try this dish with kale, but in this case choose only tender, young plants.

> *1 pound sorrel (or spinach or chard), coarsely chopped*
> *1 pound leeks, coarsely chopped*
> *4 eggs*
> *½ teaspoon salt*
> *¼ teaspoon pepper*
> *1 cup yellow cornmeal*
> *1⅓ cups cold water*
> *¾ cup Swiss cheese, finely cubed or shredded*
> *5 tablespoons oil*
> *2 tablespoons grated cheese, either Parmesan or Swiss*

Take particular care in washing the greens, as they gather a lot of soil. Leeks hide it between their rings, so you may have to rinse them again after you chop them. When the sorrel and leeks are chopped, the volume of each should be approximately the same.

Preheat the oven to 375°. Beat the eggs, adding salt and pepper. Mix the cornmeal and water and add the beaten eggs, stirring well. Thoroughly mix in the vegetables and Swiss cheese.

With 2 tablespoons of the oil, grease a baking dish, preferably about 10 inches square and at least 2 inches deep. Fill with the mixture, level the top, and dribble the rest of the oil evenly over the surface. Sprinkle with the grated cheese.

Bake for 50 minutes, then check color and consistency. If it seems all right, continue baking for another 20 or 25 minutes; if it seems too pale and liquid, raise the temperature to 400°, and check again after 20 minutes. Cooking time may vary slightly according to the amount of liquid contained in the vegetables and the quality of the cornmeal.

Serve hot or lukewarm. This is also good the following day, at room temperature.

Serves 4.

POTATO-TOMATO BAKE
Chupe

A dish from Spain.

> *2 large potatoes*
> *2 large onions, sliced thin*
> *3 large tomatoes, cut in fairly thick slices*
> *4 or 5 tablespoons butter*
> *¾ cup grated Romano or Parmesan cheese*
> *1 teaspoon cayenne pepper (or 2 teaspoons paprika,*
> *   if you don't like it hot)*
> *salt*

Boil the potatoes in their jackets until firm. Peel and slice them.

Preheat the oven to 375°. In a well-greased baking dish, place layers of onions, potatoes, and tomatoes, dotting each layer with butter and sprinkling with cheese. End with potatoes, again dotting with butter and sprinkling with the rest of the cheese and the cayenne pepper or paprika.

Bake for about 1 hour, until the onions are well cooked and the tomatoes have released their juice and reabsorbed it.

Serves 4.

ZUCCHINI-POTATO BAKE

This typical Cretan dish is rarely found in restaurants, even in Crete, but is frequently made at home. I have substituted ricotta, sour cream, and a little feta cheese to approximate the taste of the Greek anthótyro, which is a fresh cheese similar to Roman ricotta, and also made with sheep or goat's milk. You'll be able to duplicate the authentic dish if you can find anthótyro, mizíthra, or fresh Roman ricotta. Use 5½ cups of any of these instead of the feta, ricotta, and sour cream in the recipe, but if the cheese you find is too dry, you may still wish to add some sour cream. Whatever combination you use, do not decrease the amount of dill, because it is the dill that makes this dish really unusual and delicious.

> *4 medium-sized potatoes*
> *1 medium-sized onion, sliced thin*
> *1 cup olive oil (approximately)*
> *salt*
> *1 cup ricotta*
> *½ cup sour cream*
> *4 tablespoons feta cheese, crumbled, or 3 tablespoons*
>   *grated Romano cheese*
> *3 teaspoons fresh dill (or 2 teaspoons dried)*
> *2 teaspoons fresh mint (or 1 teaspoon dried)*
> *pepper*
> *4 medium-sized zucchini, sliced into rounds about*
>   *½ inch thick*

Preheat oven to 400°. Peel the potatoes and slice paper-thin (a cabbage shredder is a good tool for this), add the onion, and mix well with about ½ cup of the oil and a little salt. Spread in large shallow baking dish, and bake about 20 minutes, peeking once or twice to turn or loosen the potatoes if some are sticking to the bottom or to one another.

Thoroughly mix the ricotta, sour cream, feta, most of the dill and mint (reserving less than 1 teaspoon of each if fresh, or less than ½ teaspoon if dried), and most of the remaining oil. Sprinkle with salt and pepper, and mix in the zucchini.

Remove the potatoes from the oven, and add the zucchini-cheese mixture, stirring or turning to make sure every piece is coated. Spread evenly with a spatula. The combined mixture should be no more than 2 inches thick, preferably less. Sprinkle the remaining herbs and oil on top. Bake for about 30 minutes. The vegetables at the top should be lightly browned; if they are not, raise the temperature to 450° and bake about 15 minutes longer. It is difficult to give a precise temperature or cooking time, since the potatoes will cook slightly faster or more slowly, according to the variety you use.

Serves 4.

BUBBLE AND SQUEAK

This is a rather common dish in England but is not very well known here. It is often made the day after a big holiday, when leftover vegetables are on hand and the meal should be light after heavy holiday fare. The basic vegetables are cabbage and potatoes, but any others can be added. The name comes from the fact that, while frying, the potatoes bubble and the cabbage squeaks.

> *1 medium-sized cabbage*
> *1 pound potatoes*
> *6 tablespoons oil*
> *2 medium-sized onions, chopped*
> *salt to taste*
> *any other leftover vegetables (optional)*

Leftover cabbage and/or potatoes may be used, but if you start from scratch, shred the cabbage coarsely and peel the potatoes, cutting them into fairly thin slices.

Heat the oil, add the onions, and after a few minutes add the cabbage. When it begins to wilt, add the potatoes. Cook, uncovered, over medium heat, stirring and pressing with a spatula or wooden spoon, which will make the mixture bubble and squeak. A few minutes before the cabbage and potatoes are ready, add salt, taste, and adjust if needed. Add any leftover cooked vegetables you may have, and cook until done.

Serve very hot.

Serves 4.

HERB PUDDING

This recipe also comes from England, more precisely from Cumbria, in the Lake Region. Choose whatever greens you can find, both wild and cultivated. The list in the original recipe may be hard to duplicate, but if you are lucky enough to live in the country, the choice is yours. Some suggestions given in the original English recipe include Easter magiants (bistort), nettles, dandelion leaves, black-currant leaves; with this as a guide, make your own selection or choose your own.

In spite of the fact that the ingredients are completely different, note the resemblance between this recipe and Sorrel and Leek Bake.

> ½ *small cabbage, shredded, or equivalent amount of*
>   *tender kale*
> *3 cups wild greens of your choice, coarsely cut*
> ½ *cup oatmeal*
> ½ *cup barley*
> *salt and pepper*
> *3 tablespoons oil*
> *1 egg, lightly beaten*

Wash and dry the cabbage or kale and the wild greens. Cut them fine and put them in a deep well-greased baking dish. Add the oatmeal, barley, salt, and pepper, and cover with about ½ inch water, allowing about 2 inches space on top, as the grains swell. Let stand overnight.

Preheat the oven to 375°. Add the oil and mix thoroughly. Bake as is, for about 1½ hours or longer, until a knife inserted in the pudding comes out clean. When the dish is almost ready, add the egg on top, and bake a few minutes longer.

This pudding can also be made on top of the stove, but then you should add more oil to the mixture and stir occasionally to prevent it from sticking to the pot. Mix in the beaten egg at the end.

Serves 4.

COLD LOAF

This English dish, full of proteins, is excellent in the summer. You may serve it with a cold sauce of your choice, but use a rather mild one, as the loaf has a definite taste of its own.

> ½ *pound mushrooms, chopped*
> 1 *medium-sized onion, chopped*
> 2 *tablespoons butter*
> 4 *tablespoons beer*
> 4 *eggs*
> ½ *teaspoon dried sage*
> ½ *teaspoon thyme*
> *salt and pepper*
> ½ *teaspoon soy sauce (optional)*
> 1 *cup boiled and mashed potatoes*
> 1 *cup peeled and diced tomatoes (if canned,*
> *drain well after dicing)*
> ½ *cup chopped walnuts*
> ½ *cup chopped almonds*
> ½ *cup green pistachio nuts (optional,*
> *or substitute other nuts)*
> 1 *cup breadcrumbs*

Sauté the mushrooms and chopped onion in the butter and beer until all the liquid has evaporated. Boil 2 of the eggs for 6 minutes, cool immediately under cold water, and carefully remove the shells. (The eggs will not be completely hard.) Beat the other 2 eggs, and stir in the sage, thyme, salt, and pepper. Add the soy sauce (if used). Mix all the ingredients except the cooked eggs, and work with a wooden spoon to make a fairly hard ball.

Preheat the oven to 375°. Grease well a deep rectangular pan, such as a bread pan, and put in a little of the paste mixture, then align the cooked eggs the long way of the pan, one behind the other, and stuff the rest of the paste all around and on top, making sure that the eggs are covered. Level the top, and add a sprinkling of additional breadcrumbs.

Bake for 1 hour and allow to cool completely in the baking pan. Bang the pan on a hard surface a few times, knock it on the sides, and turn upside down on a serving platter.

Serve cold, sliced.

Serves 4.

PUMPKIN FLAN

1 pound pumpkin
1 cup flour
3 tablespoons milk
1 teaspoon grated lemon peel
¼ teaspoon nutmeg
¼ teaspoon cinnamon
¼ teaspoon coriander
salt and pepper
6 eggs, separated
1½ cups Fontina or similar tangy,
*   semi-soft cheese*
breadcrumbs

Preheat oven to 450°. Peel and cube the pumpkin, and cook it in very little water, stirring often, or bake it. Pass it through a sieve or food mill. Add the flour, milk, lemon peel, nutmeg, cinnamon, coriander, salt, pepper, and the egg yolks. Cut the cheese into very small cubes or slice it thin, then mix it into the pumpkin.

Grease a deep mold or soufflé dish with the butter, and sprinkle bottom and sides with breadcrumbs. Beat the egg whites until stiff, fold them into the pumpkin mixture, and pour the mixture into the mold. Bake for about 30 minutes, or until a knife inserted into the flan comes out clean; try not to open the oven more than once, as this dish behaves like a soufflé, puffing up, but then becoming deflated. For this reason, it is best served immediately after you remove it from the oven.

Serves 4.

SPINACH FLAN

2 pounds spinach
1 tablespoon flour
½ cup heavy cream
½ cup ricotta
5 tablespoons grated Parmesan cheese
¼ teaspoon nutmeg
3 tablespoons raisins (optional)
3 tablespoons butter
3 tablespoons cold vegetable broth
3 eggs, lightly beaten
salt and pepper to taste
breadcrumbs

Cook the spinach until it begins to wilt (see page 19); drain well, and pass through a food mill. Make a paste with the flour and a little of the cream, then add the rest of the cream, the ricotta, grated cheese, nutmeg, and the raisins (if used). Stir in the spinach, and simmer, uncovered, stirring constantly, for about 8 minutes. Remove from heat and add the butter and broth.

Preheat the oven to 350°. Allow the spinach mixture to cool somewhat, then add the eggs, salt, and pepper.

Grease an oven dish or mold, and sprinkle the bottom and sides with breadcrumbs. Pour in the spinach mixture, sprinkle with more breadcrumbs, and bake for about 45 minutes.

Allow to cool at least 5 minutes before unmolding. Serve plain or topped with a mushroom sauce (see index). Or bake in a mold with a central hole, and after unmolding fill the hole with sautéed mushrooms or with mushrooms and peas or a similar combination.

Serves 4.

FRENCH CAULIFLOWER PIE
Pain de Choufleur

This is a recipe from Brittany. Using the same method, you can substitute other vegetables according to the season. Herbs and spices may be changed to suit the vegetable you choose.

> *1 medium-sized cauliflower*
> *2 cups milk*
> *½ cup grated or shredded Swiss cheese*
> *pinch of nutmeg*
> *½ teaspoon fresh chopped tarragon*
> *(or ¼ teaspoon dried)*
> *salt and pepper*
> *4 eggs, lightly beaten*

Steam the cauliflower about 8 minutes, or until it is still rather firm. Remove the core and chop the rest coarsely. Stir the cauliflower and all other ingredients into the eggs.

Preheat the oven to 375°. Grease a mold or deep pan very well with butter, and pour the cauliflower mixture into it. Bake for about 30 minutes, or until the center seems firm when shaken and the top is beginning to turn golden.

Serves 4.

CRUSTLESS RICE AND ZUCCHINI PIE

2½ cups cooked rice
4 small zucchini, shredded or grated
4 eggs, lightly beaten
½ cup grated Parmesan cheese
½ teaspoon nutmeg
½ teaspoon grated lemon rind
¼ teaspoon turmeric powder
¼ teaspoon dried dill
½ teaspoon salt
2 tablespoons oil (approximately)

Mix the rice and zucchini, and stir in the eggs. Add all the other ingredients except the oil.

Heat the oil over high heat in a heavy skillet at least 2 inches deep. A 10-inch or 10½-inch skillet should easily accommodate this amount.

When the oil is hot, add the zucchini mixture, flattening the top. Lower the heat, and cook for about 20 minutes over moderate to low heat. When the bottom has cooked, place the pan under the broiler, several inches from the heat, for 2 or 3 minutes. Allow to cool for about 5 minutes, and turn the skillet upside down onto a serving platter.

Serves 4.

Vegetable Pies

The vegetable pies in this chapter make very satisfactory main courses for a vegetarian lunch or dinner, and when served with a salad of fresh greens are excellent meals in themselves, particularly in the summer. They can also be prepared in advance, either in part or completely. If you usually have a special time for baking bread, for example, you can prepare the dough for a few pie crusts at the same time, then freeze it in separate balls (sealed in plastic bags), each of which will yield the right amount for one pie crust. When you plan to bake a vegetable pie, allow the dough to thaw for a few hours before you proceed.

If you wish, and have ample freezer space, you can bake the entire pie and freeze it, but the results are better in terms of taste if you freeze only the pie crusts. In this case, roll out the dough and stack the crusts with sheets of plastic or waxed paper between them for easy removal, one at a time. Place them in a strong cardboard box of the right size, put the box in a large plastic bag, closing it with a twist'em so that no air will penetrate, and store in the freezer.

If you are making a pie to be eaten a few hours later, do not refrigerate but leave it at room temperature, covered. You can then reheat it in a slow oven, or serve it as it is, for vegetable pies are very tasty at room temperature. In fact, some of them taste better the day after they are made. If you refrigerate a pie, allow it to stand at room temperature at least 1 hour before serving.

140

Following the guidelines given in this section, you can substitute whatever vegetables you have at hand, use leftovers, and invent your own vegetable pies.

BASIC PIZZA

No introduction is needed for this well-known Neapolitan dish. But now that prepared frozen pizza has become so popular, we suggest you try baking your own and taste for yourself how much better it is than the commercially prepared pizza. While the real flavor and crustiness of a pizza can best be obtained if it is baked in a large professional oven, a good pizza can still be baked in the home oven. And so many people bake their own breads these days that making real pizza at home hardly means extra effort.

PIZZA DOUGH
1 ounce bread yeast
1 cup water, slightly warmed
3 cups flour
pinch salt

Dissolve the yeast in a little of the water. Mix with the rest of the water, add to the flour and salt, then knead the dough as if you were making bread, punching it and working it well, until you have a smooth and fairly soft dough, which you shape into a ball. In the bottom of a bowl twice the size of the dough sprinkle a little flour, and place the dough ball in it. Leave in a tepid place until the dough has doubled in size—between 2 and 2½ hours. Now knead it a little more, then spread it with your hands into a circle that you can easily put in a lightly greased pizza pan or on a cookie sheet. Now spread the dough to the size of the pan or sheet by slapping it with your hands to flatten it to a thickness of about ¼ inch. This amount of dough should yield a disk about 16 inches in diameter.

FILLING
½ cup olive oil (approximately)
4 ounces (about half a package) mozzarella, diced small
¾ pound fresh tomatoes, peeled and chopped coarsely
salt and pepper
1 tablespoon oregano

When preparing the pizza, preheat the oven well in advance to a temperature of 500° or a little higher. After you have arranged the dough in the pan or cookie sheet, dribble a little olive oil all over. Distribute the mozzarella on the dough, then the tomatoes. Sprinkle with salt and pepper, then with the oregano. Dribble a little more oil on top.

Bake in the lower portion of the oven for about 15 minutes. The length of baking time may vary according to the size of your oven.

Note: This is the classic filling for Neapolitan pizza. Anchovies are usually added, but as a vegetarian I have omitted them. Anyway, many Americans don't seem to like the flavor of anchovies. In the United States even in Italian pizzerie anchovies are often omitted. You may wish to substitute a sprinkling of capers.

Makes 6–8 slices.

VARIATIONS: There are countless fillings for pizza, if you simply use your imagination. A few suggestions follow. To practically any of these, fresh mushrooms, either sautéed or raw (in the latter case sliced very thin), can be added. Strips of peppers are also excellent.

PIZZA WITH RICOTTA. Often the crust for this pizza is deep-fried rather than baked, but it can also be baked as a regular pizza. In this case, just spread ricotta on the crust and grind a little pepper on top. You may also add fresh chopped herbs of your choice. Bake with the crust.

PIZZA WITH OIL, GARLIC, AND ROSEMARY. Brown a few cloves of garlic in olive oil, then pour the oil on the dough with or without the garlic. Sprinkle with fresh rosemary leaves, and bake.

PIZZA WITH TOMATO SAUCE AND FRESH BASIL.   Proceed as for the preceding recipe, adding about 2 tablespoons of tomato pulp, salt, pepper, and fresh basil to the oil and garlic. Or cook the sauce separately and spread it on the pizza dough.

PIZZA WITH CHICORY

Another Neapolitan pizza, but this one is like a double pizza, or a large sandwich.

> *1½ recipes Basic Pizza dough, rolled into*
> *   two layers*
>
> FILLING
> *4 to 6 very small heads chicory*
> *1 cup black olives (Greek or Sicilian style),*
> *   pitted and coarsely chopped*
> *3 tablespoons capers*
> *3 tablespoons pine nuts*
> *olive oil*
> *pepper*

Spread one layer of the dough in a lightly greased pizza pan or on a cookie sheet. Wash the chicory very well, but keep the heads whole. Drain well, upside down, then pat dry with a towel. Mix the olives, capers, and pine nuts with a little olive oil and pepper. Gently open the center of each chicory head, and stuff with the olive mixture. Close the heads by tying them together with string. Pan-fry them in olive oil at low to medium heat. When they are almost cooked, remove them from the pan, and allow to cool a little.

Preheat oven to 450°. Because of the double layer of crust, this pizza requires slightly lower heat and longer baking. Place the chicory heads on the bottom layer of dough, and remove the string. Cover with the other layer of dough, and press the layers together, making sure the edges are sealed. Trickle a little olive oil on top, and bake for about 30 minutes. This pizza is usually eaten warm but not hot.

Serves 6.

PISCIADELA

This pizza is a specialty from Ventimiglia, a town on the Italian Riviera, near the French border. It is similar both to Neapolitan pizza and to Pissaladière, the recipe for which follows.

> *1 recipe Basic Pizza dough*
> *¾ pound onions, chopped coarsely*
> *½ pound fresh tomatoes, chopped coarsely*
> *½ cup olive oil (approximately)*
> *salt and pepper*

Leave the dough a little thicker than for Neapolitan pizza and make the pie a little smaller—10 or 11 inches in diameter. Sauté the onions and tomatoes in half the olive oil, adding salt and pepper, then spread the mixture on the crust. Dribble more olive oil over all.

Bake a little longer than Basic Pizza and at a slightly lower temperature: about 25 minutes at 475°.

Serves 6.

PISSALADIÈRE

Legend has it that the name *pissaladière* is a French corruption of Pizza a l'Andrea, named after the famous Genoese leader

Andrea Doria, who was partial to it. This explanation makes a certain amount of sense, considering that the French find it diffi-cult to pronounce the sound *"zz"* *(ts)*, as was shown by their changing the name Nizza to Nice. Also, until about a century ago, Nice (Nizza) belonged to Italy, and the French and Italian languages could have been mixed into *pissaladière*.

Recipes for the crust vary. One calls for phyllo pastry (*mille-feuille*), which supports the belief that this is a very ancient dish originating several centuries before Christ, when the Greeks first founded Nice and imported their famous baking skills. Other recipes call for a crust made with *pâte brisée*—French Pie Crust—(perhaps a shortcut, which anyway makes it more French) and half a cup of very thick Tomato Sauce, cooked separately and placed in strips on top of the other filling.

As in the conventional Neapolitan pizza, anchovies are added to the filling. I omit these altogether or substitute capers.

> *1 recipe Basic Pizza dough, or 1 recipe French Pie Crust*
> *(see index)*
>
> > FILLING
> > ½ *pound leeks* (*only the white portion*)
> > 2½ *pounds large onions*
> > *3 cloves garlic, whole*
> > *1 bouquet garni made with thyme, bay leaves,*
> >   *and parsley*
> > *5 tablespoons olive oil*
> > *salt and pepper*
> > *12 black olives* (*Greek or Sicilian type*), *pitted*
> > *capers* (*optional*)

Chop the leeks and onions as fine as possible. Peel the garlic and then lightly press the whole clove with the flat of a knife blade. Simmer onions, leeks, garlic, and the bouquet garni in about half the oil. It is important to simmer on very low heat, covered. The vegetables should be stewed but should not pick up any color. Cook at least 1 hour, adding salt and pepper during the last few minutes.

Preheat oven to 450°. Spread the dough to about ¼-inch

thickness, and put it in a greased pie pan. Pinch the borders all around with your fingers, sticking the bottom with a fork in several spots. Spread the onion mixture on the dough, removing the bouquet garni. Top it with the olives, and capers if you use them, and dribble the rest of the oil on top.

Bake about 30 minutes, or until the crust is golden and crisp.

If you use French Pie Crust, prebake the crust for 15 minutes in a 450° oven before adding the filling and bake the whole at 450° for 15 minutes, or a little longer.

Serves 6.

POTATO "PIZZA"

Torta Tarantina di Patate

This is an authentic dish from Taranto (in the instep of Italy's boot). It is actually a false pizza, but it has the advantage of much quicker preparation than Neapolitan Pizza, and the potatoes give it a very distinctive, interesting taste.

> *½ pound mealy potatoes (1 very large potato*
> *should be sufficient)*
> *¾ to 1 cup flour*
> *¼ teaspoon salt*
> *6 ounces mozzarella, diced small*
> *3 tablespoons grated Parmesan or Romano cheese*
> *¼ teaspoon pepper*
> *2 teaspoons oregano*
> *5 or 6 fresh plum tomatoes, coarsely chopped*
> *(or canned plum tomatoes, drained*
> *after chopping)*
> *4 tablespoons olive oil (approximately)*

Boil the potatoes, mash them when still very hot, and spread out to cool. Mix the potatoes, flour, and salt, kneading well. (Add a little bit of water only if the dough is too stiff, but knead well first, to make sure.) Spread the dough to a thickness of about ½-inch in a greased pie pan (preferably a pizza pan) 11 or 12 inches in diameter. Allow the dough to dry for at least 30 minutes in a well-ventilated place. Preheat the oven to 400°. Bake for 15 minutes. Remove from the oven, leaving the heat on. Sprinkle the mozzarella all over the crust, then the grated cheese and pepper. Arrange the tomatoes on top, and dribble olive oil all over.

Bake another 20 minutes, or until the edges of the crust are golden brown and crunchy.

Note: After you have prepared this dish a few times, if you find that the crust comes out sufficiently crisp, you may skip the prebaking and simply fill the dough and bake for about 40 minutes.

Serves 4 to 6.

ITALIAN PIE CRUST
Pasta Frolla

FOR SALTY PIES
1½ cups flour
½ teaspoon salt, or a little less
5 tablespoons butter, at room temperature
1 egg

Mix flour and salt. Cut the butter in small pieces, then add to the flour, and mix quickly with two knives or a pastry blender. Mix in the egg. Act quickly, and do not work the dough more than is necessary to hold the paste together. A few drops of cold water may be needed, but go easy in adding it.

Wrap the dough in waxed paper, and refrigerate for at least 2 hours; if you can refrigerate overnight, the pastry will be even flakier.

For sweet pies, when you mix in the egg, also add to the above ingredients 2 tablespoons sugar or 1 tablespoon honey, and 1 teaspoon grated lemon peel, and reduce the amount of salt to a generous pinch. Proceed as above, and use in any pie you prepare for dessert.

Makes two 9-inch shells, or one double-crust pie.

FRENCH PIE CRUST
Pâte Brisée

This is a very close relative of the preceding Italian Pie Crust; in fact, it is almost identical.

> *1½ cups flour*
> *½ teaspoon salt*
> *¼ pound butter, at room temperature*
> *1 egg yolk*
> *1 tablespoon ice water, or more*

Mix flour and salt. Cut the butter in small pieces, add to the flour, and mix quickly with two knives or a pastry blender. Mix in the egg yolk and ice water as needed. Do not work the dough more than is necessary to make it hold together.

For a sweet crust, add a little sugar or honey.

Wrap the dough in waxed paper and refrigerate at least 2 hours, preferably overnight.

Makes two 9-inch shells or one double-crust pie.

COLD CHEESE PIE

1 recipe French Pie Crust (see preceding recipe) , chilled
4 tablespoons coarsely chopped mushrooms
2 tablespoons olive oil
salt and pepper
½ pound ricotta
5 tablespoons grated Romano cheese or crumbled
  feta cheese
4 tablespoons tiny fresh peas
3 eggs

Preheat oven to 400°. Separate the chilled dough into two pieces, one larger than the other. Grease a fairly deep pie pan. Roll out the larger piece of dough about ¼-inch thick, and line the bottom and sides of the pan with it. Bake for 10 minutes, and remove. Reduce oven to 375°.

Sauté the mushrooms in the oil, adding salt and pepper. In a bowl, thoroughly mix the ricotta with the Romano or feta cheese, then add the mushrooms, raw peas, and finally 2 of the eggs. Mix again. Fill the pie crust, then roll out the smaller piece of dough, put it on top, and close the edges by pressing with lightly moistened fingers. Lightly beat the remaining egg, brush the top with it, and then pierce the top with a fork in a few spots.

Bake for about 30 minutes. When the pie is golden, remove from the oven and let cool in its pan, putting a light weight, such as a flat plate, on top to press it down a little. When the pie has cooled to room temperature, unmold and serve.

Serves 4.

CALABRIAN SPINACH PIE

Quite probably this is derived from the Greek *spanakópita,* though the taste is quite different. It is also easier to prepare.

1 recipe Italian Pie Crust (see index)
1½ pounds, spinach, coarsely chopped
  and well drained
4 tablespoons butter
4 tablespoons raisins
4 tablespoons pine nuts
salt and pepper
¼ teaspoon nutmeg
¼ teaspoon coriander
½ cup ricotta
1 egg, lightly beaten
grated Romano cheese
milk

Preheat oven to 425°. Divide the dough into two parts, one larger than the other. Roll out the dough slightly thicker than for an average pie. Select a fairly large deep baking dish (a spring form mold is ideal). Spread out the larger piece of dough in the pan, trying not to pull it; line the sides as well as the bottom, leaving a little extra around the top, which you can fold out over the edges while you are filling the pan.

Sauté the spinach in the butter. Stir in the raisins, pine nuts, salt, pepper, nutmeg, and coriander. Allow to cool a little, then add the ricotta and the egg, and continue mixing until the paste is homogeneous.

Fill the pie dish with the mixture, pressing gently to squeeze out the air. Sprinkle with grated cheese. Roll out the remaining dough and cut it into strips about 1 inch wide. Arrange these on top in a crisscross trellis pattern. Fold in the dough around the edges to form a slightly raised border. Brush the dough with a little milk, and cover it with a sheet of waxed paper. Bake for approximately 25 minutes, removing waxed paper during the last 10 minutes.

Serves 4.

CHEESE AND ONION PIE
Zwiebelwähe

The classic pie from Switzerland.

PIE SHELL
6 tablespoons butter
2 tablespoons vegetable shortening
1½ cups flour
¼ teaspoon salt

FILLING
3 large onions, chopped
2 tablespoons butter
1½ cups Swiss cheese (8 ounces) shredded
½ cup light cream
½ cup milk
2 eggs
⅛ teaspoon ground nutmeg
¼ teaspoon salt

Cut the butter and shortening into small pieces, and chill for at least 1 hour. Mix the flour with the salt. Cut the butter and shortening into the flour and salt with two knives or a pastry blender. Pour about 3 tablespoons of ice water on the dough, mix, and make a ball. If too crumbly and dry, add more water, a little at a time. Roll the ball in flour.

A medium-sized spring form cake mold is best for this. (The sides open with a hinge and the bottom can be removed.) If you don't have one, use a deep baking dish.

Preheat oven to 400°. On a lightly floured surface, gently roll the dough in all directions with a rolling pin, without stretching it. Flatten it out to about ¼-inch thickness to fully cover the bottom of your mold or pan. Now roll out a strip of dough to line the sides of the mold. It should be a little wider than the height of the sides, so that when you press it gently all around it

Work in the butter with two knives or a pastry blender. Add the water, a little at a time (you may have to add more if the dough is too dry, but wait until you have mixed it quite well before doing so).

Roll out about two-thirds of the dough, without pulling, to a thickness of about 1/4 inch, and with it line a 10-inch pie plate. Bake the crust for 10 minutes, remove from the oven, and reduce heat to 375°. Reserve the egg and the remaining dough.

Mix the onions and scallions with half of the grated cheese, salt and pepper, and 2 tablespoons of the oil. Put into the pastry shell. Beat the eggs with the milk, add a little more salt, and pour on top. Sprinkle the remaining cheese and oil on top. Now roll out the second portion of the dough to the same thickness as the bottom half and place it on top of the pie, pressing gently between your fingers to attach it to the bottom crust. If the dough doesn't seem to stick to the baked crust, wet your fingers with water and try again. Beat the reserved egg lightly, and brush on top. With a fork, punch several holes in the surface of the dough.

Bake for 1 hour.

Serves 4.

ARTICHOKE PIE

FILLING
1 pound beet tops (spinach may be substituted)
8 small young artichokes
6 tablespoons olive oil
1 medium-sized onion, chopped
5 tablespoons grated Parmesan cheese
3 tablespoons butter
1 teaspoon marjoram, fresh (or 1/2 teaspoon dried)
salt and pepper

2 or 3 slices French or Italian bread,
  crust removed
milk

CRUST
1 cup flour
1½ tablespoons olive oil
½ teaspoon salt

Wash and clean the beet tops or spinach. Drain well and cook, uncovered, in the water that adheres to the leaves. When almost cooked, squeeze dry, and chop.

Clean the artichokes and quarter them, removing the chokes if necessary. Fry in the 6 tablespoons oil, adding the onion after a few minutes. When the artichokes begin to change color, add the beet tops or spinach. When both vegetables are cooked but still firm, remove from heat and add the grated cheese, butter, marjoram, salt, and pepper. Soak the bread in a little milk for a few minutes, then squeeze dry, and add to the mixture, blending well.

To make the crust, add the salt to the flour and mix in the 1½ tablespoons olive oil and sufficient cold water to make a rather thick dough. Mix it gently with your hands, and divide into two pieces, one slightly larger than the other.

Preheat the oven to 400°. Grease a baking dish that is at least 2 inches deep. Roll out both pieces of dough fairly thin. Line the dish with the larger layer, pour in the filling, leveling the top, then cover with the smaller layer of dough, joining the edges by pinching with your fingers. Brush the top with oil, then pierce it with a fork.

Bake for about 45 minutes.

Serves 4.

BLACK BEAN PIE

This is a very tasty English pie.

FILLING
1½ cups black beans
pinch of baking soda
2 cloves
2 cups cottage cheese
1 small onion, chopped
4 tablespoons butter
1 cup dry red wine
1 small garlic clove, minced
½ teaspoon dried fennel or dill
½ teaspoon dried tarragon
½ teaspoon dry mustard
¼ teaspoon cinnamon
¼ teaspoon thyme
salt and pepper

CRUST
½ teaspoon salt
1 cup flour
2 tablespoons vegetable shortening

Presoak the beans and cook them with the baking soda and cloves in enough water to cover. Simmer until very well done. Discard the cloves and pass the beans through a sieve or food mill, then mix in the cottage cheese.

In a medium-sized pot, sauté the onion in the butter, adding the wine and garlic when the onion is half cooked. Continue cooking at a simmer, adding the rest of the herbs and spices and the salt and pepper. Keep simmering, stirring and pressing with a wooden spoon, until you have obtained a rather thick paste. Mix this paste with the beans, blending all the ingredients thoroughly.

Preheat the oven to 425°.

To make the crust, add the salt to the flour, and mix in the shortening and just enough cold water to make a rather thick dough. Mix with your hands as little as possible, and roll to form a single crust. Put the crust in a pie pan, spoon in the filling, and bake for about 30 minutes. (If you prebake the crust for 15 minutes, you need to bake the filled pie only 15 minutes.)

Let cool, and serve lukewarm or at room temperature. A cold sauce of your choice may be served on the side.

Serves 4.

ITALIAN CHARD PIE
Erbazzone

This is a specialty from the Emilia region. It is much more tasty made with chard leaves, but if you cannot find chard, spinach is a good substitute. Or you can use equal amounts of beet tops and spinach. The same dish, without a crust, is made in the Milanese area, where it is called *scarpazza*.

CRUST
2½ cups flour
salt
2 tablespoons olive oil
2 tablespoons softened butter

FILLING
1½ pounds chard leaves (or spinach)
4 tablespoons olive oil
1 clove garlic, minced
salt to taste
pinch of nutmeg
2 tablespoons chopped parsley
3 eggs, lightly beaten
¾ cup grated Parmesan cheese

Make the crust by adding the salt to the flour and mixing in the oil and butter and enough cold water to make a rather thick dough. Knead only a little. Chill for 1 hour.

Preheat oven to 400°. Cook the chard as you would spinach (see page 19), then squeeze dry and chop. Sauté in the oil, with the garlic, salt, and nutmeg. Add the parsley during the last few minutes.

Remove from heat, allow to cool a few minutes, and then stir in the eggs and grated cheese, mixing well.

Roll out the dough to a thickness of about $\frac{1}{4}$ inch. Use two-thirds of the dough (reserving the rest for the pie top) to line a rather deep round baking dish. Fill with the chard mixture, then cover with the rest of the dough. Pinch the two sheets of dough together, pressing all around with the tines of a fork. Pierce the pie top all over with the fork.

Bake for about 1 hour, or until the top crust is golden and crisp.

Serves 4.

EGGPLANT PIE

A Roman specialty.

> *1 recipe Italian Pie Crust (see index)*
> *1 pound eggplant, peeled and cubed*
> *1 clove garlic, minced*
> *6 tablespoons olive oil (approximately)*
> *½ cup vegetable broth*
> *1 tablespoon chopped parsley*
> *1 teaspoon fresh chervil (or ½ teaspoon dried)*
> *1 teaspoon fresh tarragon (or ½ teaspoon dried)*
> *1 clove, crushed*
> *pinch of nutmeg*

salt and pepper
4 eggs, separated
1 cup Tomato Sauce
2 tablespoons heavy cream

Prepare the pie crust and bake 10 minutes in a preheated 400° oven, weighted inside with pebbles or something similar, so that it won't puff up. Remove from oven and raise temperature to 425°.

Sauté the eggplant and garlic in the oil for about 15 minutes. Make or heat the broth, adding the parsley, chervil, tarragon, clove, nutmeg, salt, and pepper. Let broth cool slightly.

Gently place the egg yolks in a bowl and pour the warm broth and the Tomato Sauce on them. Stir, then add the eggplant and the cream, and mix thoroughly.

Beat the egg whites until almost stiff, and fold into the eggplant mixture. Pour it into the crust, and bake for about 20 minutes, or until a knife inserted into the center comes out clean.

Serves 4 to 6.

LENTIL PIE

1 pound lentils
salt
1 bay leaf
1½ cups grated Parmesan or Romano cheese
½ cup hazelnuts or almonds, chopped
½ cup Marsala wine or sherry
½ teaspoon ground cumin
½ teaspoon paprika
pepper
4 eggs lightly beaten
1 recipe French Pie Crust (see index)

Cook the lentils at a very slow simmer, with the bay leaf and a little salt, in just enough water to cover them. Remove the bay leaf, then pass the lentils through a sieve or purée them in a blender. Let cool for about 30 minutes, then add cheese, nuts, Marsala or sherry, cumin, paprika, and pepper. Preheat oven to 375°. Mix the eggs, and taste, adding a little more salt if necessary. Prepare the pie crust, line a baking dish with it, and pour in the mixture. Bake for about 30 minutes.

Serve hot or cold.

Serves 4.

SPINACH ROLL
Strucolo

Strucolo (pronounced strú-colo) is a specialty from the Venetian region of Italy. It is a close relative of *rotolone* (see following recipe) and perhaps easier to prepare. I recommend both dishes as they are quite different in taste and texture.

> *2 pounds mealy potatoes*
> *1½ pounds spinach*
> *6 to 7 tablespoons butter*
> *salt and pepper*
> *1 whole egg*
> *1 egg yolk*
> *2 cups flour (approximately)*
> *½ cup grated Parmesan cheese (approximately)*
> *2 teaspoons arrowroot or cornstarch (optional)*
> *½ cup white wine (optional)*

Boil or bake the potatoes. When they are cool enough to handle, peel and mash them. (You will need rather dry potatoes for this dish, so if you are not sure of their quality, bake rather than boil them.) While the mashed potatoes are still hot, spread them out so that their moisture will evaporate, and stir them once in a while.

Wilt the spinach (see page 19), then finish cooking it by adding about 2 tablespoons of the butter and salt and pepper. Remove from heat and chop coarsely.

Make a dough with the mashed potatoes, egg, egg yolk, and flour, adding some salt. Start with about two-thirds of the potatoes, mix with the eggs and salt, then add the flour a little at a time. Gauge the proportions of flour to mashed potatoes by adding alternately as you mix. When dough is dry enough, roll it out to a thickness of about ½ inch, trying to make a slightly oval shape. Leave spread out for about 1 hour. Sprinkle half the cheese on the rolled-out dough, spread on the spinach to within 1 inch of the edges, then sprinkle more cheese on top of the spinach. Roll the dough into a cylinder, starting with a narrow end of the oval and pushing in gently around the edges so that the spinach will stay inside.

Preheat the oven to 375°. Grease a shallow baking dish. Melt the remaining butter and brush about 2 tablespoons of it on the roll. Bake for about 40 minutes; after 30 minutes, if the dough still seems very pale and soft, raise the temperature to 400°.

Pour the remainder of the melted butter on top, sprinkle with the rest of the cheese, and serve. Or mix about 2 teaspoons of arrowroot or cornstarch with ½ cup white wine, warm with the remaining melted butter, and serve the sauce on the side, together with additional grated cheese.

Serves 4.

PASTA-WRAPPED SPINACH ROLL
Rotolone

A specialty from central Italy. *Rotolone* means "big roll." This is similar to *strucolo* (see preceding recipe) except for the dough and the cooking method.

1½ pounds flour
4 eggs
salt
2 pounds spinach or chard leaves
pinch of nutmeg
pepper
1 cup chopped fresh mushrooms
1 clove garlic, whole
2 tablespoons olive oil
8 tablespoons butter (1 stick)
½ cup grated Parmesan cheese (approximately)

With the flour, eggs, and a pinch of salt, make a thin sheet of pasta, following the instructions for Homemade Pasta (see index). It should be oval-shaped. Allow to dry a little and in the meantime cook the spinach or chard leaves (see page 19), adding the nutmeg and a little salt and pepper. Sauté the mushrooms with the garlic in the oil and 2 tablespoons of the butter. Discard the garlic, and mix in the spinach. Proceed as in the preceding recipe, but after you make the roll, wrap it in a clean towel, then plunge it into rapidly boiling water. It should be ready after about 20 minutes. Remove from the water, let drip, then unwrap. Let it cool a few minutes, then cut into ½-inch slices; arrange the slices in a tight row, overlapping, on a hot serving platter. Melt the remaining 6 tablespoons of butter, dribble it on top, and sprinkle with the rest of the grated cheese.

Serves 4 to 6.

VARIATION: If you have fresh rosemary or sage or both, sauté them gently in the butter, and pour on the sliced roll before sprinkling with cheese.

TARTE RICHELIEU

Whether Cardinal Richelieu had a finger in this pie (as in so many others) is uncertain. But whether or not he invented it, this is supposed to have been one of his favorite dishes for days on which the Catholic religion forbade eating meat.

1 recipe French Pie Crust (see index)
2 pounds spinach
salt and pepper
dash of nutmeg
½ pound fresh mushrooms, sliced thin, or 1 cup imported
  dried mushrooms, rehydrated and chopped (see page 18)
3 tablespoons olive oil
½ cup hot milk
1 tablespoon flour
⅓ cup heavy cream
½ cup grated Gruyère cheese

Make the crust, adding ricotta or cottage cheese to the flour and butter instead of water, and only enough cheese to hold the dough together. Preheat oven to 400°. Bake the crust for 10 minutes. Remove from the oven and raise the temperature to 450°.

Cook the spinach (see page 19), with salt, pepper, and nutmeg, then chop coarsely and set aside. Sauté the mushrooms in the oil over a fairly high heat for about 10 minutes, stirring often. Add the milk to the flour a little at a time, and stir into the mushrooms. Stir in the cream at the last minute, and leave the sauce in the pan just long enough to heat.

Place the spinach in the pie crust, leveling the surface, then pour the mushroom sauce on top, again leveling. Sprinkle the grated cheese all over, and bake for 10 to 15 minutes.

Serves 6.

GUIDELINES FOR QUICHE FILLINGS

A quiche is usually a rather thin pie, and the amount of filling depends on the depth of the pie crust. A 9-inch pie plate is often used for four people, though a 10-inch plate would perhaps be more suitable if you plan to serve this dish as the main course of a vegetarian meal.

Fairly liquid quiches, such as cheese, require a larger amount of cream than quiches filled with diced or puréed vegetables, which should turn out more solid.

For a 10-inch quiche of the creamier type, the approximate proportions of cream, butter, and cheese should be:

> *1½ cups heavy cream*
> *1 cup grated or shredded cheese*
> *3 large eggs*
> *3 tablespoons butter*

To this you may add whatever spices or minor ingredients you wish to include, bearing in mind that cheese is salty. Adding about ¼ teaspoon of salt should be sufficient.

For a 10-inch quiche of the more solid kind, filled with diced or puréed vegetables, the average filling should be:

> *1 cup heavy cream*
> *1½ cups cooked vegetables*
> *3 large eggs*
> *3 tablespoons butter, or more*
> *spices or minor ingredients*

For any quiche, if you see when you fill the shell that the total amount is not sufficient, add about 2 tablespoons of cream. If more cream is still needed, you must add another egg to allow the filling to bind. But remember not to fill the crust too much, especially for liquid quiches.

Serves 4.

QUICHE LORRAINE

The word *quiche* is a French transliteration of the German *kuchen,* meaning cake. Perhaps the most famous quiche comes from Lorraine, which, with Alsace, lies between France and Germany and has often passed from one of these countries to the other over the centuries, with consequent mixing of the two languages. It is then not surprising that a kuchen would become a quiche, the pronunciation changing along with the spelling, and the name acquiring a more specific meaning: that of a flat, rather thin pie, filled with a variety of ingredients and often creamy and fluffy.

Here is a literal translation of a recipe for the original Quiche Lorraine, from a reputable French cookbook published in 1905. The crust called for either lard (which I have deleted from my translation) or butter, but you will notice that, unlike the more modern and Americanized versions, there is neither bacon nor cheese in the recipe.

This recipe is a little vague, as was the style then, but I thought it charming. While no mention was made in the original of how many people it would serve, the pie will serve 4 to 6. The amounts have been translated into cups and pounds.

CRUST
2 pounds flour
⅔ cup butter
2 eggs
salt
dots of butter

FILLING
2 eggs
1 cup heavy cream
salt
dots of butter

"For the crust, mix all ingredients, crumbling them, and spread out the dough, giving it the thickness of two 5-franc pieces [that is, very thin, about ⅛ inch]. Dot the bottom with butter, and make a twisted edge all around. Bake for 15 minutes, and remove it from the oven.

"For the filling, beat vigorously the two eggs with the cream and salt. Pour on the crust, and dot with butter all over.

"Bake in a moderate oven for 15 minutes on a plaque or oven dish."

Note: A moderate oven in French terms is anywhere between 300° and 375° Fahrenheit. In my opinion, baking both the crust and the pie at 375° gives the best result. Of course, instead of baking the quiche directly on a cookie sheet, you might prefer to put it in a baking dish or pie pan.

Serves 4 to 6.

FRIED SPINACH TURNOVERS
Spanakópites S'tó Tigáni

A Greek specialty, especially made on holidays.

CRUST
4 cups flour
1 teaspoon salt
2 tablespoons olive oil

FILLING
1½ pounds spinach
1 medium-sized onion, chopped
3 tablespoons olive oil
1 teaspoon fresh dill, chopped
    (or ⅔ teaspoon dried)
1 tablespoon chopped parsley
salt and pepper
4 tablespoons raisins
2 tablespoons pine nuts
oil for frying

To make the crust, mix the flour and salt, beat together with a fork the oil and about 3 tablespoons of water, and sprinkle the mixture on the flour, mixing quickly with the fork. Add more water if needed, but mix as little and as quickly as possible. Shape the dough into a ball, put into a bowl, and cover with a cloth. Refrigerate for 30 minutes.

Wash and drain the spinach, and scald it on high heat until partly wilted. Remove from heat and squeeze dry, then chop coarsely.

Sauté the onion until transparent in about 2 tablespoons of the olive oil, then add the spinach, dill, parsley, salt, and pepper, and continue to simmer for a few minutes, stirring often to make sure the spinach is well coated with the oil. Remove from heat, and add the raisins and pine nuts.

Roll out the dough to a thickness of about $\frac{1}{8}$ inch, and cut it in rounds of about 6 inches in diameter (the edge of a small bowl will do as a cutter). Fill the center of each round with about 2 tablespoons of the spinach mixture. Wet your fingers and pass them around the edges of the circle. Fold the dough in half, making sure all the spinach stays inside, and press gently all around to seal.

Fry in hot oil until each side turns a light brown color.

Serves 4 to 6.

RUSSIAN TURNOVERS
Piroshki

In this delicious Russian dish, the turnovers are filled with various types of food, including meat. In our case, use your imagination as to the filling: precooked vegetables, chopped hard-cooked eggs, chopped and sautéed mushrooms, and so on.

PASTRY
4 ounces cream cheese
1 stick (½ cup) butter
2 tablespoons heavy cream
1¾ cups flour
½ teaspoon salt
1 egg, lightly beaten with a little cold water
1 cup sour cream (approximately), at room temperature

Remove the required amounts of cream cheese, butter, and cream from the refrigerator, and allow to warm to room temperature. Mix the butter and cream cheese thoroughly, then add the cream, beating it into the mixture. Add the flour and salt, and mix. Chill the dough in the refrigerator for at least 1 hour.

Preheat oven to 425°. Roll out the dough to a thickness of about ⅛ inch. Using a pastry cutter or a small glass, cut the dough into 3-inch rounds.

Fill each round with about a teaspoonful of any mixture you desire. Fold the dough, making sure that all the filling stays inside, and close the edges with your fingers, dipping them in cold water if the dough doesn't stick together. Then press the edges with the tines of a fork all around the sealed dough.

Put turnovers in a greased shallow oven dish, paint each surface with the egg-and-water mixture, and stick a fork into each turnover without touching the bottom dough. Bake for about 20 minutes or until the crusts are golden.

Serve hot, with sour cream on the side.

Serves 4.

RICOTTA CRÊPES

4 eggs
2 tablespoons flour
1 tablespoon grated Parmesan cheese

½ *cup milk (approximately)*
olive oil
1 cup ricotta
½ *cup feta cheese (or other semi-hard*
   goat cheese), crumbled
20 capers, chopped
2 tablespoons fresh basil leaves, chopped
   (or 2 teaspoons dried)

Preheat oven to 450°. Make a batter with the eggs, flour, grated cheese, and milk. It should be as thin as the batter generally used for crêpes, and you may have to adjust the amount of milk, adding more or less according to the type of flour you use.

Using an omelet pan or crêpe pan, fry very thin crêpes in just enough olive oil to keep the batter from sticking.

Mix the ricotta, feta or other cheese, capers, and basil, making a fairly thick paste. Put about 2 tablespoons of the mixture in the middle of each crêpe, then flap the sides on top of each other. Arrange the crêpes in a single layer in a large greased baking dish (you may have to use two dishes).

Heat in the oven for about 10 minutes before serving. A sauce of your choice may be poured on top.

Note: The crêpes may be prepared and stuffed in advance, then heated in the oven at the last moment. If you have kept them in the refrigerator, they will need at least 1 hour to reach room temperature before they are put in the oven.

Serves 4.

BEAN OR LENTIL PATTIES

This dish is quite common in Poland and Germany. It is equally good made with beans, lentils, dried peas, or a combination.

2 cups dried legumes
1 bay leaf
salt and pepper
pinch cumin powder
4 tablespoons breadcrumbs (preferably
  from dark bread)
3 eggs, lightly beaten
butter or vegetable oil

Cook the legumes with the bay leaf in as little water as possible (adding more boiling water during the cooking process, if needed). Stir in salt, pepper, and cumin about 20 minutes before the legumes are done. Pass the legumes through a sieve or food mill while still hot, then spread them out on a shallow baking dish to dry the paste. If after an hour or so it still seems too loose, dry it further in a very slow oven, stirring once in a while.

Add 3 tablespoons of the breadcrumbs to the legumes and when the mixture has cooled some more, add the eggs and adjust the seasoning. Form into fairly small patties with your hands, and roll them in the additional breadcrumbs.

Fry the patties in butter or oil on both sides, briefly.

Note: This paste can be prepared in advance and refrigerated, covered, for several days. Bring it to room temperature before frying, or the patties may be cold inside.

Serves 4.

SEMOLINA SUPPLIS

Suppli is the French term for anything which is filled. These Semolina Supplis can be filled in any number of ways.

2 cups semolina
1 quart milk (approximately)
3 tablespoons butter

3 tablespoons grated Parmesan cheese
3 eggs
salt
breadcrumbs
oil for frying

Cook the semolina in the milk, together with the butter and cheese. Remove from heat, let cool a few minutes, then beat 2 of the eggs lightly, add salt to taste, and mix with the semolina. The consistency should be rather firm, but if it seems too dry, add a little cold milk, and stir.

Pour the mixture on a flat surface or large platter, spreading it until it is about ¾-inch thick. After it has cooled, cut it in rounds, using a wine glass dipped in water or a cookie cutter. Press each disk in the middle with your finger, to create a depression, and shape the disks with your hands into little bowls. Beat the remaining egg lightly, dip the disks into it, then coat them with breadcrumbs. Fry in hot oil.

Preheat oven to 425°. Grease a shallow baking dish, place the disks in it, and fill them with a thick White Sauce (see index) made with abundant grated cheese, or with small pieces of cooked vegetables, or both (or with a mixture of your own invention).

Bake for about 8 to 10 minutes before serving. These are good served on a bed of spinach.

Serves 4.

Stuffed Vegetables

STUFFED CABBAGE LEAVES

This is a composite recipe from various European countries. The cabbage to use is the open-head type, preferably green, as it is tastier. But if the only cabbage you can find is the closed-head variety, you can still manage to remove the leaves, by steaming or blanching the entire cabbage for a few minutes until the leaves become soft enough to separate easily. You will need about fourteen leaves, and you can use the rest of the cabbage for other dishes.

> *1 green cabbage, open head (about 3 pounds)*
> *5 or 6 cups Vegetable Broth II (see index)*
> *2 medium-sized onions, chopped*
> *6 tablespoons oil*
> *½ pound fresh mushrooms, chopped*
> *2 cloves garlic, minced*
> *1 teaspoon salt*
> *½ teaspoon coriander*
> *¼ teaspoon pepper*
> *1 cup rice*
> *1 medium-sized carrot, chopped*
> *4 tablespoons dark raisins*

2 cups Tomato Sauce
2 teaspoons arrowroot or cornstarch (*optional*)

Remove about 14 leaves from the cabbage, cutting them at the point where the leaf begins. In a pot in which the large cabbage leaves will fit flat, heat the broth. When it boils, put in the leaves, cover, and bring back to a boil, simmering 3 or 4 minutes, or long enough so that the leaves will bend without breaking the stems as you roll them. Drain, reserving the broth.

Preheat oven to 350°. In a skillet, sauté the onions in 3 tablespoons of the oil, then add the mushrooms, garlic, seasoning, and stir in the rice. Let it sizzle for a few minutes, stirring constantly. Then add about 1 cup of the broth, the carrot, and the raisins. Cook over medium heat for about 5 minutes.

Lay the cabbage leaves flat, stem side toward you, and put 1 or 2 tablespoons of the rice mixture on each leaf. Roll them up, folding over the stem side first, then overlapping the side flaps to enclose the filling, and roll up away from you. Arrange the rolls, top side of leaves down, in a fairly shallow baking/serving dish with a cover. They should fit snugly in a single layer. Dilute the Tomato Sauce with about 1 cup of the broth and the rest of the oil, stir, and pour it on top of the cabbage rolls, separating them gently so that the sauce reaches the bottom of the pan.

Cover and bake about 40 minutes, then uncover and continue cooking for 15 or 20 minutes, until the sauce has thickened a little. If too much liquid remains in the pan when you uncover it, spoon out a few tablespoons into a small bowl and stir in 2 teaspoons of arrowroot or cornstarch. Pour into the baking pan, gently mixing a little with the rest of the liquid. Conversely, if the sauce is too thick, add a little more broth. It is difficult to give the exact proportions of liquid, because Tomato Sauce, rice absorption, and cooking heat can vary substantially.

Serves 4 to 6.

STUFFED TOMATOES

Stuffed tomatoes and stuffed peppers recur throughout Europe. The most common version is a stuffing made with rice (see Stuffed Vegetable Medley). Here is a different one, from Italy.

4 large ripe but firm tomatoes
1 medium-sized onion, sliced
3 tablespoons olive oil
1 stalk celery, chopped
¼ pound chopped mushrooms
1 tablespoon chopped parsley
1 teaspoon chopped fresh basil (or ½ teaspoon dried)
salt and pepper
1 thin slice bread
1 egg, lightly beaten
1 tablespoon grated Parmesan cheese

Preheat oven to 375°. Wash the tomatoes and cut them exactly in half, across. Scoop out the seeds and central portion on a plate and reserve.

Sauté the onion in 2 tablespoons of the oil and add the celery, mushrooms, parsley, basil, salt, and pepper. Push aside the seeds of the tomatoes and dip the bread in the watery pulp, then squeeze, put in a large bowl, and mash with your hands. Mix in the egg and cheese. Add the onion-mushroom mixture, and mix thoroughly. If the mixture seems too thick, add a little more liquid, either water or juice from the tomatoes. Stuff the tomato halves, and arrange them in one layer on a greased baking dish. Dribble the remaining 1 tablespoon oil on top, and bake for about 20 minutes, or until the tomatoes begin to wilt and the stuffing has set.

Serves 4.

TOMATOES STUFFED WITH EGGPLANT

8 medium-sized tomatoes, ripe but firm
3 small eggplants
3 eggs
1½ cups grated Romano cheese
3 tablespoons olive oil (approximately)
¼ teaspoon oregano
salt and pepper

Partially cut off the tomato tops (the stem end), leaving a small section attached at least by the skin to serve as a hinge. Scoop out the pulp and seeds with a grapefruit spoon or teaspoon, and reserve the pulp.

Grill the eggplants either directly over a flame, turning frequently, or under the broiler, until the skin is charred. Set the oven temperature at 350°. Remove the skins and stems of the eggplants, or scoop out the pulp. Mash well with the tomato pulp. Blend in the eggs, cheese, 2 tablespoons of the oil, the oregano, salt, and pepper. Stuff the tomatoes and close their lids. Brush the outer skin with olive oil, reserving a little to grease a shallow baking dish. Place the tomatoes upright in a single layer in the dish. Bake for about 1 hour, or until the tomatoes start to shrivel and become light brown. Serve either hot or at room temperature.

Serves 4.

STUFFED SQUASH BLOSSOMS

This is a real treat in early summer. It is made at home all over Greece, but primarily in Crete. Pick the unopened blossoms with part of their stems, if possible, then wash them gently, and put the stems in water for a few hours or overnight, so that the blossoms will open. Make sure that the water does not touch the blossoms. (For more information on squash blossoms, see page 20.)

20 squash blossoms (approximately)

FILLING
1 small onion, chopped fine
4 tablespoons olive oil
1 clove garlic, pressed or minced
⅓ cup rice
½ cup Tomato Sauce
3 tablespoons chopped parsley
2 tablespoons fresh mint, chopped (or 1 tablespoon dried)
1 tablespoon fresh dill, chopped (or 2 teaspoons dried)
salt and pepper

Cut off the stems of the blossoms, taking care that the delicate flower cups remain intact. Sauté the onion in 3 tablespoons of the oil until transparent, then add the garlic, and continue cooking. Add the rice, and stir over fairly high heat. Stir in the Tomato Sauce, parsley, mint, dill, salt, and pepper. Add water to cover the rice and bring to a boil, then lower the heat and continue cooking for about 10 minutes, stirring once in a while. Remove from heat.

Using a teaspoon, stuff the blossoms with the rice mixture. To do this easily, hold a blossom in one cupped hand, open it carefully, and fill it with the other hand, then fold the petals over one another. Be careful not to overstuff the blossoms, because the rice will expand further.

Gently lay the stuffed blossoms on one side in a single layer in a skillet greased with the remaining tablespoon of oil. Pour about 1 cup of hot water into the skillet. Weight with a flat dish or board which fits inside the skillet and covers all the blossoms. Add a little extra weight on top, if needed. Cover the skillet, and simmer over very low heat for about 45 minutes. Taste one, and cook longer if it seems a bit undercooked. You may need to add more hot water after 20 or 25 minutes, so check the level a couple of times. When the blossoms are cooked they should have absorbed all the liquid.

Serves 4.

STUFFED VEGETABLE MEDLEY
Cretan Dolmádes, or Giemistá

The Greek word *dolmádes* means food that is wrapped or contained in a vegetable or leaf. The most commonly known dolmádes are wrapped in grape leaves (this version has been omitted here because, thanks to its popularity, a recipe can easily be obtained). The medley of stuffed vegetables presented here is also called *dolmádes,* or sometimes *giemistá,* which means "filled." It is a specialty from Crete, where it is never found in restaurants but only in private homes.

The filling is the same as for Stuffed Squash Blossoms (see preceding recipe), and indeed these flowers are also included in this delicious, colorful dish. However, you will need two or three times the amount of filling, and it is better to overestimate, since you can always use any excess in another dish.

This dish is usually made in large quantities, to allow each person at the table to eat at least one of each kind and to have some to serve the following day, at room temperature.

All vegetables (except the squash blossoms, of course) should be similar in size and as plump as possible, so that they will stand upright.

Although the preparation takes some time, the contrast of the various tastes makes this dish really unusual and worth trying.

> *2 or 3 recipes rice filling for Stuffed Squash Blossoms*
>   *(see preceding recipe)*
> *4 medium-sized potatoes, peeled*
> *4 medium to large fresh tomatoes, ripe but firm*
> *4 medium to large green peppers*
> *2 large wide zucchini*
> *8–10 squash blossoms*
> *olive oil*

Prepare the filling. Slice off and reserve the tops of the potatoes, tomatoes, and peppers. Cut the zucchini in half crosswise, and slice off the stem and a tiny bit of the tip. With a teaspoon or grape-

fruit spoon, carefully scoop out some of the insides of the potatoes and the zucchini (put in your soup bag) ; remove and
reserve the pulp and seeds from the tomatoes; remove and discard seeds and membranes from the peppers. Pass the tomato
pulp through a sieve or food mill, and discard the seeds. Mix
the tomato pulp and liquid into the filling.

Preheat the oven to 375°. Fill each vegetable with the rice mixture, allowing room for it to expand as it cooks. Stuff the squash
blossoms carefully, following the preceding recipe. Cover the
potatoes, tomatoes, and peppers with their own tops.

Using olive oil, grease a large baking dish, preferably round
and at least 2 inches deep. Arrange the vegetables first, alternating them so that each type is different from the next. Not only
does this make the color variety very striking, but it averages the
cooking time as well. Gently fit in squash blossoms here and there,
wherever there is a nook, but without squeezing them. Dribble
olive oil abundantly all over, using a brush to coat the exposed
portions of the vegetables.

Bake about 1½ hours, or a little longer, checking once or
twice after 1 hour by sticking a fork into a potato, since these
will take the longest to cook. During the last 20 or 25 minutes, if
the vegetables are cooking well but look a little pale, raise the
oven temperature to 425°.

Serves 4.

ZUCCHINI "BOATS"
Kolokithákia Dolmádes

This is a Greek dish, although a simplified version (usually
without the sauce) is also found in Italian homes.

6 tablespoons butter
4 medium-sized zucchini

1 cup almonds, unpeeled, measured after shelling
2 eggs
3 amaretti *(see note)*
½ teaspoon grated lemon peel
¼ teaspoon nutmeg
salt and pepper
breadcrumbs

SAUCE
½ cup yogurt, at room temperature
3 tablespoons shelled pistachio nuts (preferably untoasted and undyed) , measured after shelling
salt

Take the butter out of the refrigerator—it will be more manageable at room temperature. Slice the stems off the zucchini, then cut the zucchini in half lengthwise. Scoop out most of the pulp with a teaspoon or grapefruit spoon, making sure you don't scrape too deep at the bottom. Chop the pulp.

Chop the almonds fine. Pound the *amaretti* in a mortar (or put them between two sheets of waxed paper and roll a bottle or rolling pin over them) . Add the lemon peel and nutmeg to the amaretti. Mix the eggs, zucchini pulp, and almonds. Add the amaretti, salt, and pepper, stir, and add breadcrumbs a little at a time, until you have a rather thick paste. Fill the zucchini, pressing down gently and mounding the filling slightly.

Preheat the oven to 425°. Grease a square or rectangular baking dish large enough to accommodate all the zucchini halves fairly snugly in one layer. (Test for size with a couple of zucchini before greasing the dish.) As you arrange the zucchini boats, brush the outside of each one with some butter. Dot the rest of the butter on top, and bake for 35 to 40 minutes, or until the tops are golden brown. Test the zucchini for doneness by piercing with a toothpick. When they are done, there should be no liquid in the dish, as zucchini tend to let out their liquid and then reabsorb it.

To make the sauce, chop the pistachio nuts and stir them into the yogurt with the salt. Serve the sauce separately, at room temperature.

This dish must be served very hot. The sauce at room temperature provides contrast.

Note: Amaretti—the word means "bitter cookies"—are made with both bitter and regular almonds, and are very crunchy. If the imported Italian amaretti cannot be found where you live, a concentrated bitter-almond extract is usually available in specialized stores, and you can make a fairly good substitute for amaretti by adding a few drops of the extract to a mixture of equal quantities of wheat germ and breadcrumbs, and mixing in ½ teaspoon honey. Do not substitute macaroons, which are too sweet and gooey for this dish.

Serves 4.

Egg and Cheese Dishes

SOUFFLÉS

To make a successful soufflé is not such a tremendous gastronomic feat as many people still think. The feared disaster is that a soufflé may flatten and even sink in the middle before it is brought to the table—a visual disappointment usually not affecting the flavor. This failure can usually be avoided if a few simple rules are adhered to, especially the first few times you try making a soufflé. Later on you can be a little more daring, especially when you know how the different ingredients contained in the basic soufflé react in your oven. Here are a few basic do's and don'ts.

Do:
Preheat the oven well in advance, and maintain the same exact temperature throughout the cooking process.
Fold the egg whites into any mixture with care, gently, so as to keep the mixture fluffy.
Serve the soufflé immediately after you remove it from the oven.

Don't:
Under any circumstances open the oven door to check on the soufflé—unless it is very close to being ready—or it may flatten

out instantly. (An occasional recipe may call for something to be sprinkled on the surface a few minutes before the soufflé is removed from the oven; omit this step until you have practiced a few times.)

Be too anxious to remove the soufflé from the oven. Cooking time and temperature may vary according to the recipe. On your first attempts, bake a little longer, for it is better to risk the soufflé's being a little browner than its being underdone, which may make it deflate when removed from the oven. Of course, we are talking in terms of overcooking by just a few minutes, otherwise the soufflé may lose its inner springiness and develop too thick a crust.

The important thing is to present a soufflé at the dinner table all puffed up, not flat. After a few minutes, the change in temperature may deflate it anyway, and it will flatten out somewhat after it is cut, but don't worry about that.

There are infinite varieties of soufflé dishes, and just as many recipes. In Europe people tend to bake their soufflés at a slightly lower temperature and for a shorter time than is usual in the United States. Although the puffiness may be more precarious, the consistency and airiness are more desirable. When a soufflé contains naturally fluffy ingredients, such as mashed potatoes or chestnuts, it is more likely to remain puffy. For this reason, and to entice you to try making a soufflé if you have not yet done so, these are the two basic recipes included in this book. (Potato Soufflé follows; for Chestnut Soufflé see index) .

POTATO SOUFFLÉ

⅔ cup butter (1½ sticks)
1 pound mealy potatoes, cooked,
*   riced when still hot*
salt and pepper
2 eggs, separated
½ cup light cream
pinch of nutmeg

Preheat oven to 375°. Add the butter to the hot riced potatoes. Add salt and pepper to taste and allow potatoes to cool to lukewarm. Beat the egg yolks lightly, add to the potatoes with the cream and nutmeg, and mix well. Beat the whites almost stiff, then gently fold them into the potato mixture.

Grease a soufflé mold of about 1½-quarts capacity, and pour in the mixture, which should fill no more than two-thirds of the mold.

Bake for 20 minutes and serve immediately.

Serves 4.

PIEDMONTESE FONDUE
Fonduta

While some readers may be familiar with the Italian *fonduta* (sometimes called *fondua* in Piedmontese dialect) and most people have tasted Swiss fondue, the two dishes are quite different in taste, ingredients, and execution, and this lesser-known relative, so often made in northern Italian homes, deserves wider recognition.

Fonduta is made with Fontina, a delicious semi-soft cheese from the Alpine region of Piedmont, where Turin is located. If imported Italian Fontina is not available where you live, versions from other countries may be. Although most of these don't come up to true Italian Fontina, they are fairly good substitutes. If you can't find any kind of Fontina, do not substitute Gruyère or Swiss cheese, but use Bel Paese (either imported from Italy or domestic), Bonbel, or Muenster, in this order of preference. However, I wish to stress that it is the type and quality of the cheese which gives fonduta its characteristic flavor, so it is better to start with the right ingredient—or as close an approximation as possible.

In Italy fonduta is usually served with thinly sliced black or white truffles on top, but these don't exist in America, and canned truffles are so inferior in taste and texture to fresh truffles that this recipe omits truffles altogether.

coarsely. If the pasta was previously cooked in a sauce, reduce the amount of butter and oil in this recipe.

> *2 cups cooked pasta (approximately)*
> *8 eggs*
> *½ cup grated Parmesan cheese*
> *salt and pepper*
> *2 tablespoons butter*
> *1 tablespoon olive oil*

Mix all ingredients except the butter and oil. Heat butter and oil in a heavy skillet. When it is rather hot, pour the pasta mixture into the skillet, lower the heat, and let the mixture brown on the bottom on low to medium heat. Then run the skillet under the broiler for about 3 minutes to brown on the top. This kind of frittata should be rather crisp, so try to make it a golden-brown color.

Serves 4.

VARIATIONS. To try some of the many possible variations, you could add a couple of teaspoons of tomato paste, herbs, sautéed onions, and so on. But do not overdo the amount of sauce, or the frittata may not hold together.

GENOESE FRITTATA

> *2 pounds chard*
> *2 slices French or Italian bread, crust removed*
> *3 eggs*
> *1 clove garlic, minced*
> *1 tablespoon chopped parsley*
> *1½ teaspoons marjoram*
> *½ teaspoon nutmeg*
> *¼ teaspoon coriander*

salt and pepper to taste
½ cup grated Parmesan cheese
3 tablespoons olive oil

Wash chard and remove stalks (save them to use in other dishes). Drain well and cook as spinach (see page 19). When done, remove from heat and allow to cool until you can comfortably handle it. Squeeze as much liquid as possible from the chard, and soak the bread in the liquid.

Beat the eggs, add the garlic, parsley, marjoram, nutmeg, coriander, salt, and pepper. Squeeze excess liquid from the bread and add the bread to the eggs together with the chard and the grated cheese. Mix well.

Heat the oil in a heavy skillet, about 9 inches in diameter so that the vegetable mixture will be about 1½ inches deep. When the oil is hot, pour in the mixture, flattening the top. Reduce the heat, and cook until the sides are beginning to brown, which you can check by gently separating the mixture from the sides of the skillet with a knife. Put the pan under the broiler for 1 or 2 minutes.

Allow to cool at least 5 minutes, then turn upside down on a serving platter.

Serves 4.

SARDINIAN FRITTATA

2 medium-sized zucchini
5 eggs
1 teaspoon grated lemon peel
salt and pepper
2 tablespoons breadcrumbs, plus
*   additional breadcrumbs*
2 tablespoons milk
2 tablespoons grated goat cheese (Romano) or
*   Parmesan cheese*
2 tablespoons olive oil

Grate or finely shred the zucchini. In a separate bowl, beat the eggs lightly. Add the lemon peel, salt, and pepper, then 2 table-spoons breadcrumbs, the milk, cheese, and finally the zucchini.

Heat the oil in a heavy skillet (it should not have wooden or plastic handles, as it is to go into the oven), then sprinkle the bottom with breadcrumbs and pour in the egg mixture. Sprinkle more breadcrumbs on top, and set the oven temperature to 400°. When the bottom begins to solidify, put the pan in the oven for about 20 minutes. If after this time the top is still very soft, raise the temperature to broiling, and put the skillet under the broiler for a minute or two.

Serves 4.

VARIATION. This *frittata* can be made with other vegetables, but they should be chopped fine and pan-fried first.

ZUCCHINI OMELET
Roman Frittata

This Roman specialty has been traditional for many centuries. It is often eaten cold during the summer.

> *½ pound zucchini (approximately)*
> *3 tablespoons olive oil*
> *1 tablespoon dry white wine*
> *6 eggs*
> *1 tablespoon chopped parsley*
> *salt and pepper*

Slice the zucchini rather thin and sauté in the oil, together with the wine, in a large heavy skillet, preferably of cast iron (leave the oil in the pan). Beat the eggs, and add the cooked zucchini, the parsley, salt, and pepper. Reheat the oil left from the zucchini, adding a little more if necessary. Add the egg and zucchini mixture, and after the eggs have sizzled for a minute or two, lower the heat. When the sides and bottom are golden, place the skillet under the broiler several inches away from the heat for a minute or two. Let cool a few minutes, then turn upside down onto a serving platter. The rounds of zucchini will show through, creating a pleasant effect.

Serves 4.

VARIATION. SQUASH BLOSSOMS FRITTATA. Omit the zucchini and white wine. Tear 6 or 7 zucchini blossoms into fairly large pieces and substitute them for the zucchini.

TURNIP OMELET
Omelette de Navets

This is a French specialty, seldom found in restaurants. Being open-faced, it is actually more like a *frittata,* but the French still call it an *omelette.*

> *1 pound young small turnips*
> *3 tablespoons butter*
> *salt*
> *4 eggs*
> *½ teaspoon dry savory*
> *½ teaspoon dill*
> *½ cup chopped parsley*
> *3 tablespoons capers*
> *pepper*
> *2 tablespoons olive oil*

Scrub the turnips, then grate them coarsely. Simmer them in butter, stirring often, for about 15 minutes, adding salt during the last 5 minutes.

Just before you are ready to make the omelet, heat the oil in the skillet, and while it is heating, break the eggs into a bowl, and add the turnips, savory, dill, parsley, capers, salt (very little), and pepper. Mix vigorously, then pour into the skillet. The heat should be fairly high at first; then lower it and smooth out the mixture. You can either turn the omelet over and finish cooking it, or put it as is under the broiler for a minute or two, turning it onto a platter when it has cooled about 5 minutes.

Serves 4.

ASPARAGUS ALLA MILANESE

This specialty from Milan is often made at home but only occasionally found in restaurants.

> *2 pounds asparagus*
> *8 eggs*
> *1½ sticks (12 tablespoons) butter*
> *½ cup grated Parmesan cheese*
> *salt and pepper*

Clean the asparagus and cook until still a bit chewy (see page 13). Warm a large round serving platter in the oven, and place the asparagus on it, tips toward the center, like the spokes of a wheel. Fry the eggs sunny side up in 2 or 3 tablespoons of the butter. In a separate skillet, heat the rest of the butter until it foams, and pour about half of it over the asparagus. Sprinkle with half of the cheese. Now place the eggs, delicately so as not to break them, on the tips of the asparagus, all around. Pour the remaining butter over the eggs and asparagus, and sprinkle with the rest of the cheese.

Serves 4.

EGGS LUMBERJACK STYLE
Uova alla Boscaiola

3 tablespoons butter
1 cup dry red wine
1 cup vegetable broth or water
¼ teaspoon of each of the following spices, ground:
  coriander, turmeric, mustard seeds,
  nutmeg, pepper
¼ teaspoon each of the following dried herbs:
  thyme, basil, dill, oregano
1 clove garlic, minced
salt
8 eggs
4 slices bread, preferably Italian, toasted directly
  on the flame, if possible, rather than in a toaster
2 teaspoons cornstarch or arrowroot

Take the butter out of the refrigerator and leave at room temperature, so that it will melt quickly when needed. Pour the wine and the broth or water into a large saucepan. Add all the spices and herbs, together with the garlic and salt. Bring to a boil, and cook for 10 minutes, then lower the heat but maintain low boiling. Break the eggs into the liquid one by one, covering each egg with its own white by quickly gathering the hot liquid around it with a spoon. Place the toast on a warm serving platter. When the eggs are done, turn off the heat, remove them with a slotted spoon and put two on each piece of toast. Keep warm.

Using a fork, make a paste with the butter and cornstarch or arrowroot, add it to the wine sauce, which should have cooled somewhat, and stir. When the sauce has blended, pour it over the eggs, and serve.

Serves 4.

EGGS OYSTER STYLE
Uova all' Ostrica

This is the quickest possible way to prepare and eat eggs. It is very popular in Italy but only at home, often for breakfast.

1 egg yolk per person
salt and pepper
lemon wedge

Separate the eggs very carefully, making sure that no white is left. Save the whites for other use. Slide each egg yolk into a large soup spoon. Sprinkle salt and pepper and squeeze lemon juice on the egg yolk and pop it into your mouth whole.

If you wish to serve these at the table, perhaps as a quick "appetizer" at a salad lunch, or for breakfast, you may use egg cups. The salt, pepper, and lemon juice should be added by each person according to taste, at the very last moment.

BUCK RAREBIT

Welsh Rarebit is a well-known dish, but this rarebit has eggs added, and the taste is quite different.

2 tablespoons butter
½ pound Cheddar cheese, shredded or grated
½ cup beer or ale (ale preferred)
1 teaspoon dry mustard
pinch of cayenne pepper (optional)
white pepper
2 egg whites, beaten to a medium consistency
4 eggs
vinegar

8 slices of bread (preferably whole-wheat bread)
pinch of paprika

In the top of a double boiler, over simmering water, melt the butter, stir in the cheese, and add the beer or ale a little at a time, stirring constantly. Add the mustard, cayenne (if used), and white pepper. Keep the water in the lower half of the boiler barely simmering, as this dish has to be made very slowly and the cheese should not boil. Now fold in the beaten egg whites.

Half fill a skillet with boiling water with a little vinegar added. (This adds taste to the eggs and helps coagulate the whites.) Poach the eggs in the skillet. After a few minutes, remove the eggs and drain very well.

Toast four slices of bread, place on a serving platter, and pour the rarebit on top. Gently place a poached egg on each piece of toast. Sprinkle with paprika. Toast the other four slices of bread, cut them diagonally, and serve separately.

Serves 4.

VARIATION: Substitute 2 tablespoons of thick cream for the beer.

FRIED EGGS AND MOZZARELLA

This could be considered the Italian answer to the English Buck Rarebit.

8 slices Italian bread, about ½-inch thick
5 tablespoons butter (approximately)
1 package of mozzarella (8 ounces)
½ cup capers
8 eggs
salt and white pepper

Preheat the oven to 425°. If desired, cut the bread slices with a cookie cutter or similar tool to make rounds and remove the crust (if the bread is very fresh, an upturned large glass will do). Make the rounds 3 or 4 inches in diameter. This gives elegance to the dish, but it is not essential.

Toast the slices very lightly, then sauté them on one side in about 3 tablespoons of the butter. Slice the mozzarella about ⅓-inch thick, and slightly smaller than the bread rounds.

Using the rest of the butter, grease a very shallow baking dish or a cookie sheet. Place the bread slices on it, buttered side up, and put the mozzarella slices on top. Dot with capers, and set aside.

Fry the eggs, preferably sunny side up, until they are half done, and while they finish cooking, put the bread and cheese in the oven for about 5 minutes, or until the cheese has melted. Remove to a serving platter, top each slice with an egg, sprinkle with salt and pepper, and serve at once.

Serves 4.

PIPÉRADE

This *pipérade* comes from the Basque provinces of Spain.

> *1½ pounds fresh tomatoes, peeled, and cut into*
> *bite-sized pieces*
> *1 pound green peppers, seeded, and cut into*
> *bite-sized pieces*
> *2 cloves garlic, minced or pressed*
> *salt*
> *5 tablespoons olive oil*
> *pinch of cayenne pepper*
> *4 eggs*

In a heavy skillet—preferably of cast iron—sauté the tomatoes, peppers, and garlic in the oil for about 20 minutes, adding salt and stirring once in a while. Add the cayenne pepper, stir, then make four depressions with a wooden spoon, and break an egg into each. Cover, and continue to simmer for about 5 minutes, until the egg whites have set. (If a dryer egg white is preferred, although I do not recommend it, slide the pan under the broiler for half a minute.)

This pipérade is usually served in the skillet in which it was cooked.

Serves 4.

Side Dishes

ARTICHOKES AND FAVA BEANS

Agináres mé Kookiá

A Greek specialty.

5 medium-sized artichokes
2 tablespoons lemon juice
4 scallions, chopped
1 medium-sized onion, chopped
½ cup olive oil
1 pound fresh small tender fava beans
½ cup fresh tomatoes (or canned tomatoes, drained),
  passed through a food mill
2 tablespoons parsley
¼ teaspoon thyme or oregano
salt and pepper

Use only the tenderest part of the artichokes. Cut into quarters, lengthwise, removing the choke, and to prevent discoloration, put the artichokes immediately into a bowl with ½ cup of water and about 2 tablespoons lemon juice, rolling them around.

Sauté the scallions and onions in about 4 tablespoons of the olive oil until they begin to turn golden, then add a few tablespoons of the water in which the artichokes are soaking, and continue simmering a few minutes longer.

Meanwhile, shell the fava beans, scraping away with your nails a tiny bit of their inner skin, near the point where the "inner stem" was. This way they will cook more quickly and absorb more of the other flavors in the dish.

Add the artichokes to the onions, then add the fava beans, tomatoes, the remaining olive oil, the parsley, thyme or oregano, salt, and pepper. Cover and simmer on very low heat for about 40 minutes, or until both artichokes and beans are cooked.

This dish can also be cooked in a moderate oven, covered, but it will take about twice as long.

Note: If the fava beans are not as young as they should be, cook them with the onions for about 20 minutes before adding the artichokes and the other ingredients.

Serves 4.

ARTICHOKES AND PEAS

Agináres mé Araká

One of the most popular dishes in Greece, this must be prepared in the spring, when both vegetables are young and tender. A passable version can be obtained with frozen artichoke hearts and petit pois (tiny young peas), but the dish is much better when fresh vegetables are used.

> *3 cups very small tender fresh peas*
> *6 to 8 fresh artichokes, small and tender*
> *1 tablespoon lemon juice*
> *4 or 5 scallions, chopped*
> *½ cup olive oil*
> *½ cup Tomato Sauce (see index)*
> *1 tablespoon chopped fresh mint (or 1 teaspoon dried)*
> *½ teaspoon thyme*
> *salt and pepper*
> *3 tablespoons chopped parsley*
> *1 teaspoon arrowroot, cornstarch, or flour (optional)*

Shell the peas, clean the artichokes (see page 11), and cut in half or quarters, depending on size. After removing the choke, set artichokes aside in ½ cup water and 1 tablespoon lemon juice.

Sauté the scallions in the oil, then add the Tomato Sauce and a little water. Season with mint, thyme, salt, and pepper. Drain the artichokes and add them, with the peas, parsley, and a little more water. Cover tightly, and simmer on very low heat for about 30 minutes, or until both vegetables are cooked and the sauce has thickened. Peek into the skillet once, after about 20 minutes, to see if more water is needed. If at this point the sauce still seems very thin, continue cooking, uncovered, and after 7 or 8 minutes mix the arrowroot, cornstarch, or flour with 2 tablespoons cold water, and stir into the skillet a little at a time.

Note: If you use frozen vegetables, reduce considerably the amount of water, and reduce cooking time as well.

Serves 4.

ARTICHOKES KHÁLKIS STYLE

In Greece artichokes are often prepared in this very simple but delicious way. This particular recipe is from Khálkis.

> *10 or 12 small artichokes, fresh and tender*
> *juice of 2 lemons*
> *2 medium-sized onions, chopped fine*
> *¾ cup olive oil*
> *1 tablespoon flour*
> *salt and pepper*

Use only the hearts of the artichokes for this dish. (You may add the peeled stems, but none of the outer leaves, which you can save for other dishes.) Clean the artichokes, putting them at once into some of the lemon juice and a few tablespoons of water.

Sauté the onions in 2 tablespoons of the oil in a skillet. When they start to turn transparent, add the flour, stirring until both flour and onions are light golden brown. Then add the rest of the lemon juice and salt and pepper to taste.

In another skillet, place the artichokes with the water and lemon juice in which they soaked. Pour the onion/lemon mixture over them, adding a little more water now or later, if needed. Cover and cook over fairly low heat for about 30 minutes. Remove the cover and continue to cook until tender, the time depending on the size and quality of the artichokes.

Serves 4.

BEANS AND LETTUCE

A tasty French side dish, usually made with fresh beans. You may use any kind you like—lima, pinto, and so on.

*3/4 pound fresh beans (if dried beans are used, reduce the
   amount to 1/2 pound and rehydrate)*
1 clove garlic, minced
1/2 cup olive oil
*4 very small and tender romaine lettuce heads
   (2 or 3 if bigger)*
1 tablespoon chopped parsley
1 cup Tomato Sauce (see index)
salt and pepper
liquid from beans or vegetable broth

Cook the beans, reserving the liquid in which they were cooked. Keep warm.

In a large skillet, sauté the garlic in the oil for a few moments. Slice the lettuce fine, add it to the oil and garlic, together with the parsley, and simmer on very low heat for 15 minutes. Add the Tomato Sauce, salt, and pepper, and stir in a little of the bean liquid or a little vegetable broth, so that the lettuce is moist but not soaked with liquid (the amount depends on the quality of lettuce, the heat, and so on). Continue simmering for about 30 minutes, or until the sauce is considerably reduced. Add the beans, and simmer for a few more minutes so that they absorb the taste of the sauce.

Serves 4.

BRUSSELS SPROUTS AND CHESTNUTS

A specialty from Belgium also popular in France.

2 cups large chestnuts
1½ pounds Brussels sprouts
3 tablespoons oil
2 tablespoons butter
2 tablespoons dry white wine
salt
2 teaspoons flour or arrowroot (optional)

Boil the chestnuts (see page 15) for about 15 minutes and steam the Brussels sprouts until still quite firm.

Heat the oil and butter in a large skillet, stir in the white wine and salt, and add the chestnuts and Brussels sprouts. Simmer for a few minutes, uncovered, stirring so that the sauce coats everything.

If you wish a slightly thicker sauce, remove a couple of tablespoons of liquid from the pot, cool a bit, and mix in the flour or arrowroot. Pour this mixture back into the skillet, and stir and simmer a few minutes longer.

Serves 4.

VARIATION: FINOCCHIO AND CHESTNUTS. Substitute ½ pound finocchio for the Brussels sprouts to make a dish that is popular both in France and Italy. What makes it so special is the contrast between the anise flavor of the finocchio and the chestnut taste, which blend perfectly.

The finocchio should be small, in which case you can leave whole, after removing the outer layer and the stems. If larger, cut in half. Follow the original recipe except do not steam the finocchio first, but cook it in the sauce, and add the chestnuts when the finocchio is almost cooked. Then thicken the sauce if desired.

RED CABBAGE HUNGARIAN STYLE

1 pound chestnuts
½ teaspoon dried dill or fennel
1 medium-sized red cabbage, coarsely shredded
2 tablespoons butter
1 teaspoon fresh tarragon (or ½ teaspoon dried)
4 tablespoons red wine vinegar
1 teaspoon honey
salt and pepper
2 tablespoons dark raisins
2 tablespoons dried currants
2 tablespoons sour cream

Slit each chestnut across, and boil them (see page 15) with the dill or fennel. Remove from the pot when done, or after about 15 to 20 minutes. When the chestnuts are cool enough to handle, remove both skins and chop chestnuts coarsely.

Sauté the cabbage in the butter, mixing thoroughly. When it begins to wilt, add 1 cup warm water, the tarragon, vinegar, and honey. Stir, and continue to simmer for a few minutes. Add salt, pepper, chestnuts, raisins, and currants, and continue to simmer until the cabbage is done but still firm.

Remove from heat and stir in the sour cream, mixing well. Serve hot.

Serves 4.

RED CABBAGE WITH APPLES

This recipe is Polish, but similar versions of this dish are found in many Middle European countries.

> *2 medium-sized onions, chopped*
> *4 tablespoons butter*
> *1 small red cabbage, shredded*
> *1 medium-sized beet, peeled and grated*
> *1 cup vegetable broth*
> *3 tablespoons dry white wine*
> *2 bay leaves*
> *10 cloves, wrapped in cheesecloth and tied*
> *salt and pepper*
> *2 medium-sized cooking apples*

In a large pan, sauté the onions in the butter. When light golden, add the cabbage, and stir constantly for a few minutes over medium heat. Add the beet, broth, wine, bay leaves, cloves, salt, and pepper, mix well, and simmer for about 30 minutes, covered.

Peel and core the apples, and cut them into pieces, then add to the cabbage. Bring to a boil, and simmer, covered, for about 15 minutes, then uncover, and if the liquid seems too thin, leave uncovered. Cook about 15 minutes longer, covered or uncovered. At the end of the total cooking time (about 30 minutes) all the liquid should have been absorbed or evaporated. Remove bay leaves and cloves before serving.

Serves 4.

CARDOONS À LA LYONNAISE

1 pound young fresh cardoons
juice of 1 lemon
2 tablespoons olive oil
1 tablespoon butter
1 tablespoon flour
1 cup hot vegetable broth
1 cup dry white wine, warmed up slightly
½ cup grated Gruyère cheese
salt and pepper (preferably white pepper)

Prepare the cardoons (see page 15), then cut them in large bite-sized pieces and sprinkle with half the lemon juice. Boil them in just enough water to cover, for about 30 minutes, or until they can be pierced with a fork but are still somewhat chewy. Drain the cardoons well. In a skillet, heat the olive oil and sauté the cardoons for a few minutes over moderate heat until golden brown. Drain on a paper towel, and set aside.

Preheat the oven to 425°. In a saucepan, heat the butter and flour, as for White Sauce (see index), but add the hot broth instead of milk, then stir in the wine. Simmer for 5 minutes. Remove from heat and stir in the grated cheese and remaining lemon juice.

Put the cardoons in a fairly shallow oven-proof dish, and pour the sauce on top. Bake in 425° oven for 10 or 15 minutes.

Serves 4.

CARROT FRITTERS

A tasty dish from Perpignan, in the south of France.

> *1 pound carrots, cubed*
> *2 tablespoons flour (approximately)*
> *1 egg, separated*
> *salt*
> *pinch of nutmeg*
> *1 teaspoon brandy*
> *3 tablespoons olive oil*
> *1 tablespoon butter*

Steam the carrots until done. Mash them into a purée, and spread them out to cool and dry a little. Mix the purée with the flour, egg yolk, salt, nutmeg, and brandy. If the mixture is not sufficiently dry, add a little more flour. Make a paste which should hold together but be rather soft. Shape into patties. Beat the egg white lightly, dip the patties into it, and fry in the oil and butter.

Serve piping hot.

Serves 4.

BAKED EGGPLANT

In spite of its simplicity, this Spanish dish from Catalonia is very good.

> *8 very small eggplants*
> *6 tablespoons olive oil*
> *1 cup crumbled stale bread (French or Italian),*
> *   crust removed*
> *2 tablespoons chopped parsley*
> *3 garlic cloves, minced*
> *salt*

Preheat oven to 400°. Remove stems and peel the eggplants; then halve them, lengthwise. Sauté on both sides in half of the oil until soft but not fully cooked, and put in an oven-proof dish. Mix the bread with the parsley, garlic, and salt. Sprinkle the mixture on the eggplant halves, covering them completely, and pressing the mixture in gently. Dribble the remaining 3 tablespoons of oil on top.

Bake for 25 or 30 minutes, or until the tops begin to turn golden.

Serves 4.

FINOCCHIO AND TOMATOES

3 large onions, sliced
4 tablespoons olive oil
1 pound finocchio, stems and outer layer
  removed, quartered
1 pound fresh tomatoes, quartered
1 bay leaf
1 teaspoon thyme
salt and pepper
½ cup grated Parmesan cheese

In a heavy skillet, preferably of cast iron, sauté the onions in the oil, then add the finocchio, and sauté together for a few minutes. Add the tomatoes, bay leaf, thyme, salt, and pepper. Simmer, covered, over a low flame for about 30 minutes. Uncover and continue to simmer for about 15 minutes.

When ready to serve, if the sauce is too thin, spoon out about half, and mix the grated cheese into it, then remove the finocchio and tomato mixture to a serving platter, and pour the thickened sauce on top. If the sauce is of the right consistency, just sprinkle the cheese on top of the mixture before serving.

Serves 4.

JERUSALEM ARTICHOKES AU GRATIN

A Scandinavian specialty. This tuber, although a native of America, is much more popular in most European countries than in its native land.

> 2 pounds Jerusalem artichokes
> 1½ cups sour cream
> ½ teaspoon caraway seeds
> salt and white pepper
> 5 tablespoons hard cheese (any kind but
> with a robust taste), grated

Preheat the oven to 425°.

Scrub artichoke tubers and boil in very little water for about 10 minutes if they are not too big, a couple of minutes longer if they are larger. Peel and slice them.

Mix the sour cream with the caraway seeds, salt, and pepper. Grease an oven-proof dish, put the artichokes in it, leveling the surface, and pour the sour cream over them. Press gently with a spoon to let the cream penetrate. Sprinkle the grated cheese on top.

Bake for about 20 minutes.

Serves 4.

SPANISH BAKED ONIONS

You can serve these onions either as a side dish or accompanied by rice, if you wish to keep the meal Spanish; by pasta or polenta, for an Italian touch; or by Trahaná (see index), if you prefer to expand your gastronomic horizons. The following recipe can also be served as a main dish.

4 large Spanish onions
8 whole cloves
4 tablespoons butter
4 tablespoons Madeira wine or sherry
1 tablespoon honey
1 teaspoon salt
¼ teaspoon nutmeg
⅛ teaspoon powdered coriander
dash of cayenne pepper
⅓ cup slivered blanched almonds

Remove the outer skin from the onions, slicing off as little as possible at the ends. Then cut them across, exactly in half, and put them in a large skillet with about 1 inch of salted water. Bring to a boil, cover, and simmer for 15 minutes. Gently remove the onion halves with a slotted spoon to drain them well. Stick 1 clove in the middle of each half onion.

Preheat oven to 325°. To make the sauce, melt the butter in a saucepan, and add all the other ingredients except the almonds. Stir a few times while it is heating (it is not necessary for it to boil).

Pour a little of the sauce in a baking-serving dish that has a cover, then arrange the onions in it, and pour the rest of the sauce on top. Cover and bake for 45 minutes, basting a couple of times. At this point, if the sauce seems still rather thin, uncover, raise the temperature to 400°, and bake 5 to 10 minutes longer. Remove from the oven, sprinkle the almonds on top, and serve.

Serves 6 to 8, or 4 as a main dish.

FRIED POTATO PANCAKES

A Greek specialty, quite different from the types of potato pancakes from Middle European countries.

3 large potatoes
2 eggs
5 tablespoons grated Romano cheese
salt and pepper
6 tablespoons flour (approximately)
oil for frying, preferably olive oil

Boil and mash the potatoes and allow to cool a bit. In a large bowl, beat the eggs, then add the cheese, salt, and pepper. Mix in the mashed potatoes and, with your hands, shape the mixture into patties about ½-inch thick and no more than 2½ inches across. Dip them in flour so that it covers all sides, patting the flour in while still retaining the shape of the patties. If the mixture is too loose to handle, reshape it into balls, adding more flour, then flatten the balls out and dip in flour again.

Fry in hot oil a few minutes on each side, or until golden brown.

Serves 4.

CONVENT-STYLE BAKED POTATOES

Pommes de Terre des Nonnettes

The French name literally means "potatoes of the young nuns," maybe because the dish was invented in a convent.

2 eggs
salt and pepper
12 small round potatoes (preferably new
*   potatoes) , peeled*
¾ cup grated Gruyère cheese
1 cup breadcrumbs (approximately)
2 tablespoons butter

Preheat oven to 450°. Beat the eggs lightly with salt and pepper, and coat the potatoes with the mixture. Roll each one in the grated cheese, and finally in the breadcrumbs, pressing gently with your hands to make the crumbs stick. Melt the butter in a shallow baking dish, and arrange the potatoes in it, close together but without touching. Bake for about 45 minutes. The potatoes should have formed a crisp, golden crust.

Serves 4.

IRISH HERB SCONES

½ *pound mealy potatoes*
4 tablespoons flour, plus additional flour
¼ *teaspoon salt*
4 tablespoons butter, at room temperature
2 tablespoons chopped parsley
½ *teaspoon dried dill or tarragon*
¼ *teaspoon savory*
¼ *teaspoon marjoram*
¼ *teaspoon powdered sage*
oil or shortening for frying

Boil or bake the potatoes, then pass them through a food mill. Mix the 4 tablespoons flour, the salt, butter, and herbs, and combine with the potatoes. On a floured board, roll this dough to a thickness of about ¼ inch. Cut it into triangles 3 or 4 inches wide, and fry in very hot oil or shortening, on both sides, until light golden.

Note: You can add more herbs, dried or fresh, or change the combination of herbs to suit your taste, but a minimum of four herbs in addition to the parsley (which should always be included) is suggested.

Serves 4.

SALSIFY IN CREAM

22 to 24 small-sized salsify, scraped, then shredded
1 tablespoon butter
½ cup cream
2 teaspoons chopped parsley
salt and pepper (preferably white pepper)

Sauté the salsify in the butter for 5 or 6 minutes. Pour the cream over them, and heat, without boiling. Arrange on a hot serving platter, sprinkle with the parsley, salt, and pepper, and serve.

Note: Salsify is also excellent *au gratin,* in which case it should be cut into fairly large pieces, and prepared according to your favorite au gratin recipe.

Serves 4.

SPINACH BALL

1½ pounds spinach
½ cup crumbled stale Italian or French bread,
    crust removed
5 eggs
½ cup grated Parmesan cheese
3 tablespoons butter
1 tablespoon olive oil
salt and pepper
¼ teaspoon nutmeg
breadcrumbs

Preheat oven to 325°. Wilt the spinach in a pan for 5 minutes (see page 19). Allow to cool a bit, then squeeze it between your hands to remove as much liquid as possible, reserve liquid, and chop spinach coarsely. Soak the bread in the spinach liquid, squeeze it, and add to the spinach, making a rather thick paste. If there is not enough liquid, add a little water. Add the eggs, one at a time, mixing each egg into the paste, and then add oil, salt, pepper, nutmeg, and about 5 tablespoons of the grated cheese.

Grease a baking dish. Form the spinach mixture into a large ball with your hands, and gently place it in the dish. Sprinkle the remaining cheese on top and all around, and then sprinkle with the breadcrumbs. If the ball is not holding its shape, roll it in additional grated cheese and breadcrumbs.

Bake for about 20 minutes.

Serves 4.

TURNIP GRATIN

A very simple French dish, not to be overlooked, as it is really delicious.

> *2 cloves garlic, cut in half*
> *3 tablespoons butter (approximately)*
> *1½ pounds young turnips, scrubbed and thinly sliced*
> *salt and pepper*
> *½ teaspoon dill*
> *1 teaspoon fresh chervil (or ½ teaspoon dried)*
> *8 tablespoons thinly sliced Gruyère cheese*
> *½ cup heavy cream*
> *½ cup breadcrumbs*

Preheat the oven to 400°. Rub a shallow oven dish with the garlic; let it dry, and then grease well with butter. Arrange the turnip slices, slightly overlapping, in three layers, sprinkling salt, pepper, dill, and chervil on each layer. Cover with the cheese, pour the cream all over, sprinkle with breadcrumbs, and dot with butter.

Bake for about 45 minutes.

Serves 4.

TURNIPS IN YELLOW SAUCE

1½ pounds young round turnips, diced
2 tablespoons, plus 1 teaspoon, butter
1 tablespoon flour or arrowroot
2 cups hot milk
salt and pepper
½ teaspoon honey
1 egg yolk
1 tablespoon vegetable broth (approximately)

Sauté the turnips in the 2 tablespoons of butter, without letting them brown. Sprinkle the flour or arrowroot in the skillet, then add the hot milk, salt, pepper, and honey. Simmer on low heat for about 30 minutes, or less, according to the quality of the turnips. Remove the turnips to a hot platter, and keep warm. Turn off the heat under the sauce, stir it, and bind it with the egg yolk, the additional 1 teaspoon butter, and the broth. Turn the heat on again and warm the sauce over very low heat, without letting it boil. Pour it over the turnips.

Serves 4.

ZUCCHINI MORNAY

Another French dish, usually prepared at home.

4 medium-sized zucchini of similar shape and size
6 tablespoons olive oil
salt and pepper
½ cup French or Italian bread, crust removed
3 hard-cooked eggs, chopped
4 tablespoons grated Gruyère cheese
1 cup thin White Sauce (see index)

Cut the zucchini in half lengthwise, and scoop out part of the pulp, reserving it. Sauté the zucchini halves in 3 tablespoons of oil for about 20 minutes, or until almost done but still firm. You can either start them cooking with the cut side down, then turn them to cook on the other side, or you can start them cut side up, and cover the skillet after the bottom half has browned, removing the cover during the last 5 minutes or so.

While the zucchini are cooking, heat the remaining oil in a separate skillet, and sauté the zucchini pulp, adding salt and pepper.

Preheat the oven to 375°. Moisten the bread with water, and squeeze. In a bowl, mix the bread, zucchini pulp, chopped eggs, grated cheese, and White Sauce.

Arrange the zucchini halves, cut side up, in a baking dish, pouring the oil in which you sautéed them into the cavities. Fill them well with the mixture, and pour the White Sauce over and around them.

Bake for about 20 minutes.

Serves 4.

ZUCCHINI ÎLE-DE-FRANCE

3 medium-sized zucchini, sliced in rounds
salt
6 tablespoons olive oil
1 teaspoon curry powder
1 tablespoon flour
pepper
1 cup hot milk

Place the zucchini in a sieve and sprinkle all over with salt to draw out their liquid. After about 30 minutes, pat the slices dry, and fry in a skillet on both sides in 5 tablespoons of the oil. Remove them with a slotted spoon, and arrange them in a shallow oven dish.

While the zucchini are cooking, preheat the oven to 450°, and prepare the sauce. Put the remaining 1 tablespoon oil in a saucepan, add the curry powder, flour, and pepper, then pour in the hot milk, and stir constantly for about 5 minutes. Add whatever oil is left from frying the zucchini, stir, and pour the sauce all over.

Bake for 5 minutes.

Serves 4.

MIXED FRIED VEGETABLES
Fritto Misto

Raw, nonleafy vegetables of all kinds are used for this dish. If you can find some pumpkin or squash blossoms, wash them very gently, drip-dry them, then fry them by the method described. It is a treat well worth trying.

BATTER
1 cup flour
pinch of salt, plus ¼ teaspoon
2 eggs, separated
1 tablespoon olive oil
4 tablespoons dry white wine
⅓ cup water (approximately)
¼ teaspoon nutmeg
vegetables of your choice
oil for deep-frying

Mix the flour, pinch of salt, egg yolks, oil, wine, and about half the water in a bowl and beat until smooth. Cover the bowl, and let stand for about 1 hour. Beat the egg whites until stiff with the ¼ teaspoon of salt. Add the nutmeg to the egg-yolk paste, and gently fold in the whites.

Cut the vegetables into bite-sized pieces. Use whole flowerets of cauliflower; cut zucchini lengthwise into thin strips about 2 inches long. Dip the vegetables in the batter. Have the oil (preferably olive oil) very hot, and deep-fry the vegetables quickly until they turn a light golden color.

Note: For a more delicate taste, either cut down the amount of nutmeg or add a few gratings of lemon peel.

Serves 6–8.

Salads

Aside from the mixed salads in this section, some of which are quite unusual, salads made with only one vegetable can be very tasty. For example, try thinly shredded red cabbage dressed with olive oil and wine vinegar (or cider vinegar), salt and pepper, and allowed to marinate for about 1 hour.

Many cooked vegetables can be treated this way. To name just one, cauliflower steamed to chewy firmness, dressed while still warm, and served at room temperature, is quite a treat. Lemon may be substituted for vinegar, and a sprinkling of dill can add a subtle touch.

Such salads of a single vegetable, raw or cooked, are common throughout Europe, especially when fresh vegetables are at their peak, and I strongly recommend that you give them a try.

Even the best bottled dressings are pretty awful, and a superfluous expense. And there is no need to prepare a salad dressing in advance, using precious refrigerator space. In fact, oil coagulates and turns whitish at refrigerator temperature, and the dressing has to be re-emulsified by shaking it. It will not penetrate properly when too cold, and whatever herbs you have added will become soggy. The taste is bound to suffer. A fresh dressing of olive oil, wine vinegar, salt, and pepper is much better and is the most common in Europe. Herbs are rarely added, and only when available fresh; occasionally, a tiny bit of garlic or mustard diluted in vinegar may be included. No sugar or other sweeteners should ever be added to salad dressings. That is an unfortunate American habit which slowly crept into our sugar-loving country but certainly does not belong in a genuine salad dressing. On rare occasions, in European salads, a slight natural sweet taste is provided by the presence of certain fruits.

The best fresh dressings are made with carefully selected ingredients. The olive oil should be of the best quality, and should not have been refined—that is, it should be cold pressed oil (labeled "virgin"). The vinegar used in most of these salad dressings is red wine vinegar. White wine vinegar has a more delicate flavor and is suitable for salads which are pale in color, so as not to detract from their natural tint. In northern Europe, malt vinegar is often used, but it is hard to find in the United States. White vinegar is not recommended because in this country it is almost invariably made with artificial substances, some of which come close to being unhealthful. Cider vinegar of good, genuine quality can add a subtle flavor to certain salads, especially if the vegetable used has its own touch of natural sweetness, but in central and southern Europe wine vinegar or lemon juice is more often used.

It goes without saying that all greens used in salad, as well as other vegetables, should be washed thoroughly. Certain leafy vegetables, such as spinach, are more easily washed by immersion, changing the water twice or more times, as running water may not separate the grit from the leaves.

Drying salad greens thoroughly after draining them is not really as important as is generally believed. I have seen people religiously pat dry every single leaf of lettuce they put in their salads, only to add a third-rate vinegar to the dressing. Vinegar is always made with the addition of water, so if you use a good, strong vinegar, a few drops of water remaining in the greens won't make much difference. A good shaking while draining the greens in a sieve, then gathering the leaves in a clean dish towel and swinging it a few times, is more than sufficient.

FINOCCHIO AND RAW ARTICHOKE SALAD

This recipe comes from France, but raw artichokes, when they are still very small and have not even developed a choke, are quite common on dining tables in all European countries in which artichokes are easily grown.

> *1 large finocchio*
> *3 small very young artichokes*
> *juice of ½ lemon*
> *1 small white onion, or 2 scallions*
> *4 or 5 small red radishes, sliced thin*
> *5 tablespoons olive oil*
> *salt and pepper*

Slice the finocchio very thin, crosswise (see page 17). Also slice some parts of the stalks, if they are not too tough, and add the feathery portion.

Remove the outer leaves from the artichokes, layer by layer, occasionally tasting a leaf, until you come to the portion that is edible raw. Slice the artichokes very thin crosswise, starting from the bottom. Immediately put them in the lemon juice. Slice the onion or scallions very thin. Add the radishes, oil, salt, and pepper, toss, and serve immediately.

Serves 4.

FINOCCHIO AND GRAPEFRUIT SALAD

The origin of this salad is unknown. I tasted it at a friend's home in Italy, where the family called it "American salad"— maybe because of the grapefruit, which is not very common in Italy. However, I have never found it over here, where finocchio, until a few years ago, was even more uncommon than grapefruit in Italy. Whatever the origin, the combination of tastes is really extraordinary, and I recommend that you try it.

> *1 pound finocchio*
> *½ large grapefruit*
> *10 or 12 black olives* (*Greek or Sicilian type*)
> *4 tablespoons olive oil* (*approximately*)
> *juice of ½ lemon*
> *salt and pepper*

Slice the finocchio (see page 17). Cut the grapefruit in half and, using a grapefruit knife or spoon, remove the sections, without any skin. Remove the pits from the olives by slicing around them. Add the oil, lemon juice, salt and pepper to taste. Since Greek or Sicilian olives are very salty, go easy on the salt, or omit it altogether. Toss thoroughly.

Serves 4.

FINOCCHIO, KOHLRABI, AND ENDIVE SALAD

> *3 medium-sized kohlrabi*
> *1 medium-sized carrot*
> *3 heads Belgian endive*
> *2 medium-sized finocchio*
> *2 tablespoons capers*
> *2 tablespoons sunflower seeds* (*or other seeds*)
> *2 tablespoons assorted nuts, chopped*
> *5 tablespoons olive oil*
> *2 tablespoons lemon juice*
> *½ teaspoon mustard*
> *salt and pepper*

Peel the kohlrabi, then shred or grate them into a large bowl.

Scrape and finely shred the carrot into the bowl. Slice the endives in ¼-inch rounds and add. Slice the finocchio very thin, cross-wise, using parts of the lateral shoots, if not too tough, and the feathery green portion. Add the capers, sunflower or other seeds, and nuts.

Whip the oil, lemon juice, mustard, salt, and pepper together, using a fork or small wire whisk. Pour the dressing over the salad, and toss. Allow to rest at room temperature for at least 20 minutes before serving.

Serves 4.

RAW ZUCCHINI, TOMATO, AND CARROT SALAD

3 small zucchini, very firm
2 medium-sized tomatoes, ripe but firm
3 medium-sized carrots
1 scallion, sliced thin
½ teaspoon dill
¼ teaspoon powdered coriander (optional)
½ teaspoon fresh ginger, grated, or ¼ teaspoon powdered
5 tablespoons olive oil
2 tablespoons lemon juice
salt and pepper
sunflower seeds (optional)

Shred the zucchini. Cut the tomatoes into wedges, spread them out on a platter, sprinkle with salt, and let stand for about 20 minutes. Drain, either by pouring the juice from the platter into a bowl while holding the vegetables with your hand, or by straining through a sieve. Shred the carrots, and mix all the in-gredients together.

Serves 4.

RAW WINTER SALAD

1 medium-sized carrot
¼ small white cabbage
¼ small red cabbage
1 medium-sized turnip
1 medium-sized parsnip
2 small Jerusalem artichokes
1 medium-sized kohlrabi
2 tablespoons chopped parsley
2 tablespoons chopped chives or onion
5 tablespoons olive oil
2 tablespoons wine vinegar
½ teaspoon grated horseradish
salt and pepper

Shred both cabbages. Lightly scrape the carrot and shred it. Scrape the turnip and parsnip, peel the Jerusalem artichokes and the kohlrabi, and slice all four paper-thin. If the slices are too wide, cut them in half. Add the parsley and chives or onion. Whip together the oil, vinegar, horseradish, salt, and pepper, and pour over the vegetables, mixing thoroughly. Let stand at least 30 minutes before serving, to allow the vegetables to absorb the dressing.

Note: The combination I've given here produces interesting tastes and textures, but if some of the vegetables are not available, you can omit them or substitute others. Nuts, seeds, and herbs may be added.

Serves 4.

HEALTHY RAW SALAD

Here is a Swiss favorite, particularly in the Zurich region, where the famous health and vegetarian schools such as Bircher-Muesli originated. The vegetables must be fresh.

2 celeriac
2 small tender turnips
2 small carrots
1 medium-sized cucumber
4 tender fresh asparagus (other green vegetables may
*   be substituted if asparagus is not in season)*
1 large chunk of pumpkin or other squash
10 to 12 cauliflower flowerets
5 tablespoons olive oil (approximately)
lemon juice to taste

Grate all the vegetables, mixing in the oil and lemon juice as you proceed, to avoid oxidation.

Salt is usually omitted—the natural mineral salts in these vegetables should be sufficient.

Serves 4.

SPINACH AND YOGURT SALAD

Originally Armenian, this salad found its way into Greece, where it has become a favorite.

3 pounds spinach
1 teaspoon salt
pepper to taste
3 cups yogurt

Cook the spinach (see page 19), adding salt and pepper. Drain very well and allow to cool. Mix in the yogurt, and serve at room temperature.

Serves 4.

SPINACH SALAD

Since spinach is ubiquitous throughout the Mediterranean countries, it is hard to pinpoint the origin of this dish. It is found everywhere, although the spices vary from North Africa and the Middle East to Greece and Italy. Do not be fooled by its simplicity; the taste is really exquisite.

> *4 pounds spinach*
> *½ cup olive oil*
> *juice of 1 lemon (or to taste)*
> *salt and pepper*

Cook the spinach (see page 19). Drain very well and place in a salad bowl. While the spinach is still hot, add the seasoning. Serve lukewarm or at room temperature.

Many other vegetables are served in this way, especially in Greece and Italy. It is a slight variation on what the French have come to call vegetables *"à la grecque."*

Serves 4.

RAW SPINACH AND MUSHROOM SALAD

½ cup dried apricots
½ cup dry white wine
2 tablespoons lemon juice
1½ pounds very fresh spinach
½ pound fresh mushrooms
6 tablespoons olive oil
salt and pepper
½ teaspoon dry dill
½ cup pine nuts (slivered almonds
    may be substituted)

Into a small pot just big enough to accommodate the apricots, pour the wine and lemon juice, and heat the liquid to a bare simmer. Turn off the heat, and add the apricots. Cover tightly and allow the apricots to rehydrate for about ½ hour, turning them once or twice if the liquid does not cover them completely.

Wash the spinach and drain it well. Clean the mushrooms by wiping them with a damp cloth; remove just a thin slice from the stems if they have darkened or dried, then slice the mushrooms very thin, stem and all. If some of them are very large, cut in half lengthwise, then slice.

Over a bowl, drain the apricots through a sieve. Reserve the liquid, and cut apricots into bite-sized pieces. Add the oil, salt, pepper, and dill to the apricot liquid and whip with a fork. In a salad bowl, mix the spinach and mushrooms, add the dressing, and toss thoroughly. Sprinkle the apricots and pine nuts or almonds on top. Give a final toss at the table just before serving.

Serves 4.

VEGETABLE SALAD, GREEK STYLE

There are many tasty Greek salads, aside from the one now served under that name in Greek and Middle Eastern restaurants but often distorted beyond recognition. Here is an excellent Greek salad, often served at home.

> *½ pound green beans*
> *5 medium-sized beets*
> *½ medium-sized cabbage, shredded*
> *12 Greek olives*
> *6 tablespoons olive oil*
> *2 tablespoons wine vinegar*
> *1 tablespoon capers*
> *1 teaspoon mustard*
> *salt and pepper*

Cook the green beans until firm, and cut them in half. Cook, peel, and slice the beets. When both are cool, mix with the cabbage and olives. Whip the remaining ingredients to make the dressing, add, toss, and serve.

Serves 4.

WATERCRESS AND APPLE SALAD

In this delicious salad from France, the seemingly incongruous tastes blend with unusual subtlety.

> *1 large bunch watercress (enough to equal 2 cups)*
> *1 medium-sized finocchio*
> *2 medium-sized apples, tart variety*
> *white wine vinegar*
> *2 teaspoons fresh marjoram (or 1 teaspoon dried)*
> *5 tablespoons olive oil*
> *salt and pepper*

Wash the watercress and cut crosswise with a knife into three equal parts. Slice the finocchio very thin, but leave the feathery portion whole. Core the apples and cut them into 1-inch cubes. (If the apples are of a thick-skinned variety, peel them first; otherwise leave the skin on.) Sprinkle the apples immediately with vinegar, so that they will not darken. Add the rest of the ingredients, mix, taste, and add more vinegar if needed.

Serves 4.

ROOT VEGETABLE WHEEL
Roda Virolada

This is a salad from the Catalonia section of Spain. The Spanish name means "a wheel on its hub" and refers to the way the salad is presented.

6 very small potatoes
6 small beets
4 medium-sized turnips
6 medium-sized carrots
3 or 4 tablespoons mayonnaise
capers for garnishing
4 tablespoons olive oil
2 tablespoons wine vinegar
salt

Boil the potatoes and the beets separately; peel when cool. Scrape the turnips and carrots, and boil or steam them. Slice all the vegetables into pieces about 1/4-inch thick, keeping all vegetables separate.

To form the wheel, use a large round platter, and arrange each vegetable into wedges on the platter, alternating color and variety. Leave an empty circular center for the hub of the wheel, and here place the mayonnaise, topped with a small mound of capers. For contrast, and to delineate the hub, surround the mayonnaise with a circle of capers.

Mix the oil, vinegar, and salt in a bowl, and dribble over all the vegetables, avoiding the center.

Serves 4.

RUSSIAN SALAD I

Various versions of this very popular salad, each claiming to be the authentic one, have reached practically every European country. Actually, the original Russian salad contains a preponderance of beets and not too many other vegetables. It seems that Russian refugees at the time of the Revolution brought this dish to France and other European countries, adapting it to native vegetable fare. Strangely enough, when the salad traveled to England, though it tenaciously retained its name, the beets completely disappeared.

This first version is one of the many, and my favorite. Other recipes call for hard-cooked eggs, which I find redundant, since the mayonnaise already contains eggs.

Use the salad as a side dish, or as an appetizer, especially in the summer, or as one of the dishes for a smörgasbord-type dinner. (Then you may want to increase the amounts according to the number of people you plan to serve.)

> *1½ cups potatoes, of the firm, not mealy, type*
> *1½ cups beets*
> *1 cup carrots*
> *1 cup green beans*
> *1 cup peas*
> *1 cup baby lima beans*
> *1 cup mayonnaise (approximately)*
> *lemon juice (optional)*
> *salt and white pepper*

Cook all the vegetables separately, preferably by steaming them, but do not overcook. Dice the potatoes, beets, carrots, and green beans into rather small bite-sized pieces, about the size of the lima beans. Allow to cool, then coat the vegetables thoroughly with mayonnaise, starting with about ½ cup and adding more, to taste. Adjust with lemon juice, if desired, and salt and pepper, as you mix.

An attractive way to serve this dish is to mound it in a bowl and coat the visible surface with mayonnaise, spreading it evenly with a blunt-tipped knife. As decoration, you may add thin strips of pimiento from the center out, and put a tuft of parsley in the middle. You could also alternate the pimiento strips with rows of capers. Use your imagination, but go easy with the decoration, as the taste of this salad is rather delicate, and excessive additions may overwhelm it.

The salad tastes better if prepared at least 1 hour in advance. It also keeps for several days, refrigerated.

Serves 4.

RUSSIAN SALAD II

This version is closer to the authentic Russian salad.

> *2 cups diced cooked potatoes*
> *2 cups diced cooked beets*
> *1 cup diced cooked carrots*
> *¼ cup minced raw onion or thinly sliced scallion*
> *½ cup peeled and diced raw cucumbers*
> *½ cup peeled, cored, and diced raw apple*
> *salt and pepper to taste*
> *½ cup mayonnaise or sour cream (more or less*
> *according to taste)*

When the cooked vegetables have cooled, mix all ingredients

with the mayonnaise or sour cream, and allow to marinate for at least 1 hour. Serve at room temperature.

This salad will keep in the refrigerator for several days.

Serves 4.

SWISS SALAD

This very refreshing salad comes from the Jura Alps in Switzerland.

> *2 cups small, tender fresh green beans*
> *2 cups Swiss cheese*
> *2 teaspoons mustard*
> *1 cup Green Sauce (see index), approximately*
> *1 hard-cooked egg*

Steam the green beans until still firm. If they are very small, keep them whole, otherwise, cut in half.

Slice the cheese about ¼-inch thick, then cut into strips the size of the green beans. Add the mustard to the green sauce, and mix well with the beans and cheese. Chop the egg very fine, or pass it through a sieve, and sprinkle on top.

Serves 4.

POTATO AND ONION SALAD

> *5 large potatoes of a nonmealy variety*
> *10 small onions*
> *olive oil*
> *salt*
> *wine vinegar (preferably white wine vinegar)*
> *3 tablespoons chopped parsley*
> *pepper (preferably white pepper)*

Boil the potatoes in their skins. Remove only the outer skins of the onions and cut a thin slice off the ends. Boil them separately over low heat until cooked but still firm. (Reserve the water from both potatoes and onions, to be used in soups.)

When potatoes and onions are cooked, peel and slice the potatoes while still warm; quarter the onions, discarding one or two additional layers of the outer skins if they seem too tough (or adding them to your soup ingredients, if you wish) .

Mix onions and potatoes gently but thoroughly, adding oil and salt to taste while they are still warm. After they are coated with the oil, add the vinegar. Allow to cool, then add parsley, pepper, and more oil and vinegar to taste, since the potatoes will have absorbed some of the dressing. The amount of seasoning depends on how much the potatoes have absorbed while cooling. Allow to rest at room temperature for at least 1 hour before serving.

This salad will keep in the refrigerator for several days; in fact, its taste improves if served a day or two after you make it.

Serves 4.

VARIATION.   Boil, peel, and slice 5 or 6 medium-sized beets and mix them with the potatoes and onions. The tastes of these three vegetables blend very well.

POTATO SALAD, FRENCH STYLE

Although this is the "classic" French potato salad, the habit of seasoning cooked potatoes (and other vegetables) while still hot is common throughout Europe, because the taste of the seasoning blends more thoroughly with the hot vegetables.

1½ pounds potatoes of a nonmealy variety
6 tablespoons olive oil (approximately)
2 tablespoons wine vinegar (preferably white wine vinegar)
1 teaspoon fresh chervil, chopped (or ½ teaspoon dried)

1 teaspoon fresh dill (or ¾ teaspoon dried)
salt and pepper (preferably white pepper)

Boil the potatoes in their skins. While the potatoes are cooking, whip together the oil, vinegar, chervil, dill, salt, and pepper. Peel the potatoes, holding them with a fork if too hot to touch. Slice them about ¼-inch thick, and add the dressing immediately, even as you are still slicing. Mix well. Allow to cool, and serve at room temperature, or while still lukewarm.

Serves 4.

OLD ENGLISH POTATO SALAD

This English recipe dates back to the beginning of the nineteenth century. The original recipe called for anchovies, for which I have substituted Worcestershire or soy sauce, but it is otherwise unchanged. Note how the taste for the best Italian olive oil had already reached the shores of England and was beginning to be appreciated by the local epicures.

Even if cold mashed potatoes do not seem too appealing to you, try this salad, as it is really quite good.

6 large potatoes, cooked and mashed
2 teaspoons finely chopped onion
9 tablespoons olive oil (preferably from Lucca)
4 tablespoons cider vinegar
2 teaspoons Worcestershire sauce or soy sauce
3 teaspoons English mustard
salt
6 hard-cooked eggs, chopped

Mix the potatoes and onion. Vigorously whip together the oil, vinegar, Worcestershire or soy sauce, mustard, and salt. Pour the dressing on the potatoes, and toss. Allow to rest 15 or 20 minutes, then sprinkle the chopped eggs on top, and serve at room temperature.

Serves 4.

LETTUCE, CHICORY, AND ORANGE SALAD

Another old English salad. Oranges had been recently introduced into England and were just a little more common than Italian olive oil when this salad was invented.

1 head curly chicory
1 small open-head lettuce
1 bunch watercress
3 tablespoons chopped chives, parsley, or half and half
3 oranges, peeled, separated into sections, and seeded
8 tablespoons olive oil
3 tablespoons cider vinegar
salt and pepper

Tear the chicory, lettuce, and watercress with your hands, or cut into 2-inch pieces. Arrange the greens in a salad bowl, together with half the chives or parsley. Cut the orange sections in 2 or 3 pieces and drop them on the greens, with whatever juice oozed out while you were slicing them.

Whip the oil, vinegar, salt, and pepper in a separate bowl, pour on top of the salad, and serve topped with the rest of the chives or parsley. Toss at the table.

Serves 4.

RICE SALAD CAPUCHIN MONK STYLE

Some readers may be surprised to learn that the word *cappuccino* in Italian simply means a Capuchin monk. It is derived from *cappuccio,* meaning "hood" and generally referring to the hood on top of a cape (*cappa,* same word root). The popular coffee-and-milk mixture takes its name from the color of the robe worn by the Franciscan Capuchin monks.

This salad has nothing to do with either coffee or milk but was invented in a Capuchin monastery several centuries ago, and was eaten by the monks during Lent. Later, with a few variations, it became a favorite outside the Italian monasteries.

> *2 cups rice*
> *1½ cups imported dried mushrooms, rehydrated and*
> *   liquid reserved (see page 18)*
> *4 cups vegetable broth (approximately)*
> *15 very small onions*
> *4 artichoke bottoms, or 10 asparagus tips, both fresh*
> *juice of ½ lemon*
> *4 tablespoons butter or oil*
> *15 black olives, Greek or Sicilian type*
> *3 tablespoons mayonnaise*
> *1 teaspoon dry mustard*
> *½ teaspoon paprika*
> *2 small dill pickles, chopped fine*

Heat the oven to 400°. Add the mushroom liquid to the vegetable broth to make about 4 cups of liquid altogether. Bake the rice in the liquid, covered, for about 30 minutes, or until the liquid has been absorbed and the rice is cooked but still firm.

While the rice is cooking, coarsely chop the mushrooms, onions, and artichoke bottoms or asparagus tips. Mix the artichokes with the lemon juice to prevent oxidation. Sauté the vegetables in the butter or oil, adding a part or all of the lemon juice (taste as you add). Coarsely chop the olives, and mix them and the vegetables into the cooked rice. Blend together the mayonnaise, mustard, paprika, and pickles, and stir into the rice.

Allow to cool to room temperature, and serve.

Serves 4.

HUNGARIAN SALAD

1 cup cooked rice
2 medium-sized tomatoes
3 small celeriac
2 hard-cooked eggs
2 hot red peppers (see note)
4 or 5 tablespoons mayonnaise
salt
2 teaspoons paprika

Cut the celeriac into very thin strips. Cut the tomatoes into bite-sized pieces. Chop the hard-cooked eggs and the red peppers very fine. Mix with the rice and mayonnaise, adding salt to taste, and sprinkle the paprika on top.

Note: The hot peppers should be of the Hungarian type, rather than the very hot Mexican variety. If the Hungarian peppers are not available, or if you don't like a very spicy taste, use only 1 pepper, or none, and double the amount of paprika, using half while mixing the salad, and sprinkling the rest on top.

Serves 4.

BLACK-EYED PEA SALAD

Although the Greeks seldom prepare spicy foods, this salad is an exception. Occasionally, chick-peas are substituted for the black-eyed peas and cooked in the same manner. The amounts of spices may be increased or decreased according to taste.

> *2 cups black-eyed peas*
> *3 teaspoons ground coriander*
> *3 cloves garlic, minced or crushed*
> *3 tablespoons fresh ginger, grated*
>   *(or 1½ teaspoons powdered ginger)*
> *½ red pepper, chopped, or cayenne pepper to taste*
> *olive oil*
> *wine vinegar*
> *salt*
> *paprika*

Soak the peas (see pages 13, 19). Put them in a pot with water to cover, plus 1 inch, and add the coriander, garlic, ginger, and chopped red pepper or cayenne. Cook for a little over 1 hour, or until still a little chewy. While the peas are cooking, prepare a dressing by mixing together oil, vinegar, salt, and paprika. Add to the peas as soon as you remove them from the heat. Allow to cool to room temperature, and correct the seasoning just before serving.

Serves 4.

CHICK-PEA SALAD

Ensalada de Garbanzos

This salad is originally from Spain, but chick-peas appear in salads or are served with drinks before dinner in many southern European countries. In Greece, dried chick-peas are slowly toasted, then eaten like peanuts. One must have good teeth to eat them, but the taste is delicious with drinks.

> 2 cups chick-peas
> 1 bay leaf
> salt
> 4 spring onions, sliced thin
> 1 large sweet pepper (preferably red), coarsely chopped
> 3 tablespoons chopped fresh parsley
> 4 tablespoons olive oil
> 2 tablespoons lemon juice
> paprika, or dash of cayenne pepper

Presoak the chick-peas, and cook them in water to cover plus about 1 inch, adding the bay leaf at the beginning and the salt after they have simmered for about 30 minutes. They should be ready in a little over 1 hour, but check now and then, and add a little more boiling water if necessary. Cooking time varies according to the quality of the chick-peas and whether they have been soaked in hot or cold water, but do not overcook them, as they are much tastier if still a bit chewy. For this reason, I do not recommend canned chick-peas, which are overcooked as a safety precaution.

Drain the chick-peas. Combine all ingredients and allow to stand at least ½ hour at room temperature before serving.

Serves 4.

BEAN SALAD

Another favorite in most southern European countries. Use any kind of large bean, fresh or dried. In Italy, this salad is usually made with large white beans, preferably fresh, and is dressed with wine vinegar instead of lemon.

> 3 cups large beans
> 1 large onion, chopped fine
> salt and pepper (preferably white pepper)
> ⅓ cup olive oil

> *juice of 1 lemon (or to taste), or wine*
> *vinegar, to taste*

If dried beans are used, presoak them. Cook them, barely covered with water, until tender but not mushy. Drain, and put in a large bowl, adding the onion, salt, and pepper, then the oil and lemon juice or vinegar. Toss lightly. Serve lukewarm or at room temperature.

Serves 4.

ESAU SALAD

This recipe owes its name to the Biblical story of Esau and Jacob. Esau, the first-born son, is reported to have sold his birthright to clever Jacob, his brother, for nothing more than a dish of lentils.

> *2 cups lentils*
> *1 bay leaf*
> *1 large tomato*
> *1 medium-sized green pepper*
> *2 medium-sized celeriac (or 3 celery stalks,*
> *   if celeriac is unavailable)*
> *Green Sauce (see index)*
> *2 hard-cooked eggs*

Cook the lentils with the bay leaf, until they are done but still a bit firm. Cool. Cut the tomato into bite-sized pieces and the pepper and celeriac into thin strips. (If celery stalks are used, chop them coarsely.) Combine lentils and vegetables, and mix in the Green Sauce; marinate for at least 1 hour. Just before serving, slice or chop the eggs and sprinkle or spread on top.

Serves 4.

BULGUR SALAD

This, or a similar version of bulgur salad, is made in Greece, the Middle East, and parts of North Africa, where it must have originated. It is a very simple but delicious salad.

1 cup bulgur
1 medium-sized onion, minced
4 tablespoons chopped parsley
3 tablespoons fresh mint (or 2 tablespoons dried),
  chopped or crumbled
4 tablespoons olive oil
3 tablespoons lemon juice
salt and pepper
1 small head of lettuce (preferably romaine)

Put the bulgur in a fairly deep, heavy pot. Add enough boiling water to cover, plus 1 inch. Let stand for 30 minutes, covered, after which time the bulgur will have swelled considerably. Drain, and press the ball of bulgur between your hands to squeeze out as much water as possible. Place in a salad bowl, and mix in the onion, herbs, oil, lemon juice, salt, and pepper. The lettuce can either be sliced very thin, crosswise, and tossed with the other ingredients, or the leaves may be left whole, and the salad served on top of them.

Serves 4.

CHRYSANTHEMUM SALAD

This salad has a very distinctive taste which may not appeal to everybody, and even the enthusiasts admit that it can be eaten only in small quantities. The following amount is sufficient as a side dish or second salad.

2 cups petals of large yellow or white chrysanthemums
4 tablespoons olive oil
1 tablespoon lemon juice
salt and pepper

Bring a pot of water to a boil, and switch off the heat. Plunge the petals into the hot water for no more than 1 minute. Drain and dry thoroughly by gently patting them with a towel. Whip together the oil, lemon juice, salt, and pepper, and pour over the petals. Toss the salad at the table very delicately, so that the petals won't be damaged.

Serves 4.

DAISY SALAD

2 cups daisy petals
1 tablespoon each lemon juice and orange juice
3 medium-sized potatoes, boiled, peeled, and cubed
½ pound fresh green beans, steamed, then
  cut in 1-inch pieces
1 cup small tender peas, steamed
4 tablespoons olive oil
3 tablespoons dry white wine
1 teaspoon mustard
salt

Soak the daisy petals in the juices for about 20 minutes. Drain, leaving some of the juices with the petals, and reserving the rest.

While the petals are soaking, prepare the potatoes, beans, and peas. Make a dressing with the oil, wine, mustard, and salt. When the vegetables have cooled, toss them in a bowl with the dressing, and sprinkle the daisy petals on top. Pour on the reserved juice, and serve.

Serves 4.

GLADIOLUS SALAD

Like Chrysanthemum Salad, a little of this dish goes a long way. Here, make sure that the gladioli bulbs have not been treated with any chemicals.

30 gladioli bulbs (approximately)
vinegar to taste
3 tablespoons olive oil
½ cup port wine
1 teaspoon strong mustard (Dijon or similar)
salt and pepper
50 gladioli flowers, freshly picked and in full bloom

Wash the bulbs, and cook them in their own skins, just covered with water and the vinegar, for 10 to 20 minutes, depending on size and freshness. Peel and slice them while still hot. Prepare the dressing by whipping together all the other ingredients except the flowers. Toss the bulbs in the dressing, and arrange them in a salad bowl. Coarsely chop the gladioli flowers into fairly even pieces and arrange gracefully on top.

Serves 4.

Sauces

This section contains a variety of sauces, both cold and warm, with suggestions on how to use them, although by no means should you confine your choice to the dishes mentioned. Some of these sauces are good for pasta or dumplings; others are best suited for vegetables; still others can give an unusual taste to an omelet or may be used as sandwich spreads, salad dressings, and so on.

Whenever no specific suggestions are made, experiment. You'll be surprised how much a compatible or even a contrasting sauce can enhance some foods.

At times a sauce can be an afterthought, in a sense, and in fact this is how some famous sauces have been invented. Let's say you made a nice vegetable pie, but it came out a little too dry or tasted a little too bland. Make a sauce and serve it on the side, and you have invented a new twist on an old dish.

A good sauce can add elegance to a simple meal, give a different taste to leftovers, turn an insipid dish into an interesting gustatory experience, or improve the appearance of a dish that has accidentally turned out misshapen or unattractive.

Sweet sauces appear, as appropriate, in the Dessert Section.

WHITE SAUCE

This is the basic sauce for many dishes, and if you follow the method explained here, it is easy to make. Many cookbooks still call this modern simplified version Sauce Béchamel, though that is really a misnomer. The Marquis of Béchamel, who invented the sauce that took his name, was majordomo to King Louis XIV of France. His was a much more complicated dish; it contained more ingredients, and took at least an hour to cook. But the simpler white sauce which we know today, like its illustrious ancestor, still remains a classic. According to the demands of the dishes in which you are going to use this sauce, it can be made thinner or thicker.

This recipe yields a white sauce of medium consistency. For a thinner sauce, either add more milk or reduce the amounts of butter and flour; for a thicker one, do the reverse.

> *2 tablespoons butter*
> *2 tablespoons flour*
> *1 cup milk, heated almost to boiling point*
> *¼ teaspoon salt*
> *powdered white pepper (optional)*
> *nutmeg (optional)*

In a heavy saucepan, melt the butter and flour over low to moderate heat, making sure that it does not brown by removing the pan from the heat a few times. Mix vigorously with a whip or a wooden spoon. After 2 or 3 minutes, raise the heat slightly and immediately pour the hot milk into the sauce, stirring very quickly and thoroughly. The sauce will begin to thicken when it reaches a boil. Add salt, the pepper, and nutmeg, if used; stir, lower the heat, and simmer 2 or 3 minutes, then remove from heat.

To keep warm, put the saucepan, covered, in a pan of hot water. If a film forms on top, add a few dots of butter, which you will stir into the sauce just before you use it.

For a thin sauce, either reduce the flour and butter to 1 tablespoon each or, if you need a larger quantity, increase the milk to 2 cups.

For a thick sauce, you can simply cook it longer. However, you can also thicken it by increasing the flour and butter to 3 tablespoons each or decreasing the milk to ⅔ cup.

Makes about 1 cup.

VARIATIONS. As is the case with mayonnaise, there are many variations on this main theme. In France these often take completely different names. You can add 2 or 3 tablespoons of thick Tomato Sauce and make a Sauce Aurore, or to make a Sauce Mornay, add about ⅔ cup grated semi-hard cheese, ½ teaspoon prepared mustard, and 1 teaspoon Worcestershire sauce. Or, by substituting hot vegetable broth for the milk in the original recipe, you'll have a Sauce Veloutée.

BURNED BUTTER SAUCE FOR PASTA OR RICE

There are a few dishes in both French and Italian cooking that break the usual rule to use low heat when cooking butter. Here is one of them. Of course, you will want to try this dish only if you have no qualms about using a lot of butter.

Cook the pasta or rice, and when it is almost ready, put about 2 sticks of butter in a small pan, cut the butter into cubes so it will cook more evenly, and put in a pan on fairly high heat, moving it often with a circular motion, until the butter is well browned. Drain the pasta or rice, and pour on the butter while very hot—it must sizzle. Mix quickly, and serve immediately with abundant grated Parmesan cheese.

Serves 4.

VARIATION. If you have fresh sage and/or rosemary, put a few young sprigs in the butter, and fry them to a crisp. No need to discard the herbs, as they taste very good.

TOMATO SAUCE

There are no definite rules for making a good tomato sauce. After you have made it a few times you will be able to tell what to do and when.

In case you wish to make a large batch of sauce to refrigerate, or to serve many guests, it will take longer to cook. In this case, a good shortcut is to use two middle-sized pots instead of a large one.

1 small onion, chopped
1 clove garlic, minced or pressed
3 tablespoons olive oil
1 tablespoon butter
1½ pounds fresh tomatoes, peeled, or canned
*   tomatoes, chopped*
1 small can tomato paste
salt and pepper
2 teaspoons fresh basil, chopped (or 1
*   teaspoon dried)*
½ teaspoon oregano
milk (optional)

Sauté the garlic and onion in the olive oil and butter until very light brown. Add the tomatoes, and simmer, uncovered, for a few minutes, then stir in the tomato paste, making sure it blends well. Continue to simmer, uncovered, stirring once in a while, until about half the liquid has evaporated. The time varies according to the original liquidity of the tomatoes, but this should take about 15 minutes. If the sauce tends to become too thick, you may have to add a little hot water a few minutes after you have added the tomato paste. Add salt, pepper, basil, and oregano, stir, and continue to simmer for about 10 minutes. Taste, and if the tomatoes have given an acid taste to the sauce, stir in a couple of tablespoons of milk.

Total cooking time is about 30 minutes, and generally a tomato sauce should not be cooked any longer, or it may become bitter. The density depends on individual taste—I prefer it rather thick, while others like it better if it is on the thin side.

Serves 4.

VARIATIONS. The old-fashioned tomato sauce calls for the addition of chopped celery and chopped carrots (for this amount of sauce about 2 tablespoons), to be sautéed with the onion and garlic. Adding a couple of tablespoons of red wine about 10 minutes before the sauce is ready is another interesting touch. The classic sauce was strained, but I prefer it unstrained—the choice is yours.

QUICK FRESH-TOMATO SAUCE

To be tried when fresh tomatoes are at their peak. It can be prepared in less than 30 minutes, including peeling and chopping the tomatoes.

> *4 tablespoons olive oil*
> *2 tablespoons butter*
> *medium-sized fresh tomatoes, peeled and chopped*
> *6 or 7 fresh basil leaves, chopped*
> *salt and pepper*

Heat the oil and butter in a skillet wide enough to accommodate the tomatoes in a fairly thin layer (this will help them cook faster), add the tomatoes, salt, pepper, and basil. Simmer, uncovered, no longer than 15 minutes.

Note: Some people prefer to strain this sauce, because there may be too many tomato seeds in it. If you opt for this method, you don't have to peel the tomatoes first, as the skin will also be strained out.

Serves 4.

EMERGENCY TOMATO SAUCE

A method I sometimes use when I find myself with unexpected guests and have to prepare a meal quickly. This sauce is still infinitely better than store-bought sauce.

> *4 tablespoons olive oil*
> *1 tablespoon butter*
> *1 teaspoon dried onion flakes or onion powder*
> *1 medium-sized can tomato paste (12 ounces)*
> *hot water or vegetable broth*
> *1 teaspoon garlic powder*
> *1 teaspoon dried basil*
> *½ teaspoon dried thyme or oregano*
> *1 bay leaf*
> *salt and pepper*
> *3 tablespoons milk (approximately)*

If you use onion flakes (which I find tastier than the powder) heat the oil and butter, add the flakes, and stir. Be careful, because they brown quickly. As they begin to change color, add some hot water or broth. Keeping the heat low, add the tomato paste, with more hot water or broth, and stir. (If you are using onion powder, heat the oil and butter, add hot water or broth, the tomato paste, and the onion powder, and stir.) Add a little more liquid, always stirring. The pot should be uncovered. When the sauce is of the desired consistency (like a thin white sauce), add all the seasoning. Simmer for a few minutes, then add the milk, stir, and taste. You may have to add a little more milk if the sauce seems a bit tart. About 10 minutes, or less, of simmering should be sufficient. Remove the bay leaf before serving.

Serves 4.

PINK SAUCE FOR GNOCCHI OR PASTA

1½ cups milk
1½ tablespoons flour
3 tablespoons butter
1 medium-sized onion, chopped fine
3 tablespoons dry white wine, or more
3 tablespoons tomato paste
1 tablespoon fresh sage (or 1½ teaspoons dried)
1 tablespoon grated Parmesan cheese
salt (optional)

Make a White Sauce (see index), using the milk, flour, and 2 tablespoons of the butter.

In a separate skillet, sauté the onion in the remaining butter, adding 1 tablespoon of the wine. Mix the tomato paste with the rest of the wine, then add to the onion when it becomes transparent. Add the sage, and simmer for 3 or 4 minutes. If the sauce gets too thick, add a little more wine or a little water. Now stir the White Sauce into the red sauce, add the grated cheese, stir again, taste, and add salt if necessary.

Note: If you use fresh sage, the sauce will be much tastier, but you will have to strain the red sauce in order to remove the pieces of sage before you add the White Sauce. Do not decrease the amount of sage, as this is what gives the sauce its special taste.

This sauce is really excellent. Served with tiny Green Gnocchi (see index), it becomes a Tuscan specialty.

Serves 4.

RED SAUCE

An unusual cold sauce from the Milanese region. It is good on poached or hard-cooked eggs, and makes a nice contrast served with green vegetables, such as steamed string beans. The heat of the food with which it is served brings out its pungent sweet-and-sour taste.

> *3 medium-sized ripe beets, baked and peeled*
> *2 tablespoons parsley, chopped very fine*
> *2 cloves garlic, pressed*
> *2 teaspoons finely chopped capers*
> *3 tablespoons wine vinegar*
> *½ teaspoon salt*
> *freshly ground pepper*
> *olive oil*

Slice the beets very thin. In a small bowl, beat all the other ingredients, except the oil, using a fork or whisk. Put the beets in a jar where they will fit snugly, alternating each layer of thin slices with some of the sauce. Pour olive oil up to the top of the jar, and seal well. Let stand at least overnight before using.

Serve at room temperature, and add more oil to the jar, if needed, after you have removed some of its contents.

This sauce can be preserved for many weeks, either in a cool place or in the refrigerator.

Makes about 2 cups.

GREEK EGG AND LEMON SAUCE
Avgolémono

This well-known Greek sauce is usually added to a rice soup at the last moment, but it can also be used to impart a very special taste to many cooked vegetables, especially those with a delicate flavor.

> *2 eggs, separated*
> *juice of 2 lemons, strained (can be reduced to 1 lemon,*
> *if this amount seems too lemony)*
> *2 cups hot vegetable broth*

Beat the egg whites until they are stiff. Beat the yolks lightly, and stir into the whites, using a wire whisk or egg beater. Continue to beat, adding the lemon juice a little at a time, and then the broth, a few drops at a time, especially at the beginning, then a little more.

If you are using this sauce in a soup, transfer the soup to a tureen, stir it to cool it, and after a few minutes stir in the sauce.

If you are making the sauce for hot vegetables, put it in a double boiler after stirring in about 1 cup of the broth. Make sure that the water in the bottom pot does not reach the boiling point. Stir for a couple of minutes, until the sauce becomes foamy and thickens a little.

Note: If a thicker sauce is desired, omit the broth, and make a roux with 1 tablespoon butter and 1 tablespoon flour in the top of the double boiler. Then lower the heat and slowly add the sauce. Serve immediately, either in a warm bowl or poured on the vegetables.

Makes 2 cups.

PORTUGUESE SAUCE

A good sauce for artichokes, peas, Jerusalem artichokes, carrots, beets, salsify, and Brussels sprouts.

> *1 large Spanish onion, sliced very thin*
> *4 tablespoons butter*
> *1 cup dry white wine*
> *6 tablespoons flour*
> *1 cup water*
> *bouquet garni (see index)*
> *1 teaspoon tomato paste*
> *1 cup Madeira wine (or port)*
> *salt and pepper*

Sauté the onion in the butter in a saucepan on very low heat.

Add ¼ cup of the white wine to the flour, mix with a fork, and stir the paste into the onions. Continue cooking until the sauce turns a light golden brown. Add the rest of the white wine and the water, stir, and bring to a boil. Now add the bouquet garni, and simmer for about 10 minutes. Pass the sauce through a sieve or food mill, add the tomato paste, mix, and return the sauce to the pan. Simmer awhile longer, stirring occasionally. A couple of minutes before serving, add the Madeira or port, salt, and pepper, and heat without allowing the sauce to boil.

Makes about 3½ cups.

VARIATION. Sauté in butter about 1 cup chopped mushrooms, and add after the sauce has been strained. If the sauce seems too thick, cover the pot after adding the mushrooms, and proceed as in main recipe.

UKRAINIAN SAUCE

This sauce is frequently used by peasants in southern Russia, especially on boiled grains.

> *2 tablespoons butter*
> *2 tablespoons flour*
> *1 cup milk (hot)*
> *½ cup vegetable broth (hot)*
> *1 tablespoon fresh dill (or 2*
> * teaspoons dried)*
> *1 teaspoon fresh mint, chopped (or 1 teaspoon*
> * dried, crushed)*
> *salt and pepper*
> *6 tablespoons sour cream*
> *6 tablespoons yogurt (at room temperature)*

In a heavy skillet, make a roux with the butter and flour as for White Sauce, and when butter and flour begin to foam, add the hot milk all at once, stir, and add the broth, also all at once. Raise the heat slightly, and keep stirring until sauce thickens. Add the dill, mint, salt, and pepper, lower the heat, and simmer 3 or 4 minutes. Stir in the sour cream, and when it is well blended and heated, remove from heat. After a few minutes stir in the yogurt, and serve.

Makes about 2½ cups.

WINE SAUCE

Excellent on any steamed or boiled vegetable, this sauce is particularly suitable for artichoke bottoms or cauliflower.

> *4 tablespoons butter*
> *1 tablespoon flour*
> *2 medium-sized carrots, thinly sliced or grated*
> *1 bay leaf*
> *1 teaspoon ground coriander*
> *2 cups dry white wine*
> *salt and pepper (preferably white pepper)*
> *2 tablespoons heavy cream*

In a saucepan, make a paste with the butter and flour. Add the carrots, bay leaf, and coriander, and sauté, adding about ½ of the wine. Stir in the rest of the wine after a couple of minutes, add salt and pepper, and simmer, uncovered, stirring often, for about 10 more minutes, or until the carrots are done. Remove from heat, and pass through a sieve or food mill. Put the sauce back on very low heat, and gradually stir in the cream. If the sauce seems too thick, add a little more wine. Heat without letting boil, stirring constantly until smooth.

Remove from heat, and serve immediately.

Makes about 2½ cups.

AROMATIC VEGETABLE SAUCE

This is a good sauce to use with pasta, leftovers, or any bland-tasting vegetables that need to be perked up. It can also be served cold, over cold cooked vegetables, and it makes a good sandwich spread.

> 2 pounds tomatoes, chopped
> 1 medium-sized head lettuce (open-head type), chopped
> 1 medium-sized carrot, chopped
> 1 small onion, chopped
> 2 stalks celery, chopped
> 1 clove garlic, minced or pressed
> 1 tablespoon chopped parsley
> 1 teaspoon mustard
> 1 teaspoon mayonnaise
> 4 tablespoons olive oil (approximately)
> 1 tablespoon wine vinegar
> salt and pepper

Place the first seven ingredients in a pot, and add a very little water—just enough to prevent the vegetables from sticking to the bottom. At the beginning the tomatoes may provide enough liquid so that you do not need to add any water. Cover and simmer, checking and stirring once in a while, and adding a little water if necessary. When the vegetables are cooked and have absorbed quite a bit of the liquid, pass them through a sieve or food mill. Mix in the mustard and mayonnaise. Add the oil a little at a time, stirring it vigorously into the sauce. When you have used all the oil, beat in the vinegar and salt and pepper to taste.

Makes about 3 cups.

ARTICHOKE-MUSHROOM SAUCE

Serve this sauce on a plain omelet, on boiled rice or Feathered Rice (see index), or on dumplings (especially German Dumplings).

½ cup imported dried mushrooms
3 medium-sized artichokes
½ medium-sized onion, chopped
3 tablespoons olive oil
1 tablespoon chopped parsley
1 clove garlic, minced
2 teaspoons flour
1 tablespoon tomato paste
salt and pepper
2 tablespoons dry white wine

Rehydrate the mushrooms (see page 18) and save the liquid. Cut off tips from artichokes and remove outer leaves, then quarter the artichokes, remove the chokes, and slice into thin strips. Sauté the onion in the oil, add the artichokes, parsley, and garlic, then add the mushrooms in the liquid in which they have been rehydrated. Simmer on very low heat, uncovered, stirring once in a while.

Make a paste with the flour and tomato paste, adding a little cold water and salt and pepper. Stir into the sauce, and continue simmering. When the sauce is almost done (which you can test by trying one piece of artichoke), raise the heat, add the wine, and stir well. Allow the sauce to thicken a little longer. Remove from heat and either serve immediately or keep very warm, as this sauce is particularly good hot.

Makes about 3 cups.

CREAMY MUSHROOM SAUCE

This delicious sauce comes from the Lake Garda section of Italy, where it is made with one of the local light-red wines. Because these wines may not be readily available here, we suggest using Lambrusco, even though it comes from another part of Italy; it is now widely imported in the United States. This sauce is equally good with pasta or vegetables.

> *2 cups chopped mushrooms*
> *5 tablespoons butter*
> *½ cup Lambrusco or other light-red wine*
> *3 tablespoons flour*
> *2½ cups milk*
> *½ cup grated Parmesan cheese*
> *¼ teaspoon saffron, crushed or powdered*
> *¼ teaspoon nutmeg*
> *¼ teaspoon savory*
> *salt and pepper*

Sauté the mushrooms in 2 tablespoons of the butter, adding a little of the wine if they seem to need some liquid. Simmer for about 6 minutes, stirring occasionally.

While the mushrooms are cooking, make a White Sauce in a fairly large saucepan, using the remaining 3 tablespoons butter, the flour, and the milk. When the sauce thickens, add the grated cheese, and continue stirring until the cheese has melted. Stir in the rest of the wine, a little at a time, then stir in the seasoning. When the sauce seems well blended, add the mushrooms. Simmer a few minutes longer, and serve immediately.

Note: To shorten cooking time and to make sure the sauce will not cool off suddenly when you add the wine, reheat the mushrooms briefly, add the wine to them, and then slowly add both to the sauce.

Makes 3 cups.

MILANESE CAPER SAUCE

This sauce is excellent on hard-cooked eggs or on steamed new potatoes (served hot, in their jackets), but it is also a versatile sauce that can be used on many other vegetables, such as green beans, cauliflower, and lima beans. For contrast, try serving this sauce hot on cold vegetables, or vice versa.

2 tablespoons butter
2 tablespoons olive oil
½ medium-sized onion, minced
4 tablespoons capers, chopped
1 cup vegetable broth or water (approximately)
2 teaspoons arrowroot or cornstarch
½ teaspoon fresh tarragon, chopped (or ¼ teaspoon dried)
1 teaspoon chopped parsley
½ teaspoon marjoram
⅛ teaspoon nutmeg
pinch of powdered cumin
pepper
salt (optional)

Leave the butter at room temperature while you prepare the other ingredients for the sauce.

Heat the oil, add the onion and capers, stir to blend, then add half the broth or water, and simmer for about 20 minutes. With a fork, make a paste of the arrowroot or cornstarch and the butter, then beat into it the rest of the broth or water (either cold or lukewarm) a little at a time. Add the paste to the sauce, together with the spices, and stir. Simmer for about 3 minutes, stirring often. Taste, and add salt only if needed (the capers are usually salty enough to season the sauce).

Makes about 1½ cups.

SPINACH SAUCE

This is particularly good with previously boiled or steamed cardoons, chard stems, or finocchio. Serve hot on hot vegetables.

> ½ pound spinach
> 3 tablespoons butter, melted
> ½ cup chopped parsley
> 1 tablespoon Anisette, Pernod, or Ouzo
> ½ teaspoon Worcestershire sauce or soy sauce
> salt and pepper
> ½ cup light cream

Cook spinach (see page 19), drain well, and allow to cool a little. While spinach is cooling, melt the butter and allow it to cool.

Put the spinach in a blender, together with parsley, liqueur, Worcestershire sauce or soy sauce, butter, salt, and pepper. Blend at high speed for about 1 minute, or until the mixture seems smooth.

Put the mixture in a saucepan, stir in the cream, and set pan on moderate heat until the contents barely simmer. Serve immediately.

Serves 4.

MALTESE SAUCE

This is an excellent sauce for cold boiled asparagus and many other cooked and cooled vegetables.

> ½ teaspoon dry mustard
> ¼ teaspoon salt
> 1 teaspoon lemon juice

1 cup mayonnaise
juice of ½ a juice orange
¼ teaspoon powdered or crushed saffron

Make a paste with the mustard, salt, and lemon juice, adding the juice a little at a time. Mix in the mayonnaise, orange juice, and saffron.

Makes about 1½ cups.

SWEDISH MUSTARD SAUCE

As with the preceding sauce, you can use this one for any cold vegetables, but it is particularly good with cold boiled artichokes. You may serve large artichokes, to be eaten individually, leaf by leaf, dipping the leaves in the sauce, or you may quarter small, tender artichokes, cook them, and mix them with the sauce. The choke can be removed after quartering, and the stems can be used also.

2 teaspoons mustard (preferably Dijon
    or Düsseldorf)
juice of ½ lemon
1 cup light cream
salt to taste

Mix the mustard and lemon juice, and gradually mix in the other ingredients, including the small artichokes, if used.

Makes about 1¼ cups.

OIL AND LEMON SAUCE

Call it a sauce or a dressing, this is the simplest combination you can find, either to dress salads or to pour on plain steamed vegetables. It is what I frequently use, served on the side, with whole artichokes eaten leaf by leaf. Oil and lemon juice, or oil and vinegar, when whipped with a fork or whisk, become emulsified, at least temporarily. For a thicker, more successful sauce, the ingredients should be cold, but not chilled. When oil is kept in the refrigerator, it forms lumps. For best results with this simple sauce, do not refrigerate the oil longer than ½ hour.

For most dishes, the following amounts will yield enough sauce for four people.

> *1 cup olive oil*
> *3 tablespoons lemon juice or vinegar (or to taste)*
> *1 teaspoon salt*
> *¼ teaspoon pepper, preferably white*

Put all ingredients in a bowl, and whip vigorously until they emulsify. Do this at the very last minute before serving the vegetables.

To prepare in advance, proceed as above, then pour into a jar and cover tightly. Refrigerate for no more than 30 minutes, then shake the jar vigorously before pouring out the sauce.

Makes about 1¼ cups.

VINAIGRETTE SAUCE

The French classic sauce, for salads or vegetables.

> *¾ cup olive oil*
> *¼ cup lemon juice or vinegar*
> *¼ teaspoon dry mustard*
> *1 tablespoon chopped capers*
> *1 tablespoon chopped cucumber pickles*
> *1 teaspoon chopped parsley*

½ teaspoon chopped chervil
½ teaspoon chopped chives
½ teaspoon chopped shallots
salt and pepper

If you wish to have a warm sauce, place all ingredients in the top of a double boiler and warm over hot but not boiling water.

For a cold sauce, whip together the first three ingredients, as for Oil and Lemon Sauce, then mix in the remaining ingredients. Chill only briefly, or serve at room temperature.

Makes approximately 1¼ cups.

COLD GREEN SAUCE
Salsa Verde

This sauce is particularly good with Raw Fresh Vegetables (*Crudités*), boiled cold vegetables, or boiled cold rice.

3 slices Italian or French bread, crust removed
wine vinegar
1 hard-cooked egg
4 tablespoons parsley
10 capers
olive oil
pepper

Soak the bread thoroughly in a little vinegar. Remove, and squeeze out most of the vinegar. Separately, finely chop the egg, parsley, and capers, adding oil and vinegar to taste. Mix thoroughly with the bread, and add pepper to taste.

Makes about 1 cup.

TARTAR SAUCE

3 yolks of hard-cooked eggs
1 tablespoon finely chopped parsley
½ medium-sized onion, chopped fine
1 small cucumber pickle, chopped
grated peel of ½ a small lemon
1 teaspoon mustard (preferably Dijon)
salt and pepper
4 tablespoons olive oil
2 tablespoons white wine vinegar or lemon juice

Press the egg yolks with a fork until completely crumbled. Add parsley, onion, pickle, lemon peel, mustard, salt, and pepper. Mix well, then add a little oil, whip with a wire whip, and keep whipping as you add more oil, a little at a time. After you have used about half the oil, start adding the vinegar, alternating with more oil, still proceeding a little at a time. The sauce should be smooth and have a whipped, fluffy appearance.

Makes about 1 cup.

MAYONNAISE

This is the recipe for authentic French mayonnaise. It is almost foolproof; if you follow these instructions carefully, it will be almost impossible for the mayonnaise to curdle. Success is practically guaranteed because the emulsifying process takes place at the beginning by the addition of hot vinegar, lemon juice, or water to the egg yolks.

2 egg yolks
½ teaspoon salt
1 teaspoon prepared mustard

1 teaspoon hot wine vinegar or hot water
1½ cups olive oil (approximately)
1 tablespoon wine vinegar or lemon juice
½ teaspoon white pepper (optional)

For mayonnaise not to separate, all the ingredients and utensils should be at room temperature. A rotary beater gives better results both in taste and consistency than a blender does. Put the egg yolks, salt, and mustard in the bowl, and start beating at low speed. When well blended, add the 1 teaspoon hot vinegar or hot water, beating constantly at low speed. Immediately start adding the oil, about a drop at a time at first, then by pouring it in a thin thread. When the sauce has thickened somewhat, you can add the oil a little more generously, but always make sure it is blended before you add more. When the sauce is still on the thin side, add the 1 tablespoon vinegar or lemon juice, a little at a time, and add the pepper, if you wish. If you allow the sauce to thicken too much before adding the vinegar or lemon juice, it may separate at this point. After you have added the vinegar or lemon juice, you can beat in a little more oil if the sauce seems to have lost consistency.

Makes about 2½ cups.

TO REINSTATE MAYONNAISE. If you are particularly unlucky and your mayonnaise has separated, you can still put it back together. Put another egg yolk (at room temperature) in a bowl, and add a little salt. Whip the curdled mayonnaise into it, one tablespoonful at a time. Or heat a couple of teaspoons of water or vinegar, whip them into the extra yolk, and immediately start whipping in the curdled mayonnaise, a little at a time.

STORAGE. It is better to make this amount of mayonnaise rather than a smaller amount, which may not turn out as well. Even without the preservatives of store-bought mayonnaise, homemade mayonnaise can be kept in the refrigerator for at least several days, but store it on the bottom shelf, where it is less cold. I keep mayonnaise in the vegetable drawer, in a hard plastic container put into another, larger plastic container, both tightly covered, and in this way it keeps well. However, after a certain amount of time the mayonnaise may curdle, as oil tends to separate at low temperatures; if it does, you can leave it at room temperature for about 30 minutes, then whip it with a whisk, and it often re-emulsifies. If it does not, try to reinstate it by one of the methods described.

VARIATIONS. The variations are almost infinite. You can fold in any one of the following: capers, finely chopped pickles, chopped raw spinach, finely chopped herbs (preferably fresh), or beat 1 egg white until stiff and fold into 1 cup of mayonnaise. The latter is especially good on asparagus. Many sauces based on mayonnaise have been invented in France and other European countries. A few follow.

SAUCE MOUSSELINE. Fold 1/2 cup whipped heavy cream into 1 cup mayonnaise. This is good as a salad dressing or on hard-cooked eggs. (It is a shortcut version of real Mousseline, but in my opinion just as good.)

SAUCE NIÇOISE. To 1 cup of mayonnaise add 1 medium-sized sweet red pepper, minced, and a couple of tablespoons of thick Tomato Sauce, plus 1 teaspoon of fresh tarragon and 1/2 teaspoon paprika. Also good on hard-cooked eggs or any cold vegetable. This sauce may very well be a French version of the Andalusian sauce of Spain, or vice-versa. In Spain, 1 hot red pepper, chopped, is often added, as well as chopped chives or onions.

FRENCH GARLIC SAUCE. See Garlic Sauces in this section.

ROQUEFORT MAYONNAISE. Crumble 2 tablespoons Roquefort, Gorgonzola, blue, or similar cheese into 1 tablespoon milk, mixing with a fork. When well blended, add 1/2 cup whipped cream and 1 cup mayonnaise, and mix gently until blended. (Sour cream may be used instead of whipped cream, for a more pungent taste.)

GREEN MAYONNAISE. Add 1 teaspoon dry mustard, 1/2 teaspoon freshly ground pepper, 1 chopped scallion, and 2 tablespoons chopped parsley to each cup of mayonnaise.

Garlic Sauces

It is said that the Roman legions brought garlic-and-oil sauce to France and Spain. The Greeks insist that they taught it to the ancient Romans, and archaeologists discovered its presence in ancient Egypt. By now there are dozens of recipes; in fact, every southern European, Middle Eastern, and North African country seems to have one or more versions of garlic sauce.

Sometimes lemon juice or wine vinegar is added; other recipes call for egg yolks, mashed potatoes, nuts, breadcrumbs, mashed cooked chick-peas, or tomatoes, individually, or in combinations. The quantity of garlic varies from 2 to 12 or more cloves per ½ cup olive oil. Garlic sauces are used for salads or on cold boiled vegetables.

The system of preparation varies little from country to country. Usually a garlic paste is made in a mortar with a pestle, and the other ingredients added. The oil is dribbled very slowly, mashing always in the same direction, either clockwise or counterclockwise, and the salt is added near the end, according to taste. Today, garlic sauces can be made quickly in a blender.

GREEK GARLIC SAUCE
Skordaliá

1 large head garlic
½ teaspoon lemon juice or wine vinegar
1 cup olive oil
salt

Separate the garlic into individual cloves, and peel. In a blender, combine the garlic and lemon juice or vinegar. Add about ¼ of the oil, and blend. Add about half the remaining oil, blend; add the rest of the oil and salt to taste, and blend.

GREEK GARLIC SAUCE WITH POTATOES. Same ingredients as for the basic recipe for Skordaliá, plus 1 cup mashed potatoes, added with the final amount of oil.

GREEK GARLIC SAUCE WITH BREADCRUMBS. Add 1½ cups moist breadcrumbs instead of the mashed potatoes.

MIDDLE-EASTERN GARLIC SAUCE. Follow the basic recipe, but add ½ cup blanched almonds, walnuts, or pine nuts. Since the blender may not grind the larger nuts evenly if put in whole, chop them coarsely before adding.

ITALIAN GARLIC SAUCE (AGL-I-OLI) AND FRENCH GARLIC SAUCE (AÏOLI)

The Italian name is a dialect contraction of *aglio e olio*, which simply means garlic and oil. There are various types of garlic-and-oil sauces, and they vary from very simple to fairly elaborate. A common agl-i-oli sauce is made by pounding garlic with olive oil (plus a pinch of salt) in a mortar, or mixing these ingredients in a blender, the proportions being left to individual taste.

In Italy garlic-and-oil sauces are popular in Sicily and some southern regions, then they seem to skip, and reappear along the Ligurian coast, where the famous Genoese Pesto Sauce, which follows, is, in fact, based on the ubiquitous garlic-and-oil sauce. In parts of Spain (where it is called *ajo y aceite*), as well as in Italy and southern France, peasants rub this sauce on freshly baked bread for a delicious snack.

In southern France, agl-i-oli has acquired the French spelling of aïoli. Basically, this sauce is very similar to the Italian one just described, but it acquires a definite French taste by the addition of an egg yolk and lemon juice, so that it becomes essentially a garlic mayonnaise.

Purists insist that the taste and consistency of the real aïoli sauce can only be achieved by using mortar and pestle, so we give this method. All ingredients must be at room temperature, or the sauce may separate.

FRENCH GARLIC SAUCE (AÏOLI)
2 cloves garlic per person
pinch of salt
1 egg yolk
1 cup (or more) olive oil
juice of 1 lemon
1 teaspoon lukewarm water, plus a few drops

Peel the garlic cloves and pound them in the mortar. Add salt and egg yolk, and start pouring in the oil, a few drops at a time at first, then in a thin thread, as you keep turning with the pestle. When mixture is fairly thick, add the lemon juice and the luke-warm water, and continue to stir and to add the oil little by little. When the sauce has thickened again, add a few more drops of lukewarm water.

Note: If the sauce separates, it can be put together again by adding another egg yolk (also at room temperature) and a few drops of lemon juice, stirring constantly, the same method used to rescue a mayonnaise that has separated.

Serves 3 or 4.

VARIATIONS. Add a couple of tablespoons of crumbled French or Italian bread without crust (previously moistened with a bit of water, then squeezed) to the garlic and egg yolk before adding the oil. Or, add a medium-sized boiled potato, cooled to room temperature, instead of the egg yolk.

QUICK AÏOLI. Use a rotary beater rather than a blender. Put crushed garlic and egg yolk into the bowl, add other ingredients as in main recipe, and proceed as in Mayonnaise (see index).

PESTO

This well-known Genoese basil and garlic sauce is used with thin long pasta (spaghetti, linguine, noodles, and so on), potato gnocchi, or occasionally boiled rice. It is also added to Genoese-style minestrone. As already mentioned, *pesto* literally means pounded, and that's exactly how this sauce has been made for centuries—with mortar and pestle. Recently, however, the blender has supplanted the mortar, and if good ingredients are used, there is little difference between the two methods, except that the blender is much quicker.

The following recipe is sufficient for pasta for 8 persons, as only a small amount should be used. However, this sauce keeps very well in the refrigerator for several months, so you may wish to take advantage of the fresh basil season and make a large batch to be used later. After a time the surface of the stored Pesto will darken, but this in no way affects the taste.

> *1 cup fresh basil leaves (young and tender)*
> *6 cloves garlic*
> *4 tablespoons grated Romano or Sardo cheese*
> *4 tablespoons grated Parmesan cheese*
> *2 tablespoons chopped walnuts*
> *1 tablespoon chopped pine nuts*
> *8 tablespoons olive oil (approximately)*
> *¼ teaspoon salt*

Put the first six ingredients in a blender, add a little of the oil, cover, and blend at low speed for about 15 seconds. Add the rest of the oil, and blend at low or medium speed only until small pieces of basil are still visible. Make sure not to heat or homogenize the sauce. Better to underblend than to overblend.

When pasta or gnocchi are cooked but before you drain them, take a couple of tablespoons of the hot water in which they were cooked and mix into the sauce. Some people like to mix in some butter at this point. Always serve the sauce at room temperature.

If you plan to store the Pesto in the refrigerator, stuff it into a jar, pushing it down as you fill it to remove air pockets, add a little more olive oil on top, and seal well. It can keep up to several months this way, but it does not freeze well. Freezing makes it lose its flavor and become bitter, so I don't recommend it. If you prefer, you can simply store the fresh basil or make Winter "Pesto" using dried herbs (see the following recipe).

Note: There are several variations for Pesto. Some recipes omit the nuts or use only pine nuts or only walnuts; others call for much less garlic. Originally, Pesto was made only with Sardo cheese (a Sardinian sheep's milk cheese); now the mixture of Romano or Sardo with Parmesan is more common.

Makes 8 servings.

WINTER "PESTO" SAUCE

Fresh basil can be preserved easily for about 1 year, so if you like the real Pesto sauce, you may pick fresh, tender basil leaves still green and young and stuff them in a jar, covering each layer with some salt and olive oil, pressing down the leaves, and covering the top layer with oil nearly to the top of the jar. Another system is to prepare "half" a pesto by chopping finely fresh basil leaves, sprinkling them with salt, then mixing them with the same amount of grated cheese, and putting the mixture, covered with olive oil, into a jar kept in the refrigerator. In this case, the sauce can be finished when needed, using fresh garlic, more oil, and other ingredients. Whichever method you opt for, the basil should be held down by a light weight (a flat stone just a little smaller than the jar neck works fine) so that it won't float above the oil. (See also preceding recipe.)

The first method is preferable if you wish to use fresh basil throughout the year, as basil preserved this way can be used in any recipe, as well as for Pesto. However, some people may not have fresh basil leaves handy in the winter, and the following is a fairly good substitute for real Pesto.

> *3 cups fresh spinach leaves, stems removed*
> *4 cloves garlic*
> *1½ cups fresh parsley*
> *4 tablespoons grated Romano cheese*
> *4 tablespoons grated Parmesan cheese*
> *2 tablespoons chopped walnuts*
> *2 tablespoons chopped pine nuts*
> *1½ teaspoons dried basil*
> *2 tablespoons butter*
> *8 tablespoons olive oil*

Chop the spinach coarsely; peel the garlic, and chop or press, then put all ingredients in the blender and blend until smooth.

Desserts

This section contains a modest sampling of European desserts, many of which are based on fresh fruit. As mentioned in the introduction, cheese and fresh fruit in season commonly end a meal in Europe, especially in the central and southern countries, and since this book aims to give a glimpse of daily European culinary habits, it would be out of place to include many of the desserts reserved for special occasions.

Those among you who have been vegetarians for some time must have noticed a marked lessening of the craving for sugar and sweet substances that meat eating seems to stimulate. A piece of fruit in its natural state is the best way to close a meal. A more elaborate prepared dessert can be enjoyed once in a while, for a change, rather than out of a habit which is in some ways a form of addiction.

The American habit of eating pies, cakes, and other desserts as a steady fare was inherited from the English, and goes back to pre-Revolutionary times. In England, the climate precluded the growth of most fresh fruits for many months of the year; therefore fruits were preserved and used in pies and other baked dishes. Also, to import fresh fruit from the continent was difficult and expensive. But in this century, in the United States, to hold stubbornly to that habit is an anomaly. Fruits of all kinds grow in one part of the country or another throughout the year, and modern methods of transportation have made them more accessible. To relegate fruit eating to an occasional snack is really nonsensical.

While I don't suggest that you abstain completely from eating prepared desserts, I do strongly recommend that you curb this habit considering the large amounts of sugar, depleted flour, and other non-nutritious substances which are the basic ingredients of most desserts. Instead, try some of the simpler desserts in this section.

APRICOT SANDWICHES

In the spring, when apricots are in season, this makes a very good and simple dessert.

> *2 pounds very ripe apricots*
> *1 pound (approximate total) assorted semi-soft*
> * cheeses such as Bel Paese, Fontina, Bonbel,*
> * Monterey Jack*

Wash the apricots and pat them dry. Open them lengthwise, but not completely, with your thumbs or a knife, and remove the pits. Insert in each apricot a piece of cheese about the same size and shape as the pit. Close the apricots again, gently squeezing the edges so that the fruits will seem untouched.

If you wish, bring unopened apricots to the table with three or four varieties of cheese, so that your guests can experiment on their own.

Serves 4.

FIGS IN WINE

A simple but delicious French dessert. In spite of its simplicity —or maybe because of it—do not change the ingredients. Thyme and figs go very well together; in fact, in Mediterranean countries, figs are often strung together with a straw or string and packed to dry with thyme sandwiched between them.

1 pound dried figs
2 cups sweet red wine
2 small branches thyme (or ½ teaspoon crumbled dried),
*   wrapped in cheesecloth and tied*
2 tablespoons honey

Cut off the tips of dry stems from the figs, then simmer with the wine, thyme, and honey, in a covered pot, for about 30 minutes. Now and then, stir and turn over the figs, especially if the wine does not cover them completely.

With a slotted spoon, remove the figs, and remove and discard the thyme. Turn up the heat and continue to cook the syrup, uncovered, for a few minutes, stirring until it thickens a bit.

Pour the syrup on the figs, and serve.

Serves 4.

VARIATION. Add coarsely chopped almonds or other nuts to the syrup at the last moment.

STUFFED MELONS

Originally from Iran (then known as Persia), melons were exported to southern European countries many centuries ago. In Europe, the most famous center for the cultivation of at least one variety was Cantalupo in central Italy. It is from this town that the cantaloupe has taken its name.

For this dish, any berries can be used as a filling, but they should be small. Tiny wild strawberries, if you can find them, make an excellent filling, as do blueberries, raspberries, currants, and so on, but all of them must be fresh.

> 2 *cups berries (approximately)*
> 2 *tablespoons lemon juice*
> 1 *tablespoon honey*
> 2 *tablespoons Cointreau or any sweet liqueur*
>   *of your choice*
> 2 *medium-small cantaloupes, very ripe*

Wash, hull, and drain the berries. In a bowl, mix the lemon juice, honey, and liqueur, and pour it on the berries. Mix very gently, so as not to damage them. Cut the melons exactly in half, across, scoop them out and discard the seeds. With a blunt-tipped knife, score the flesh in several places, crisscross, without piercing the skin. Fill the halves equally with berries and juice. Carefully but quickly, join the halves of each melon together, fastening them shut with bits of tape. Refrigerate for at least 2 hours before serving, turning the melons over once.

When ready to serve, separate melon halves, and set them in bowls, surrounded with shaved ice. If ice is not available or not desired, and the melon halves don't stand up by themselves, stick three or four pieces of toothpick at a slant around the bottom of each melon half, giving it legs to stand on.

Serves 4.

VARIATIONS. Using smaller melons (1 per person), slice off a cap, scoop out and discard the seeds, and proceed as described in recipe, recapping the filled melons. Serve with caps on. This is often called Melon Surprise.

Another suggestion is to use the melons as bowls to contain a fruit salad. In this case, especially if you plan to include fruits that oxidate easily, such as apples, pears, or bananas, increase the amount of lemon juice.

ORANGES SUN STYLE

This method of preparing oranges, although the slicing requires some skill, is so striking visually and so elegant that it can be offered at an important lunch or dinner, perhaps accompanied with assorted small pastries or cookies.

4 large juicy oranges
3 tablespoons honey
1 tablespoon liqueur—Cointreau, Grand Marnier, or
whatever you prefer (optional)

You will need a very sharp paring knife or a small knife with a serrated blade—whichever works best for you.

Scrub the tops of the oranges, on the side opposite the stem. Slice off a small circle and reserve it. Peel the rest of the orange, and then stick a fork into either the top or the bottom to act as a handle. Working away from you, and following the contours of the orange from top to bottom, peel off the thinner skin over a deep dish, so that you will collect all the juice. You may rest the orange on the dish if you find it easier. Then, always holding the orange with the fork, make two cuts very close to the membrane separating each section, as if you were cutting a wedge. Gently remove the wedge with the knife and place it on a dessert plate. Remove all the wedges in this way, and when you have finished, keep the fork in place and squeeze out whatever juice is left by pressing the knife all around the membranes. Use a new plate for each orange, and when all the oranges have been separated into wedges, arrange the wedges of each one on its plate in a circle, each wedge following the next in the same direction. Leave enough room in the center for the reserved round of orange peel.

Mix the honey and the liqueur (if you use it) with the juice you collected in the bowl, and pour on the oranges. Refrigerate. Place the circle of peel (the "sun disk") in the middle of each plate just before serving.

Serves 4.

VARIATION. If you think that too much orange juice is splashing about on the plates, place a cookie the approximate size of the orange peel under it. The cookies should be of a type that absorbs liquid easily. A round piece of cake, such as pound cake, can be used instead of a cookie; by cutting it slightly larger than the peel you can make a two-toned sun disk.

PEACHES IN LEMON JUICE

One of the simplest desserts—if you can call it that—is a specialty from Rome, now popular throughout Italy. It is a summer favorite, when peaches are abundant and at their peak.

> *3 tablespoons honey*
> *2 or 3 lemons, depending on juice yield and personal taste*
> *2½ pounds very ripe peaches*
> *1 cup slivered almonds (optional)*

At least 1 hour before mealtime, dilute the honey with the juice of 2 lemons. This can be done in the bowl in which you plan to serve the peaches. Peel the peaches; if they are ripe enough the peel should slide off easily without any of the pulp, leaving a smooth surface. Cut them into large bite-sized pieces, and discard the pits. Mix them immediately with the lemon juice and honey. Taste the juice, and add a little more honey, if needed, but don't overdo it, because the peaches will add their own sweetness as they marinate. At this point, depending on the quality of the peaches, the juice of the third lemon may be added, to make sure the peaches don't darken.

Mix well but gently, cover, and refrigerate. Take the bowl out of the refrigerator at the beginning of the meal, mixing once more. By now, there should be quite a bit of juice, drawn out by the lemon. Add the almonds, if you wish.

Serves 4.

VARIATIONS. Cut the amount of lemon juice in half, and add an equal portion of Marsala wine or a liqueur such as Cointreau. Or add a few drops of bitter almond essence, which would give this dessert an interesting touch; the taste of almonds goes very well with that of peaches.

PEARS IN WINE ON PARADISE RICE

RICE
2½ cups milk (or same amount of liquid
  recommended on the rice package)
2 tablespoons honey
¼ teaspoon powdered cinnamon
few drops vanilla extract
1½ cups rice
pinch of salt
2 tablespoons butter
1 egg yolk

PEARS
8 small pears
about 1 cup red wine
3 tablespoons honey
1-inch stick of cinnamon
2 cloves
2 pieces lemon peel
2 pieces orange peel

To cook the rice, pour the milk into a pot, adding honey, cinnamon, and vanilla. Bring to a boil, add the rice, salt, and butter, and simmer for about 20 minutes, or until cooked but still firm. Turn it into a serving bowl, allow to cool a bit, and mix in the egg yolk.

Wash the pears (peel only if the skins are very tough) and stand them up in a pot in which they fit snugly. In a smaller pot gently heat ½ cup red wine with the honey, and mix until the honey dissolves. Pour the wine and honey on the pears, add the other ingredients and enough additional wine barely to cover the pears. Simmer, uncovered, until most of the wine has evaporated, or until the pears seem cooked when you pierce them with a toothpick. Make sure the pears don't stick to the pan. You may need to add a little more wine during the cooking process, if it seems to evaporate quickly. Let the pears cool, and remove cinnamon, cloves, and lemon and orange peel.

Arrange the pears on top of the rice, pour whatever wine sauce remains in the pot on top, and serve, either lukewarm or at room temperature.

Serves 4.

FRUIT FRITTERS

Many fruits make excellent fritters, especially when dipped in the batter described here, and then deep-fried in very hot oil (preferably olive oil) until the batter turns light golden in color. Vegetable shortening can also be used for frying, if a lighter taste is preferred.

BATTER
1 cup flour
2 tablespoons melted butter
2 eggs, separated
2 teaspoons honey
½ teaspoon grated lemon peel or orange peel
2 tablespoons brandy, rum, or liqueur
½ cup water
pinch salt

Mix flour, butter, egg yolks, honey, lemon or orange peel, brandy, rum, or liqueur (if desired), and water, and beat until smooth. (If liquor is not desired, mix a few drops of vanilla extract or almond extract in 2 tablespoons water and add to batter.) Let stand for 1 hour or more. Beat the egg whites until stiff, adding the salt, then fold delicately into the egg yolk paste.

FRUIT
apples, pears, slightly unripe peaches, apricots, bananas,
* or other fruit*

oil for deep-frying (preferably olive oil) ,
  or vegetable shortening
confectioners' sugar or honey

While batter is standing, prepare the fruit. For apples and pears, peel, core, and slice about ¼-inch thick, horizontally— leaving a hole in the middle where the core was. Other fruits can be sliced or cut into bite-sized pieces. Dip each piece of fruit into the batter. Heat the oil or shortening and fry the fruits until batter turns a light golden color.

Serve hot, sprinkled with confectioners' sugar or honey. Honey may be diluted with a little water or liqueur if it seems too thick.

Serves 4–6.

PEACH BLOSSOM OMELETS

This dessert, as some of the ingredients will indicate, comes from the eastern Mediterranean countries, between Bulgaria and Sicily. Of course, it is not absolutely essential to have branches of a myrtle tree or a lemon tree in order to whip the eggs, though this little touch adds a distinct aroma to the omelet. But you might wish to add a pinch of grated lemon peel when you add the honey to the eggs, to approximate the flavor of lemon leaves.

10 eggs, separated
1 bunch of small branches of lemon or myrtle (optional)
¾ cup peach blossoms (approximately)
5 or 6 tablespoons champagne or any sparkling
  white wine
2 tablespoons honey
2 tablespoons fresh pistachio nuts (undyed) ,
  finely chopped
butter

Beat the yolks and whites separately with a wire whisk or with the bunch of lemon or myrtle branches (if available) . Wash the blossoms very gently, and only if insecticide was used on the tree. Remove the pollen, and put the blossoms carefully into a glass with the champagne or sparkling wine. Let soak at room temperature for at least 1 hour.

Preheat the oven to 450°. Mix the egg yolks and whites, adding two teaspoons of the honey. Make four omelets, rather large and thin. As soon as the eggs have coagulated at the bottom, remove the blossoms from the champagne and place in the middle an equal amount for each omelet, and fold the two sides over each other. Remove the omelets to an oven-proof dish in which they can be served, pour in the rest of the honey, and sprinkle the nuts on top. Put in the oven for about 5 minutes, and serve hot.

Serves 4.

FRIED MAGNOLIA BLOSSOMS

While magnolia trees originated in America, they were imported to southern Europe by the Spaniards centuries ago and are now quite common in Mediterranean countries. It is not certain when or where the idea of frying magnolia flowers originated, but the following recipe comes from Yugoslavia.

There are several species of magnolia, but the blossoms which are used in this recipe must come from the *Magnolia Grandiflora* or Southern Magnolia, which grows throughout the South, and as far north as the Washington, D.C., area.

> *3 egg whites*
> *½ cup honey, preferably of a rather thin type*
> *1 cup flour*
> *¾ pound very fresh magnolia flowers (approximately)*
> *3 tablespoons hazelnuts*
> *oil*

Prepare a batter by beating the egg whites lightly, mixing in the honey, and finally adding the flour, a little at a time. The batter should be fairly thick, but if it seems too thick, add a little water.

Gently submerge the magnolia blossoms in cold water, pull them out, and allow them to dry, upside down, in a towel-lined strainer.

Chop the hazelnuts very fine—they should be almost pulverized. Heat the oil in a small heavy skillet, dip the blossoms in the batter, and fry them quickly, turning them as one side becomes golden. It is easier to fry them one or two at a time in a small skillet, and to keep them warm as you go. Put them on absorbent paper as you remove them from the skillet. Sprinkle them all over with the nuts, and serve.

Serves 4.

RICOTTA DESSERTS

There are two basic types of ricotta in Italy. The more widespread of the two (used from north of Rome and even Tuscany through the south of Italy, including Sicily and Sardinia) has probably never reached your table. It is usually called Roman ricotta. The other type is found in some parts of northern Italy and is called *ricotta piemontese* because it originated in Piedmont, the region in which Turin is located. This type, which is made with cow's milk, is the ricotta commonly used in the United States.

Roman ricotta is made from goat's milk, sheep's milk, and sometimes even buffalo milk, although this milk is more often used to make the old-fashioned—and more authentic—mozzarella. Goat's or sheep's milk ricotta has a completely different taste from that of the cow's milk ricotta, and is firmer. Many of the Italian dishes that have become popular in this country—lasagne, for example—are made with Roman ricotta in Italy, which gives them a more robust taste and a more compact consistency.

Roman ricotta is similar to the Greek *mizíthra* (but is more creamy) and is even closer to the more delicate Greek *anthótyro*. Both of these can occasionally be found in Greek-American markets. Unfortunately, very often what is sold as Roman ricotta even in the best Italian food stores in the United States has very little resemblance to the real thing, either in taste or consistency. Instead of being absolutely fresh and pasty, it looks, tastes, and smells like a semi-aged cheese, so I don't recommend it. You would be better off using cow's milk ricotta.

The variations for desserts with a ricotta base are infinite. Ricotta is usually sold in 15-ounce containers, and on the basis of about 1½ containers you can make a sufficient amount for 4 to 6 people. Because of the difficulty in finding true Roman ricotta, I suggest that you stick to the ricotta found in most markets. Make sure it is fresh, keeping well within the expiration date allowed by the manufacturer. Use a fairly large bowl, working with a fork, and mix or combine any of the following, or invent your own dessert.

Start by adding about 3 tablespoons of honey, more or less, to taste, to about 22 ounces ricotta. To this base, add any or a few of the following: 6 or 7 tablespoons carob powder, adding it a little at a time, and mixing in between, until it tastes like a chocolate mousse, or even better in the opinion of many gourmets. Raisins, coarsely chopped nuts, bits of dried fruits, such as dates, apricots, pears, apples (if you are adding dried fruits, omit the carob). It is a good idea to rehydrate the bits of dried fruits. In a small pot, soak them in sherry, Marsala, port, a liqueur, or water mixed with almond extract or vanilla extract, then warm them up, turn the heat off, and cover the pot for about 30 minutes before draining and mixing the fruit into the ricotta. Save the liquid in a well-sealed jar, to be reused, or add some to the ricotta, tasting as you mix, but do not add so much liquid that it would make the mixture too thin.

For thicker desserts, omit any liquid, and stir in some wheat germ, crushed Graham crackers, or crushed cookies. Recently, a new method of preparing commercial ricotta (as well as cream and other products) seems to have changed the consistency slightly, although the taste has remained fairly close to that of genuine fresh ricotta. This new ricotta is thicker, and you may like its consistency even after adding some liquid.

Let your imagination go, but always test a small quantity if you are trying something new, and don't forget that it is easier to add than to subtract. A final touch can always be given after you have finished mixing. In Italy a few tablespoons of very strong Italian coffee, or even finely ground, dark, toasted coffee, dry, is sometimes mixed into ricotta. A pinch of cinnamon, nutmeg, powdered coriander, ginger, or other spice may be added or substituted for the coffee.

Whatever you do, mix the ricotta at least 1 hour before serving to allow all elements to blend. This can be done in the bowl in which you are planning to serve it, but cover it, especially if you added wine or liqueur, so that the surface won't become crusty or the aroma evaporate.

Of course, you can use any of these suggestions as fillings for a pie, if you wish, but first try them as simple spoon desserts.

Serves 4 to 6.

YOGURT DESSERTS

In the Middle East, Greece, and the Balkan countries, yogurt is a very common food. Plain yogurt is usually eaten as a side dish or, less often, as a dessert with the addition of a little honey. In that part of the world it is more frequently made from goat's or sheep's milk, which gives it a different taste and consistency from the cow's milk yogurt to which we are accustomed.

Yogurt has become such a popular food here in recent years that many people make their own. If you use commercial brands, I suggest that you stay away from the premixed varieties and instead start with plain yogurt. It is healthier and more fun to mix plain yogurt with your own combination of small bite-sized pieces of fresh fruit or any of the ingredients which I suggested for ricotta desserts. If the taste of yogurt is too sour for you, add some honey.

The consistency of yogurt is thinner than that of ricotta. For a thicker dessert, strain the yogurt by wrapping and tying it in muslin or several layers of cheesecloth, and suspending it over a bowl for a few hours. Do not discard the whey which drips out, as it is very healthful and can be used in other dishes, such as cold soups or salad dressings.

Yogurt should never be added to hot foods, since heat destroys the healthiest bacilli it contains. However, yogurt can be added after the cooked food is removed from the heat and has cooled somewhat.

CHESTNUT FLOUR

Chestnut flour is a rarity in most of Europe but is a favorite ingredient in isolated areas. For example, it is very popular in Tuscan home cooking, yet almost completely unknown in northern Italy; it is used in certain parts of Greece, the Balkan countries, and here and there in the Middle East, but unknown in the Mediterranean islands, even where chestnut trees flourish in abundance, as in Crete. And I have never heard of it being used in France.

To make desserts with chestnut flour is easy, and the results are usually delicious. Frequently, nuts or grains have different flavors in their various states. For example, think of how different in taste are fresh corn, polenta, and cornflakes. Chestnut flour is no exception. It has a very distinct flavor only vaguely reminiscent of fresh chestnuts. If you have never tried it, you're in for a treat.

While it is not always easy to find chestnut flour in the United States, it is available in specialized stores. Buy only relatively fresh flour, as it tends to become bitter when it has been ground for some time.

If chestnut flour is not available where you live, and you have a grain grinder, you can make your own. Use dried chestnuts and grind them to as fine a powder as your machine will allow.

Fresh chestnuts can easily be dried: put them in a 150° oven for an hour, then peel them, and leave them spread out in a warm dry place, away from rodents, for a few weeks. They can also be dried unpeeled, but this is not advisable, and it takes longer.

CHESTNUT FRITTERS

¾ pound chestnut flour
2 or 3 tablespoons Anisette, Ouzo, or any strong
  anise-flavored liqueur (see note)
1 tablespoon raisins
1 tablespoon pine nuts
1 egg white, beaten stiff
oil for frying

Put the flour in a bowl, add the liqueur, raisins, and pine nuts, and then start adding lukewarm water, a little at a time, mixing until you have a soft but sticky paste. Fold in the beaten egg white.

Heat about 1 inch of oil in a heavy skillet, and when it is very hot, pour in blobs of the chestnut mixture (about 2 tablespoons at a time), making a few fritters at a time. Remove them to absorbent paper, and keep them warm. Continue until you have used all the batter.

Serve hot. For sweeter fritters, sprinkle with confectioners' sugar or honey.

Note: If you don't wish to use liqueur, substitute about ¼ teaspoon of crushed fennel seeds, or even dill powder.

Serves 4.

CHESTNUT PIE
Castagnaccio

1½ cups chestnut flour
1 cup ice water (approximately)
4 tablespoons raisins
3 tablespoons pine nuts and/or chopped walnuts
5 tablespoons olive oil
½ teaspoon fresh rosemary leaves
pinch of salt
ricotta

Preheat oven to 375°. Add the water to the chestnut flour a little at a time, along with the raisins and nuts, making a paste a little thicker than that for Chestnut Fritters. Grease a shallow baking dish with half the oil, pour the chestnut mixture in it, dribble the rest of the oil on top, and sprinkle with the rosemary. Bake for 45 minutes to 1 hour. The top crust should be dark and crisp. Serve hot with fresh ricotta on the side to be spread on individual slices.

Serves 4.

VARIATION. Instead of the ricotta, use any fresh creamy cheese, even one that is a little salty or sour. Or try plain cream cheese, softened with a little milk, and worked into a soft paste with a fork. The sour taste of yogurt also goes very well with this pie (see Yogurt in index).

CHESTNUT SOUFFLÉ

Chestnuts can be served either in the middle or at the end of a meal. Because of their natural sweetness, they make a very nice dessert. This soufflé can be used either way. For a middle course, add vegetable broth to the purée; if you plan it as a dessert, substitute milk for the broth and add 1 tablespoon of honey.

> *1 pound chestnuts*
> *pinch of salt*
> *1 tablespoon butter*
> *1½ cups vegetable broth (a clear, light type) or milk*
> *1 tablespoon honey (for dessert version)*
> *2 egg whites*

Boil the chestnuts (see page 15), add salt, and mash when still hot. Melt the butter in a saucepan, add the chestnut purée, then the broth or milk (depending on the occasion) a little at a time, stirring, until the consistency is that of a potato purée. Stir in the honey if for dessert. Cool to lukewarm. Preheat the oven to 375°. Beat the egg whites almost stiff, then gently fold into the purée. Pour into a greased soufflé dish which will hold about 1½ quarts. Fill the mold only two-thirds full. Bake for 20 minutes, and serve immediately.

Serves 4.

CREAMY EGG CUSTARD
Crema Pasticcera

This soft custard can be served by itself in individual glasses or cups, with or without the addition of finely chopped nuts, crumbled *amaretti,* whipped cream, or other decoration. It can also be used as a filling for cakes or pastries.

> *4 egg yolks*
> *2 teaspoons potato flour or cornstarch (approximately)*
> *½ teaspoon grated lemon peel*
> *¼ teaspoon powdered vanilla bean, or ½ teaspoon*
> *   vanilla extract*
> *1 tablespoon honey*
> *2 cups milk*
> *1 tablespoon butter (optional)*

Put the egg yolks, potato flour or cornstarch, lemon peel, vanilla, and honey in a saucepan, and mix before you turn on the heat. You can adjust thickness by using more or less potato flour or cornstarch. A thinner custard may be preferable if it is to be used as pastry filling. In this case, reduce the amount of thickener to 1½ teaspoons.

In a separate pot, heat the milk to scalding point, then add it to the egg mixture, beating constantly with a rotary beater or stirring vigorously with a wooden spoon. Cook on very low heat, stirring constantly, and remove from heat 3 or 4 minutes after it has reached the boiling point.

Add butter, if you wish, and allow the custard to cool somewhat before pouring into individual bowls. Level the tops with a wetted spoon. If you are using nuts or a similar topping, let the custard cool a little longer; if it is too hot, the topping will sink. Refrigerate the custard at least 1 hour. If you use whipped cream as a topping, add it just before serving.

Serves 4.

FRIED CUSTARD

Crema Fritta

This dessert is very popular in northern Italy, especially with children. It is almost unknown in restaurants except around Venice, where the dish originated.

> *¾ cup plus 1 tablespoon flour*
> *2 eggs*
> *1 cup milk*
> *2 teaspoons honey*
> *1 egg yolk*
> *½ teaspoon grated lemon peel*
> *additional flour*
> *breadcrumbs*
> *oil for frying*

Select a large serving platter, and chill it by putting a couple of ice cubes on it.

In a small pot, combine the flour and one of the eggs and mix well with a wooden spoon. Add the milk, a little at a time, stirring until all lumps are dissolved. Put the pot on the heat, raising the heat slowly and stirring constantly. When the sauce has thickened and the flour has lost its raw taste, remove from heat, add the honey, allow to cool a little, then add the egg yolk and lemon peel, and stir well.

Remove the ice from the platter, leaving it moist. Immediately pour the sauce on the plate, spreading it out to a thickness of about ½ inch and flattening the surface with a wet knife or spatula. Allow to cool.

When cold, cut the cream with a knife, scoring it diagonally to make diamond shapes about 2 inches on each side. Lightly beat the remaining egg. Carefully lift each piece of custard with a knife and dip it first in flour, then in the beaten egg, then in breadcrumbs. If the cream seems a little soft, it doesn't matter. Press each piece gently with a knife or spatula, so that the bread-crumbs stick to the custard, and reshape into diamonds with knife and fingers if it seems to lose its shape.

In a heavy skillet, heat enough oil for deep-frying. When it is very hot, fry a few pieces of custard at a time, remove them as they become light and golden, and dry them on paper towels.

Serve hot or warm.

Note: You can prepare this dessert 1 or 2 hours in advance, but do not refrigerate if you plan to reheat it soon. Just leave at room temperature, covered with a towel. Reheat in a very slow oven (about 250°) for about 15 minutes.

A sauce made with honey diluted in a little Marsala, port wine, or a similar dessert wine may be served on the side, but these fritters are excellent just as they are.

Serves 4.

GREEK RICE PUDDING
Rizógalo

Rizógalo is the Greek version of rice pudding, and one of the best. It is also one of the oldest, rice having reached Greece from the Middle East earlier than other European countries. As was mentioned earlier, rice was first used exclusively as a dessert.

> ¾ *cup long-grain rice*
> *9 cups milk*
> *grated peel of 2 oranges*
> ½ *cup honey, or a little more*
> *2 teaspoons powdered cinnamon (approximately)*
> ¼ *teaspoon freshly ground nutmeg*

Preheat oven to 375°. Warm a heavy casserole and put the rice in it. Scald the milk, then pour it on the rice. Cover, and put in oven. After 20 minutes, remove the casserole, closing the oven door to maintain the temperature, stir the grated orange rind and the honey into the rice, and taste for sweetness, adjusting if needed. Cover the casserole again, and continue cooking for 25 to 30 minutes more, or until the milk has been absorbed.

Serve in a large bowl or individual bowls, sprinkled with the cinnamon and nutmeg.

Serve warm (not hot) , or at room temperature.

Serves 4.

SWEET PILÁF WITH ALMONDS

This rice dessert arrived in Greece during the Turkish occupation; the Turkish version, in turn, seems to have originated elsewhere in the Middle East.

¾ cup long-grain rice
12 tablespoons (1½ sticks) butter
1 cup honey
8 cups orange juice, or a little more, freshly squeezed
1½ cups blanched almonds, slivered

Preheat oven to 375°. In a heavy oven-proof casserole with a lid, sauté the rice in the butter on medium heat, stirring until the rice turns brown and opaque. Stir in the honey, remove the pot from the heat, and bake, uncovered, for about 20 minutes, stirring once after 10 minutes. The rice should be toasted.

Heat the 8 cups orange juice in a saucepan, then stir it into the rice, cover, and bake for 30 minutes, then check and if the rice is too dry, add a little more warm orange juice. At this point, stir about half the almonds into the rice. Return casserole to the oven and continue baking for 15 minutes, or until rice is tender but still a little chewy. Then sprinkle the remaining almonds on top, and serve after a few minutes. Also good at room temperature.

Note: The rice is usually served in the casserole in which it was baked, but you may wish to remove it to individual bowls or to a large serving bowl, making a mound. In either case, sprinkle with the remaining almonds after you have arranged the rice.

Serves 4.

WHEAT PUDDING
Assouréh

This pudding seems to have been invented by the Jewish community in Greece. The combination of wheat and pomegranate seeds gives it its special flavor, but if you can't find pomegranates, which unfortunately are rather uncommon in the United States, or if they are not in season, you may substitute other tart fruits, such as coarsely chopped strawberries.

pinch of salt
½ cup wheat kernels, whole
1 teaspoon powdered cinnamon
3 tablespoons honey (approximately)
¼ cup pomegranate kernels
¼ cup chopped walnuts
2 tablespoons dark raisins

Boil 3 cups of water with the salt. Keep another pot of water boiling. Add the wheat to the first pot, and stir. When the water comes to the boiling point again, lower the heat, cover, and simmer for about 1½ hours, stirring frequently, and adding more boiling water from the other pot, if needed. Gauge both cooking time and the addition of water so that the result will have the consistency of a fairly stiff pudding. Taste occasionally to see whether it is done, and add the cinnamon during the last 15 or 20 minutes of cooking.

Remove from heat, stir in the honey, adding more or less according to taste. Pour into a serving bowl, and decorate with the pomegranates, walnuts, and raisins. This can be served either hot or at room temperature.

Serves 4.

SEMOLINA PUDDING I

Gurievskaia Kasha

This is a very common dessert in Russia, but many versions of semolina pudding are found in other European countries. I am giving you the authentic old-fashioned recipe, and because of the elaborate way in which it is cooked, the taste is unique. Do try it —it is really worth the effort.

4 cups milk
½ cup semolina
½ teaspoon salt

1 tablespoon butter, plus butter for greasing
   baking dish
½ cup chopped blanched almonds
½ cup raisins
⅓ cup honey
2 eggs, separated

SAUCE
1 cup chopped dried apricots, presoaked
   in 1½ cups hot water
2 teaspoons honey

Preheat the oven to 500°. Bring the milk to a boil in an oven-proof casserole, and put it in the oven. Check it frequently, opening the door just a little (if you don't have a glass door on your oven), so as not to lose too much heat. When the surface of the milk turns golden brown, push the film down until a new surface also browns. Repeat at least 5 times, acting quickly each time to maintain the temperature. This should take about 30 minutes.

Remove the milk from the oven and boil it once more on top of the stove. Add the semolina, a little at a time to avoid lumps, and the salt, and lower the heat. Simmer for about 10 minutes, stirring constantly, especially from the bottom. Add 1 tablespoon butter, the almonds, raisins, and 3 tablespoons of the honey. Remove from heat.

Lower the oven temperature to 400°. Beat the egg whites until they form peaks. Break the yolks and gently mix with the whites. Fold the eggs into the semolina. Grease a baking dish with butter, pour in the mixture, and bake for 15 minutes, or until the top begins to turn golden.

Heat the apricots in the water in which they were soaked, add the remaining honey, bring to a boil, and simmer for a few minutes.

The sauce should be served on the side, very hot.

Serves 4.

SEMOLINA PUDDING II

This version of semolina pudding is more compact than the preceding one, and much easier to prepare. It comes from Italy, where it is almost never found in restaurants but very often served at home.

¾ cup semolina
1½ cups milk
2 tablespoons butter
4 teaspoons honey
2 tablespoons raisins
2 tablespoons rum
2 eggs, separated
1 whole egg, lightly beaten
1 teaspoon grated lemon peel
1 teaspoon grated orange peel

Mix the semolina with a few tablespoons of the milk, and bring the rest of the milk to a boil. Add the semolina, bring back to a boil, stirring, and simmer for about 5 minutes, stirring constantly. Pour the mixture into a bowl, and mix in the butter and the honey. Allow to cool a little, stirring once in a while to quicken the process.

Soak the raisins in the rum for at least 20 minutes. (If you don't want to use rum, soak them in water mixed with a few drops of vanilla extract or almond extract.)

Preheat the oven to 375°. When the pudding has cooled to lukewarm, mix in the 2 egg yolks, one at a time, and the beaten whole egg, then the raisins and their liquid, and the lemon and orange peels. Beat the egg whites until they form peaks, then fold them into the pudding.

Grease an oven-proof dish, such as a 10-inch pie pan, and pour in the mixture without filling the pan to the top, as the pudding may puff up a bit while baking. The container should allow the pudding to be between 1 and 2 inches thick. Bake for 1 hour.

Allow to cool for at least 10 minutes, then either unmold onto a serving plate or serve in the pan in which it was cooked.

An orange sauce or other sauce of your choice can be served on the side.

Serves 4.

PEASANT GRAPE PIE

The Italian peasants often make this pie at grape harvest time. In many southern European countries, one can buy fresh bread dough (for Italian-style loaves) from the local baker, who always reserves some just to sell. While this simplifies the preparation of many dishes requiring dough, you may still wish to prepare this simple tasty pie, especially if you bake bread at home.

> *3 pounds seedless grapes, preferably dark*
> *1½ pounds bread dough, or 1 recipe Basic Pizza*
> *   dough (see index)*
> *honey*

Wash the grapes and separate them from their stems. Roll out the dough to a thickness of about ½ inch, and put it in a square or rectangular baking dish, allowing the dough to fill the sides and overflow the edges slightly. Fill with the grapes, pushing them slightly into the dough, not only at the bottom but also around the sides. Set the pie in a warm place and allow the dough to rise for about 1 hour. Preheat the oven to 450°. Pour a little honey all over the grapes, and bake for about 30 minutes, or until the crust has browned at the edges. Serve hot or luke-warm.

Serves 4 to 6.

APPLE CHARLOTTE

This is a very simple version of the classic French dessert.

8 slices of Italian or French bread,
  crust removed
butter, at room temperature
5 large apples
1½ tablespoons lemon juice
honey to taste (according to tartness of apples)
1 teaspoon grated lemon peel

Preheat oven to 425°. Grease a fairly deep round oven-proof pan. Butter the bread slices lightly. Peel and core the apples, reserving some of the peel. Slice the apples thin, and dip the slices in the lemon juice. With whatever juice is left, mix the honey and lemon peel, and set aside. Place one even layer of bread slices on the bottom of the pan, cutting them to fit, if necessary. Add a layer of apple slices. Sprinkle lightly with the lemon-and-honey mixture, and continue to make layers in this fashion, ending with apples. Cover the top surface with the apple peel. Bake for about 50 minutes, or until the apples are done, which you can easily check by lifting the peel and eating one piece.

Turn the Apple Charlotte into a serving bowl, or leave in the oven dish, if it is presentable.

Serves 4 to 6.

HONEY CAKE

½ cup butter, at room temperature
1 cup honey
4 eggs, separated
3 cups flour

2 tablespoons baking powder
pinch of salt
½ cup chopped walnuts
½ cup dried currants
½ cup raisins
1 tablespoon lemon juice
1 teaspoon grated lemon peel
pinch of powdered coriander

Cream the butter and honey with a fork. Lightly beat the egg yolks, and add them. Combine the flour, baking powder, and salt, mixing well. Gently stir in all the other ingredients except the egg whites.

Preheat the oven to 350°. Beat the egg whites until almost to peaking point, then fold into the mixture. Line a deep, rectangular bread pan with waxed paper cut to shape. Pour the mixture into the pan, and bake at 350° for about 1 hour. Serve in the same dish, or unmold onto a platter.

Serves 4 to 6.

CARROT ALMOND CAKE

½ pound peeled almonds
¾ pound carrots
1 teaspoon lemon juice
1½ cups flour (approximately)
2 teaspoons baking soda
½ cup thick honey
3 eggs, separated
½ teaspoon grated lemon peel
½ teaspoon grated orange peel
few drops of bitter almond extract (optional)

Preheat oven to 350°. Reserve about 15 of the almonds. By hand or in an electric mixer, chop the rest of the almonds very fine. Mince the carrots (they can be grated by hand or in a food processor). Mix the carrots with the lemon juice immediately.

Combine the flour and baking soda, stirring well, and divide in half. To one half, add the chopped almonds. Separately, mix the honey with the egg yolks, and add to the almond-flour mixture, blending everything well with a fork or pastry blender. Add the rest of the flour, the lemon peel, orange peel, and almond extract. Beat the egg whites to the peaking point, and gently fold them into the mixture. Butter a cake mold, sprinkle with flour, and turn upside down to remove excess flour. Pour in the cake batter, and bake for 30 minutes or until the blade of a knife comes out clean.

Allow to cool 10 minutes, then unmold, and finish cooling on a rack. Put the whole almonds on top of the cake in any design that pleases you. If they don't stick properly, dip each one in honey on one side.

Serves 4.

CORNMEAL CAKE

Information about cornmeal is given under Polenta (see index).

1 cup butter
4 tablespoons honey
5 eggs, separated (at room temperature)
1 envelope yeast
2 tablespoons lukewarm water
5 tablespoons yellow cornmeal
¼ teaspoon salt
½ teaspoon grated orange peel
½ teaspoon grated lemon peel
pinch powdered coriander
flour

Slowly melt the butter in a saucepan. Add the honey and stir until blended. Remove from heat and add the egg yolks, one at a time, stirring well after each addition. (During this process you may have to put the pot back on very low heat to keep it warm, or you can use a double boiler.)

Preheat the oven to 375°. Mix the yeast with the lukewarm water, let stand 5 minutes, and add to the yolks. Stir in the cornmeal, salt, orange peel, lemon peel, and coriander. Beat the egg whites to peaking point, then gently fold into the cornmeal mixture.

Grease a 1-quart cake pan and sprinkle with flour, removing any excess. Pour the cornmeal mixture in the pan, and bake for 45 minutes.

Tap the cake out of the pan and let cool. It can be served lukewarm or cold, plain or with a warm or cold sauce.

Serves 4.

STRAWBERRY PIE

1 pint strawberries
2 tablespoons honey
4 tablespoons sweet white wine
½ recipe Italian Pie Crust (see index) for sweet pies
    or 1 cup crumbled graham crackers and
    2 tablespoons melted butter
2 eggs, separated
½ pound ricotta
2 teaspoons lemon juice
3 tablespoons yogurt

Wash the strawberries, trim off the stems, and place the berries in a small bowl. In another bowl, stir the honey and wine until the honey dissolves. Pour over the strawberries. If they are not completely covered, gently mix once or twice. Allow to soak for about 30 minutes.

Preheat the oven to 400°. If pie shell is used, line a pie pan with the dough. Otherwise, mix the cracker crumbs with the butter, and press the crumbs and butter on the bottom and along the sides of an 8-inch round oven dish. Bake pie shell or crumb crust for 7 or 8 minutes, remove it, and reduce the temperature to 350°. Beat the egg yolks, stir in half the ricotta, the lemon juice, a little marinade from the strawberries, then the rest of the ricotta. Beat the egg whites until almost stiff, and fold into the ricotta mixture. Pour into the pie crust, and bake for 30 minutes. Drain the strawberries over a bowl. Mix the yogurt with their juice, and pour on top of the pie. Let cool. Arrange the strawberries in an orderly or geometric design on top, points up. Serve at room temperature.

Serves 4.

Dessert Sauces

The dessert sauces that follow provide varied possibilities, not only for the desserts in this book but for other end-of-meal treats you may invent. Added to your own favorites, they can provide a refreshing change.

According to the dessert, you can add chopped almonds or chopped walnuts, hazelnuts, or green pistachio nuts to the sauces as you make them.

Here are a few general suggestions: Orange- or grape-flavored sauces blend very well with semolina puddings. For cakes use a slightly sweetened whipped cream instead of icing. Not only will it enhance the flavor, but it is healthier as well. If you plan this addition, bake the cake in a square mold, unmold it, cut it in flat slices rather than sections, and serve the slices horizontally rather than standing up. The whipped cream can then be added individually. Whipped cream is also a good topping for any unsweetened fresh berry dessert, especially strawberries. Use practically any of the warm dessert sauces given here over Fried Custard, Fruit Fritters, or Cornmeal Cake (see index).

HONEY SAUCES

A very simple but delicious dessert sauce can be made by diluting honey with an equal amount of Marsala, sweet sherry, Madeira, port, or a mild liqueur. Warm the sauce slowly in a small pot, stirring until blended, and use warm. Milk or cream, either cold or warm, mixed with honey also makes a nice sauce. If the honey is thick, use warm milk or cream.

JAM SAUCE

Using the same method as for honey sauces, slowly heat equal amounts of jam and your choice of a fortified wine or a liqueur and a little water.

Marmalade made with any citrus fruit blends well with Cointreau and a little water or wine. A touch of almond extract can add a pleasant aroma. Serve warm.

GRAPE SYRUP

Grapes, considered by many the perfect fruit, are usually so sweet that you can make a syrup without the addition of any sweetener.

Boil the desired quantity of a sweet variety of table grapes very slowly until they begin to thicken. Pass through a sieve to remove the skins, then continue to simmer until the syrup is of the desired consistency. Remember that it continues to thicken while cooling. Use warm or cold.

WHIPPED CREAM

If you like whipped cream but don't want to use sugar, add honey instead. For a faint but very pleasant sweetness, use 1 teaspoon honey for ½ pint of heavy cream, adding the honey slowly after the cream begins to thicken.

Makes about 1 cup.

WINE AND ORANGE SAUCE

A variation of a classic Greek dessert sauce, this is excellent on cakes or cold desserts and makes a good marinade for fruit salads. Because of its dark color, it is preferable, if you care about appearance, to use it with colorful fruits, as it may look unappealing on apples, pears, bananas, and such.

> *1 cup red sweet wine*
> *1 cup orange juice*
> *3 tablespoons thick honey*
> *1 tablespoon grated orange peel*

Warm all ingredients slowly in a small pot, stirring to blend. Simmer, uncovered, for about 10 minutes.

Serve immediately if you want a warm sauce. Or allow to cool, pour in a jar, seal well, and refrigerate. It will keep for months, and can be reheated. If it has become too thick, add a little wine to reheat.

Makes approximately 1½ cups.

Wines

While some vegetarians completely abstain from any form of alcoholic beverage, wine drinking is enjoyed by many others, and a word should be said about the types of wines that are best suited to complement vegetarian meals.

Drinking wine with meals is a relatively new habit in the United States, and many people are overly concerned with what kind of wine to serve. Rather than make a mistake, hosts frequently avoid any definite choice by serving a mediocre rosé wine, because rosé is supposed to be compatible with any type of meal. But the choice of rosé is much more difficult than that of red or white wine, as there are so few rosés that are really good.

For vegetarian meals the rules are much less strict than for other meals. In fact, there are no rules at all, but a few guidelines ought to be followed.

In general, imported wines are to be preferred to domestic wines, as the rules against the adulteration of wine are much more strict in Europe than in the United States, wine being so widely used there but until recently not here, so that the federal regulatory agencies have not yet quite caught up with specific standards of purity. The same holds true for beer. For example, in Germany, England, and some other countries, it is strictly forbidden to add sugar to beer, while there are no such rules here, and most domestic brands contain sugar.

Pasteurization of wine is another American process that domestic wines, especially the less expensive varieties, seldom escape.

Aside from the fact that pasteurization considerably alters the taste of any wine, it is totally superfluous. To my knowledge, it has not been adopted in Europe, especially for good vintage wines.

For vegetarian meals, very dark, thick red wines should generally be avoided, as they tend to cover the taste of the food rather than enhance it. Clarets, light Burgundy, Bordeaux, Chianti, Valpolicella, Bardolino, Rhine wines, and the like are good dry red wines that are indicated to complement dishes such as pasta with tomato sauce, eggplant dishes, beans, spinach, kale, cabbage—robust menus comprised of stronger-tasting vegetables or containing a strong flavor of garlic—although white wines also do very well with this type of meal.

Red wines are to be served "at room temperature," especially if they are good wines. However, the temperature of a European room is considerably cooler than the 75° to 80° of many American homes and I find that in the United States red wines are served too warm. It is therefore advisable to keep the red wine you are planning to serve in the coolest place in your home, to be served at a temperature no higher than 65°.

Chilled dry white wines are better suited to accompany meals that include more-delicate-tasting vegetables and dishes. There is a great variety of excellent imported wines: you may choose practically any French, Italian, Greek, Spanish, or Portuguese white wine that is considered "table wine." Sometimes the label states this, sometimes not. French Chablis can be dry or a little fruity in taste, and certain brands are not very dry at all. German white wines that are popular here are often on the sweet side, even when they are sold as dry. There are some excellent Rhine wines, both red and white, but for the white types it is suggested you try a bottle before you pass judgment. Riesling is usually a good dry white wine, whether it is made in Germany or in other countries. There are some good Spanish, Chilean, and Argentinean Rieslings that are quite palatable, without being absolutely superb, and they are often available in wine stores in this country. Italian white wines are quite good and almost always very dry, unless the label states *"semisecco"* (semi-dry) or *"abboccato"* (semi-sweet). Two dry white wines that have encountered great favor in the United States are Soave and Verdicchio, but there are dozens of other varieties to choose from. Aside from Chablis, which can often be borderline dry, among the many excellent dry wines from France are Pouilly Fuissé and Pouilly Fumé, either of which is always a good choice, unless it is of a poor vintage year.

This is not the place to elaborate further on wine, especially since some varieties may be more available in one part of the country than in another. Again, experiment and try to acquire a taste for good wines. They don't have to be expensive. Once your taste is more secure, you will be able to judge for yourself and buy very good imported wines that are often cheaper than many of the domestic varieties.

For vegetarian meals there is only one absolute must: Artichokes should always be served with a dry white wine. Try a little test yourself, and have a sip of a good dry white wine after a mouthful of artichoke. You will be pleasantly surprised at the effect. The taste of artichokes fills your mouth while blending exquisitely with the taste of the wine, and both are enhanced. Vegetables that are similar to artichokes in taste—Jerusalem artichokes, cardoons, and the like—also go very well with dry white wine. And so do the more delicate vegetables, as well as rice.

Aside from this, it is worth repeating that there are no definite rules. If you plan to serve only one type of wine at a party, though, you would be better off choosing a white wine than a red, unless the entire menu consists of the stronger-tasting dishes mentioned earlier.

Vintage is much more important with French, German, Hungarian, and northern Swiss wines than for wines made with grapes grown in countries below the Alps. This is mostly a matter of the climate, which is more stable in southern regions than farther north, where, because of unpredictable rains, strong winds, and other factors, the same vineyard can produce an excellent wine one year and a rather poor wine the next.

The sweeter wines, as well as the fortified wines, should be served with dessert or after dinner, and they are especially favored as an after-dinner treat by people who don't drink hard liquor or strong liqueurs.

Menu Planning

As I explained in the Introduction, the vegetarian meal is not necessarily separated into courses as are meals dominated by meat or fish. Many complementary dishes may be served all at once, or you can serve a succession of dishes with contrasting flavors. To help you get started with planning your own vegetarian meals, I have put together some sample menus to suit different occasions and tastes. But I urge you to experiment on your own and use your imagination to create meals which will reflect your own personal preferences.

LUNCHES

Ovolactovegetarian

Eggs Oyster Style (served in small egg cups or shot glasses)
Dark-bread sandwiches: Cucumber Dip as a spread, watercress or tender lettuce leaves, and slices of Swiss cheese
Fruit in season

Quiche Lorraine
Finocchio, Kohlrabi, and Endive Salad
Fruit salad

Buck Rarebit
Raw Zucchini, Tomato, and Carrot Salad
Apricot Sandwiches (if in season) , or berries and yogurt

304

Rice Salad, Capuchin Monk Style, served with Lentil Pâté
Stuffed Melons

Open cheese sandwiches (Muenster or other semi-soft cheese,
either on dark bread previously toasted lightly, or inserted in
previously toasted whole-wheat pitta bread which is then
warmed in 425° oven for 5 minutes)
Marinated beets
Fruit in season

Hard-cooked eggs, halved, with Red Sauce
Russian Salad (either)
Cheese and fruit

Egg-filled Tomatoes
Marinated Zucchini
Greek Rice Pudding, or fresh fruit

Slices of any vegetable pie, at room temperature
Green salad
Fruit salad

Artichoke Frittata, or other frittata
Tomato salad
Bananas and berries in lemon and orange juice

Lactovegetarian

Cold Borscht
Esau Salad (omit eggs)
Peaches in Lemon Juice (if in season) , or fresh fruit

Bread and Tomato Soup
Mixed Greens Salad
Yogurt and nuts

Assorted cheeses with assorted breads
Raw Spinach and Mushroom Salad
Peasant Grape Pie, or fruit

Cereal Broth
Cherry tomatoes stuffed with Gorgonzola Spread
Melon and watermelon chunks (if in season) , or other fruit

Rice and Peas
Assorted cheeses and fruit

Cornmeal and Spinach Soup
Fruit salad

Melted cheese and tomato sandwiches
Bulgur Salad
Strawberries with whipped cream

Rice and Milk Soup
Raw Zucchini, Tomato, and Carrot Salad
Fruit juice (freshly squeezed)

Strict Vegetarian

Stricter vegetarians can choose from practically any of the salads in the book, with or without minor adaptations, but should try to add some proteins to their lunches unless a full-protein dinner is planned. Pitta bread can be stuffed with practically any salad, and this will constitute a healthy, nourishing meal. Or two complementing salads can be selected.

DINNERS

While the following dinners have been selected from the viewpoint of compatibility of foods, color combination, and variety of taste, and with an eye on nutrition, if your standards are stricter we refer you to *Diet for a Small Planet* by Frances Moore Lappé, *Recipes for a Small Planet* by Ellen Buchman Ewald, and similar books, where you can find specific charts about nutrition. You can then use the following guidelines with your own variations.

Ovolactovegetarian

Minestrone
Spinach Mold filled with sautéed Mushrooms
French Potato Salad
Ricotta dessert

Spanish Garlic Soup
Bean or Lentil Patties
Shredded Carrot Salad
Greek Rice Pudding

Roasted Peppers
Potato Soufflé
Spinach Ball
Mixed salad
Apple Charlotte

Tomatoes Stuffed with Eggplant
German Dumplings
Chick-Pea Salad
Green salad
Semolina Pudding (either)

German or Italian ravioli
Mixed Vegetable Mold
Tomato and Greens Salad
Pears in Wine on Paradise Rice

Baked Pasta and Tomatoes
Raw Spinach and Mushroom Salad
Fried Custard

Rice and Milk Soup
Stuffed Tomatoes
Swiss Salad
Honey Cake

Tuscan Rice Soup
Cheese and Onion Pie
Raw salad—any kind, but colorful
Fruit salad

Lactovegetarian

Imám Baialdí (cold)
Rigatoni au gratin
Finocchio and Artichoke Salad (if in season) , or
    Mixed Green Salad
Yogurt with berries and nuts

Corsican Vegetable Soup
Potato Pizza
Shredded Turnip and Carrot Salad
Chestnut Pie (served with ricotta)

Vermicelli Sicilian Style
Stuffed Tomatoes
Green Salad
Greek Rice Pudding

Spanish Vegetable Soup
Mixed Green Salad, or Spinach and Mushroom Salad
Stuffed Melon, or Apricot Sandwiches (if in season)

Cream of Lentil Soup
Dutch Taart
Finocchio and Grapefruit Salad, or Red Cabbage Salad
Fruit salad

Chick-Pea and Spinach Soup
Black Bean Pie
Vegetable Salad, Greek Style
Assorted cheeses and fruits

Crudités
Polenta with Sage and Rosemary
Red Cabbage Salad
Ricotta or yogurt dessert

Rice and Asparagus Soup
Zucchini-Potato Bake
Steamed vegetable in season
Fruit salad

Strict Vegetarian

Minestrone
Four steamed vegetables in season, with a sauce
Fried or broiled polenta
Mixed Green Salad
Fresh or stewed fruit (according to season) , with nuts

Pasta with Garlic and Oil
Two or three salads, with different dressings
Peaches in Lemon Juice, or Stuffed Melon

Kasha with Spinach
Spanish-Style Onions (oil instead of butter)
Irish Herb Scones (oil instead of butter)
Mixed salad, your choice
Fruit salad

Vegetable Broth (either)
Pipérade
Boiled Rice, or Feathered Rice
Assorted fruits and nuts

Spaghetti with Pesto
Red Cabbage and Apple Salad
Figs in Wine

Potato "Pizza," or Pizza with Chicory
Finocchio and Grapefruit Salad
Chestnut Fritters

Risotto with Vegetables
Potato-Onion-Beet Salad
Oranges and bananas in lemon sauce or sparkling white wine

DINNER PARTIES

These menus are planned to be served to six to eight guests seated at the table. Quantities given in recipes should be increased proportionately.

Ovolactovegetarian

Artichokes with Lemon and Oil Sauce
Semolina Gnocchi
Zucchini Boats
Root Vegetable Wheel
Fruit Salad

Celeriac in Sour Sauce
Piedmontese Fonduta, served with boiled rice
Rutabaga and Carrot Casserole
Convent-Style Baked Potatoes
Green salad
Honey Cake, with sauce of your choice

Eggplant Appetizer (Caponatina or Melitsanosaláta)
Pasta-Spinach Roll (either Rotolone or Strucolo)
Two steamed vegetables in season, with Egg-Lemon Sauce
Assorted cheeses with assorted breads
Carrot-Walnut Cake

Rice and Asparagus Soup
Vegetable Mold (Far du Poitou)
Brussels Sprouts and Chestnuts, or Finocchio and Tomato
Raw Zucchini, Tomato, and Carrot Salad
Semolina Pudding with honey-wine sauce

Minestrone with Pesto
Polenta Pasticciata
Red Cabbage Salad, or Mixed Greens and Red Cabbage Salad
Creamy Egg Custard

Pasta with Broccoli Sauce
Buck Rarebit
Steamed artichokes or Jerusalem artichokes in Wine Sauce
Shredded Carrot Salad
Greek Rice Pudding

Lentil Pâté
Calabrian Spinach Pie
Finocchio and Grapefruit Salad
Pears in Wine on Paradise Rice, or Peaches in Lemon Juice

Egg-Filled Tomatoes
Pan-Fried Rice
Herb Pudding, served with one vegetable in season
English Potato Salad
Apricot Sandwiches, or assorted cheeses and assorted fruit

Lactovegetarian

Pepper Zakuski
Black-Bean Pie
Healthy Raw Salad, or Winter Salad
Ricotta dessert

Artichokes with Lemon-Oil Sauce
Pasta al Gratin
Root Vegetable Wheel, or Mixed Green Salad
Peasant Grape Pie, or Strawberry Pie

Risotto with Vegetables
Turnip Gratin, or other vegetable au gratin
Lettuce, Chicory, and Orange Salad
Yogurt with berries or cut-up fruit

Pasta with Ricotta Sauce
Raw Zucchini, Tomato, and Carrot Salad
Red Cabbage and Apples
Strawberries with whipped cream

Goat Cheese and Herb Spread
Greek Vegetable Stew, served with Polenta and
    Cheese Croquettes
Chick-pea Salad, or Black-Eyed Pea Salad
Chestnut Pie, or fresh fruit

Strict Vegetarian

Onions in Sweet-and-Sour Sauce
Pizza with Chicory
Red Cabbage Salad
Chestnut Pie

Fried Peppers, or Roasted Peppers
Spanish-Style Rice (omit butter)
Artichokes and Fava Beans, or Artichokes and Peas
Wheat Pudding

Eggplant Appetizer (Caponatina)
German Vegetable Stew, served with Feathered Rice
Oranges Sun Style

Green Rice
Brussels Sprouts and Chestnuts, or Bubble and Squeak
Watercress and Apple Salad
Figs in Wine

Vegetable Broth (very small pasta may be cooked in it)
Polenta with Onion and Pea Sauce
Sautéed mushrooms
Winter Salad, or Root Vegetable Wheel
Fruit salad

BUFFET-STYLE PARTIES

Multiply the recipes according to the number of guests you expect. People's tastes are often unpredictable, and you will notice that certain foods will quickly disappear, while you'll be staring at abundant leftovers of other dishes after the party. It is a good rule to make more food than for other parties, as people often tend to stay at buffets longer than expected, and their appetites increase in the late hours, especially if the party is successful.

You will usually have sufficient food if you add a little to your multiplication. For example, if you expect ten people and the original recipe is meant for four, treble it rather than multiplying it two and a half times.

Raw Vegetables (*Crudités*). To be served with drinks, as appetizers. Make a large batch, colorful and varied. Serve with two or three sauces: Aïoli; chili sauce with a little soy sauce and lemon; Green Sauce. Or mayonnaise and mustard (one-fourth mustard in proportion to three-fourths mayonnaise); Red Sauce; Maltaise Sauce. Select only fairly thick sauces, so that drippings won't decorate your carpets and furniture.
Pastitsio
Spinach Ball
Mixed Raw Salad (try not to repeat any vegetable that was used as an appetizer)

Fried Custard (make smaller pieces than suggested in the recipe, to be eaten in one bite, so you will not need dessert plates)
Assorted fruits

Deviled Eggs and Melted Cheese Canapés
Polenta Pasticciata (the pyramidal shape), with mushroom sauce, or Peas and Onions Ragout, or both
Lettuce, Chicory, and Orange Salad
Strawberry Pie

Lentil Pâté and Gorgonzola Spread (or Celery and Tomatoes stuffed with Gorgonzola Spread)
Zucchini and Rice Pie
Jerusalem Artichokes au Gratin (or Cardoons or other vegetables in season, also au gratin)
Mixed Green Salad
Shredded Carrot Salad with Dry Currants
Ricotta dessert

SMORGASBORD-TYPE PARTY

Egg-Filled Tomatoes
Roasted Peppers
Marinated beets
Chick-peas and Sesame Paste
Sicilian Eggplant Appetizer
Spanish olives and Greek olives
Assorted cheese and assorted breads (cut in bite-sized pieces)
Genoese Frittata, cut in separate portions, either at room temperature or kept barely warm
Artichoke Pie, or Eggplant Pie, served as previous dish
Lentil Pie, warm, and Creamy Mushroom Sauce
Zucchini Boats (use small zucchini which are more manageable)
Assorted salads (avoid salad greens that may wilt or become soggy if previously dressed)
Russian Salad (either)
Carrot and Walnut Cake (sliced)

Strawberry Pie or Peasant Grape Pie
    (according to season)
Fresh fruit (select types of fruit that can be eaten easily;
    if in season, Apricot Sandwiches would be a good choice)

Index